Microsoft 365 Copilot and Agent Administration Fundamentals

Build practical skills and confidently prepare for the Microsoft AB-900 certification exam

Steve Miles

<packt>

Microsoft 365 Copilot and Agent Administration Fundamentals

Portfolio Director: Pavan Ramchandani
Relationship Lead: Mohd Riyan Khan
Program Manager: Divij Kotian
Content Engineer: Rounak Kulkarni
Technical Editor: Vidhisha Patidar
Indexer: Tejal Soni
Proofreader: Rounak Kulkarni
Production Designer: Shankar Kalbhor
Growth Lead: Nivedita Singh

First published: July 2026

Production reference: 1160626

Published by Packt Publishing Ltd.
Grosvenor House
11 St Paul's Square
Birmingham
B3 1RB, UK.

ISBN 978-1-80730-651-9
`www.packtpub.com`

To everyone learning how Microsoft 365, Copilot, and agents are changing the way people work, and to those building the knowledge needed to support trusted, responsible, and well-governed AI adoption.

- Steve Miles

Contributors

About the author

Steve Miles works in a senior partner technology enablement role within the cloud practice of a multi-billion-euro European IT distributor.

He is a Microsoft **Most Valuable Professional** (**MVP**), **Microsoft Certified Trainer** (**MCT**), and an Alibaba Cloud MVP. He has more than 25 years of technology experience spanning hosted datacenter services, hybrid and multi-cloud platforms, as well as a previous military career in engineering, signals, and communications.

Steve is the author and technical reviewer of numerous books on Microsoft technologies, with a particular focus on security, Azure, AI, and data.

LinkedIn Profile: `https://www.linkedin.com/in/stevemiles70`

I want to thank the people who have been close to me and supported me, professionally and at home, especially my wife, Pippa, aka Mrs. Smiles, and my family.

About the reviewers

Thiago Beier is a Cloud Solution Architect at Microsoft, serving as a trusted advisor and technical leader across Microsoft 365, Intune, Entra ID, Azure, Security, and AI-powered solutions.

With more than 25 years of experience spanning consulting, architecture, operations, and customer success, he has led enterprise-scale modernization, security, identity, and endpoint management initiatives worldwide.

An active community contributor, blogger, GitHub maintainer, and technical reviewer, Thiago is passionate about automation, PowerShell, Generative AI, Microsoft Copilot, Claude, and emerging AI technologies. He enjoys helping organizations accelerate cloud adoption and digital transformation.

Andrew Wood is the Head of Cloud Platform and Security at Simpson Associates, a Microsoft Solutions Partner based in York. With over 15 years of experience in IT, he started in on-premises systems administration before moving into cloud platform engineering and security architecture.

He has worked across a range of roles within the Microsoft ecosystem, from platform and DevOps engineering to infrastructure architecture and security consultancy, spanning Azure, Microsoft 365, and the Microsoft security stack.

Holding a broad range of Microsoft certifications across Azure, security, and Microsoft 365, he is passionate about identity and access management, agentic AI governance, and infrastructure automation. He writes about cloud and security topics at awood.tech and is driven by helping clients adopt best practices and modernize their infrastructure and security in the right way.

Table of Contents

Preface xix

Free benefits with your book xxii

Chapter 1: Identifying the Core Features and Objects of Microsoft 365 Services 1

Explaining how licensing affects access to Microsoft 365 features 3

Identifying user-based and group-based license assignment • 3

Identifying license components that affect service access • 5

Exploring organization configuration in the Microsoft 365 admin center 7

Identifying the Microsoft 365 tenant model • 8

Identifying domain types • 8

Default tenant domain • 10

Custom domains, verification, and DNS records • 11

Identifying organization-wide settings • 13

Organization profile settings • 13

Tenant-wide access and sharing settings • 14

Identifying configuration objects in the Exchange Online admin center 16

Exploring mailbox types • 17

User mailboxes • 17

Shared mailboxes • 19

Resource mailboxes • 20

Comparison • 21

Identifying distribution lists • 22

Identifying configuration objects in the SharePoint admin center 24

Identifying SharePoint site types • 25

Team site • 25

Communication site • 26

Identifying document libraries • 26

Identifying folders within libraries • 27

Identifying SharePoint site roles and permissions 28

Identifying permission inheritance • 28

Inherited permissions • 28

Breaking inheritance • 28

Identifying default SharePoint roles • 29

Owners • 30

Members • 30

Visitors • 30

Identifying permission scope levels • 31

Site-level permissions • 31

Library-level permissions • 31

Folder-level permissions • 32

Item-level permissions • 32

Identifying configuration objects in the Teams admin center 32

Identifying teams • 33

Identifying channels • 34

Standard channels • 35

Private channels • 36

Shared channels • 36

Identifying Teams policy types • 36

Meeting policies • 37

Messaging policies • 38

App permission policies • 38

Summary 38

Core Microsoft 365 objects reference 39

Key terms and acronyms 41

Exam readiness drill – chapter review questions 43

Link to this chapter's quiz • 44

Chapter 2: Understanding Microsoft 365 Security Principles 45

Explaining Zero Trust principles 46

Traditional perimeter-based security • 46
The Zero Trust security model • 47
Core principles of Zero Trust • 48
Zero Trust in Microsoft 365 • 49
Understanding authentication methods **49**
Understanding identities • 49
Types of identities • 50
The purpose of authentication • 50
Authentication versus authorization • 51
Authentication methods • 52
Multi-factor authentication • 52
Authentication factors • 52
Passwordless authentication • 53
Understanding authorization **54**
The purpose of authorization • 54
Role-based access control • 54
Benefits of role-based access control • 55
Managing permissions with groups • 55
Understanding threat protection and intelligence **56**
The modern threat landscape • 56
Common attack techniques • 57
Threat detection and intelligence • 57
Security alerts and investigation • 57
Understanding Microsoft Defender XDR capabilities **58**
Security signals and telemetry • 58
Alert correlation and incidents • 59
Investigation and response capabilities • 59
Summary **59**
Microsoft 365 security principles reference **60**
Key terms and acronyms **62**
Exam readiness drill – chapter review questions **64**
Link to this chapter's quiz • 65

Chapter 3: Identifying Core Security Features of Microsoft 365 Services 67

Understanding features and capabilities of Microsoft Entra 68

Understanding conditional access and policies • 70

Identifying the appropriate security object to use in an organization (users and groups) 74

User identities in Microsoft Entra • 74

Groups as identity containers for managing access • 75

Common group types used in Microsoft environments • 76

Understanding the purpose and benefits of single sign-on (SSO) 78

Understanding App registrations and Enterprise applications 79

App registrations • 80

Enterprise applications (service principals) • 80

Relationship between an app registration and an enterprise application • 81

Identifying the role of Privileged Identity Management (PIM) in an organization. 81

Just-in-time privileged access using Privileged Identity Management • 82

Controlling and monitoring privileged role activation • 82

Interpreting Identity Secure Score in Microsoft Entra ID 82

Using Identity Secure Score to improve and monitor security posture • 84

Using the appropriate tools to review audit logs for user and admin activity 84

Reviewing sign-in logs in Microsoft Entra • 84

Reviewing audit logs for administrative and configuration activity • 85

Identifying the appropriate tools to troubleshoot common sign-in issues (MFA, Conditional Access, and risky sign-ins) 86

Investigating sign-in issues using Microsoft Entra tools • 87

Understanding sign-in results and resolving issues • 87

Summary 87

Core Microsoft 365 objects reference 88

Key terms and acronyms 90

Exam readiness drill – chapter review questions 94

Link to this chapter's quiz • 95

Chapter 4: Understanding Microsoft Purview 97

Introduction to Microsoft Purview and data governance 98

What is Microsoft Purview • 98

Key Microsoft Purview capabilities • 99

Understanding data classification in Microsoft Purview 100

Detecting sensitive information • 100

Sensitive information types • 101

Trainable classifiers • 101

Exact data match • 101

Identifying the use cases for sensitivity labels in Microsoft Purview 102

Understanding sensitivity labels • 102

How sensitivity labels support data protection • 103

Understanding data lifecycle governance • 104

Understanding retention 104

Retention labels • 105

Retention policies • 106

Summary 107

Microsoft Learn reference links.. 107

Key terms and acronyms.. 110

Exam readiness drill – chapter review questions.. 112

Link to this chapter's quiz • 113

Chapter 5: Understanding Data Security Implications of Copilot 115

Understanding how Copilot Accesses Data.. 115

Microsoft 365 data sources accessed by Copilot • 117

User identity as the data access context • 117

Prompt-driven data retrieval in Copilot • 118

Copilot limitations • 118

Understanding how Microsoft Graph Influences Copilot Responses 118

Microsoft Graph as the data aggregation layer • 119

Prompt grounding using Microsoft Graph • 120

Permissions trimming in Microsoft Graph data retrieval • 120

Microsoft Graph limitations • 120

Understanding how Copilot uses permissions and controls 121

Microsoft 365 permissions model • 121

Copilot enforcement of existing permissions • 122

Data protection using Microsoft Purview • 123

Data loss prevention using Microsoft Purview DLP • 124

Risk detection using Microsoft Defender • 124

Security control limitations in Copilot • 125

Understanding responsible AI principles 125

Enterprise guardrails controlling Copilot behavior • 126

Prompt filtering in Copilot • 127

Policy-aligned response generation in Copilot • 127

System messages and grounding controls in Copilot • 128

Summary 128

Microsoft Learn reference links 129

Key terms and acronyms 132

Exam readiness drill – chapter review questions 135

Link to this chapter's quiz • 136

Chapter 6: Identifying Data Protection and Governance Risks for Microsoft 365 and Copilot 137

Identifying compliance risks and recommendations using Microsoft Purview Compliance Manager 138

Compliance posture through control-based assessments • 139

Compliance scores and control responsibility • 140

Improvement actions for control gaps • 140

Compliance posture compared to detection and enforcement • 141

Identifying sensitive information by using Microsoft Purview Data Explorer 141

Classification signals from labels and sensitive information types • 142

Aggregated insights from classified data • 143

Distribution of classified data across services • 143

Data Explorer limitations • 143

Identifying risks using Insider Risk Management 144

User-centric risk model • 145

Signals and indicators from user activity • 145

Behavioral patterns from correlated activity signals • 146

Risk scenarios and policies • 146

Cases for investigation and management • 146

Insider risk limitations • 147

Identifying and responding to alerts generated by Microsoft Purview DLP • 147

Policy conditions based on classification signals • 148

Policy matches for classified or sensitive data • 148

Alerts for sensitive data events • 149

Enforcement actions for data protection • 149

DLP limitations • 149

Identifying policy violations generated by communication compliance............... 150

Message content analysis across communication channels • 151

Conditions for non-compliant communication content • 151

Violations as reviewable items • 151

Structured review workflows for investigation • 152

Communication compliance limitations • 152

Identifying user activities reported by Microsoft Purview Activity Explorer 152

Audit-derived activity events • 153

User interactions with data • 154

Activity events: users, actions, and context • 154

Activity timelines for investigation • 154

Event-level activity compared to aggregated data insights • 155

Activity Explorer limitations • 155

Discovering and managing AI Activity by using DSPM for AI 155

Data exposure from AI access • 157

AI access to data through existing permissions • 157

Exposure risk from classification and access • 157

AI exposure scenarios for sensitive data • 158

Governance through classification and access • 158

DSPM limitations • 159

Searching data using content search in Microsoft Purview eDiscovery 159

Query-based data retrieval across Microsoft 365 • 160

Filtering using keywords, locations, and conditions • 161

Indexed data in Microsoft 365 services • 161

Content retrieval to support investigation workflows • 161

Item-level retrieval compared to aggregated insights • 162

Content Search limitations • 162

Summary 162

Microsoft Learn reference links 163

Key terms and acronyms 165

Exam readiness drill – chapter review questions 168

Link to this chapter's quiz • 169

Chapter 7: Identifying and Monitoring Oversharing in SharePoint in Microsoft 365 171

Understanding oversharing risks in SharePoint 172

What oversharing means in SharePoint environments • 173

Common oversharing scenarios and business risks • 174

Identifying the tools to troubleshoot oversharing in an organization 175

Sharing reports in Microsoft 365 and SharePoint • 176

Auditing and monitoring sharing activity • 176

Running a data access governance report in SharePoint 177

Understanding Data Access Governance (DAG) reports • 178

Using DAG reports to identify and remediate risky sites • 179

Understanding the features and capabilities of SharePoint Advanced Management (including restricted access control) 180

Overview of SharePoint Advanced Management • 181

Summary 182

Microsoft Learn reference links 183

Key terms and acronyms 185

Exam readiness drill – chapter review questions 186

Link to this chapter's quiz • 187

Chapter 8: Understanding Features and Capabilities of Copilot and Agents 189

Comparing built-in capabilities of Copilot and Agents 190

Copilot and agent limitations • 190

Comparing Copilot's monthly licensing and pay-as-you-go 191

Licensing model limitations • 191

Identifying Copilot features that can be enabled or disabled 192

User-level access assignment controlling Copilot availability • 192

Service-level enablement controlling where Copilot is active • 192

Environment-wide compared to service-level control scope • 193

Copilot control limitations • 193

Identifying use cases for Researcher 193

Multi-source content aggregation • 194

Cross-source content synthesis • 194

Exploratory Research Scenarios • 194

Structured output generation • 194

Researcher limitations • 195

Identifying use cases for Analysts 195

Structured dataset analysis • 196

Pattern, trend, and anomaly detection • 196

Data-driven insight generation • 196

Multi-source dataset handling • 196

Analyst limitations • 197

Identifying use cases for custom agents 197

Execution of predefined workflows • 198

Automation of repetitive tasks • 199

Continued task execution beyond the initial trigger • 199

Application of custom business logic • 199

Custom agent limitations • 199

Summary **200**
Microsoft Learn reference links **200**
Key terms and acronyms **202**
Exam readiness drill – chapter review questions **204**
Link to this chapter's quiz • 205

Chapter 9: Performing Basic Administrative Tasks for Copilot 207

Assigning Copilot licenses **208**
License assignment as the control for Copilot access • 208
Individual license assignment behavior • 209
Group-based license assignment and inheritance behavior • 209
Copilot licensing limitations • 209
Monitoring and managing pay-as-you-go billing policies **210**
Pay-as-you-go: a consumption-based billing model • 210
Usage-driven cost behavior in pay-as-you-go • 211
Billing policy controls for pay-as-you-go usage • 211
Pay-as-you-go billing limitations • 211
Monitoring Copilot usage and adoption **212**
Enabled and active users as core adoption metrics • 212
Usage analysis across users, applications, and time • 212
Monitoring surfaces for Copilot usage visibility • 213
Copilot Analytics for feature-level insights • 213
Copilot usage monitoring limitations • 214
Managing prompts in Copilot **214**
Prompt lifecycle management • 215
Risks from prompt sharing and repeated execution • 215
Governance controls for prompt lifecycle management • 215
Prompt management limitations • 216
Summary **216**
Microsoft Learn reference links **216**
Key terms and acronyms **218**
Exam readiness drill – chapter review questions **219**

Link to this chapter's quiz • 220

Chapter 10: Performing Basic Administrative Tasks for Agents 221

Identifying how to configure user access to agents 222

Licensing controls access to agents • 223

Role assignment controls agent management permissions • 223

The environment defines agent scope and data access • 223

Combined licensing and role requirements for agent access • 224

Agent access limitations • 224

Creating an agent 224

Instructions define agent behavior • 225

Configuration defines agent structure and capabilities • 225

Creation methods define how agents are instantiated • 225

Knowledge sources ground agent responses • 226

Testing validates behavior and knowledge before deployment • 226

Editing modifies the agent and resharing controls visibility • 226

Agent creation limitations • 227

Understanding the agent approval process 227

Governance defines approval criteria • 227

Approval controls release, not build or access • 228

Approval transitions to monitoring after deployment • 228

Monitoring agents using admin center 228

Monitoring begins after deployment • 229

Usage monitoring tracks adoption and interactions • 229

Operational monitoring evaluates performance and reliability • 230

Lifecycle monitoring manages agents over time • 230

Monitoring identifies drift, risks, and resource impact • 230

Agent monitoring limitations • 231

Summary 231

Microsoft Learn reference links 231

Key terms and acronyms 233

Exam readiness drill – chapter review questions 235

Link to this chapter's quiz • 236

Chapter 11: Unlock Your Exclusive Benefits 237

Unlock this Book's Free Benefits in 3 Easy Steps.......... 238

Other Books You May Enjoy 242

Index 247

Preface

Microsoft 365 Copilot and agents are changing how organizations work with Microsoft 365 data, apps, and business processes. Rather than treating AI as a separate tool, Microsoft 365 brings AI into the services people already use every day, including Teams, Outlook, Word, Excel, SharePoint, and Microsoft 365 Copilot Chat. This creates new opportunities for productivity, automation, and insight, but it also introduces new responsibilities around identity, data access, security, governance, and administration.

This book provides a practical introduction to the Microsoft 365 and Copilot fundamentals covered by the AB-900 exam. It explains the core objects and services in Microsoft 365, the security and identity principles that protect them, and the administrative tasks needed to manage Copilot and agents safely. It also explores how Microsoft Purview, Microsoft Defender, SharePoint, Teams, Exchange, and Microsoft Entra support secure and governed AI adoption.

The book is structured to build from Microsoft 365 foundations through to Copilot and agent administration. You will first learn how Microsoft 365 tenants, users, groups, licenses, and workloads are organized. You will then explore security principles, identity controls, data protection, oversharing risks, Copilot capabilities, agent features, usage monitoring, pay-as-you-go billing, prompt management, and agent lifecycle administration.

Who this book is for

This book is written for learners preparing for the AB-900: Copilot and Agent Administration Fundamentals exam. It is designed as an exam study guide for readers who need to understand the Microsoft 365 services, identity concepts, security principles, governance features, Copilot capabilities, and agent administration topics covered by the AB-900 Skills Measured.

Readers do not need deep technical experience, but basic familiarity with Microsoft 365 services such as Teams, SharePoint, Exchange, and Microsoft Entra will help them connect the exam concepts to real administrative scenarios.

What this book covers

- *Chapter 1, Identifying the Core Features and Objects of Microsoft 365 Services*, introduces Microsoft 365 tenants, users, groups, licenses, organization settings, and core workload objects

- *Chapter 2, Understanding Microsoft 365 Security Principles*, explains Zero Trust, authentication, authorization, threat protection, threat intelligence, and Microsoft Defender XDR
- *Chapter 3, Identifying Core Security Features of Microsoft 365 Services*, covers Microsoft Entra features, Conditional Access, security objects, sign-in troubleshooting, audit logs, PIM, and app registrations
- *Chapter 4, Understanding Microsoft Purview*, introduces Microsoft Purview capabilities for information protection, DLP, insider risk, communication compliance, and compliance management
- *Chapter 5, Understanding Data Security Implications of Copilot*, explains how Copilot uses Microsoft 365 data and how permissions, security, governance, and Responsible AI controls affect Copilot responses
- *Chapter 6, Identifying Data Protection and Governance Risks for Microsoft 365 and Copilot*, goes into data classification, DLP, Activity Explorer, eDiscovery Content Search, DSPM for AI, and governance risks across Microsoft 365
- *Chapter 7, Identifying and Monitoring Oversharing in SharePoint in Microsoft 365*, explains how oversharing occurs in SharePoint and how reports, access governance, and SharePoint controls help reduce risk
- *Chapter 8, Understanding Features and Capabilities of Copilot and Agents*, explores Copilot and agents, licensing models, feature controls, Researcher, Analyst, and custom agent use cases
- *Chapter 9, Performing Basic Administrative Tasks for Copilot*, covers Copilot licensing, usage monitoring, pay-as-you-go billing, adoption reporting, prompt management, and scheduled prompts
- *Chapter 10, Performing Basic Administrative Tasks for Agents*, explains user access, agent creation, approval processes, monitoring, and lifecycle management for agents

To get the most out of this book

To get the most out of this book, you should have a basic familiarity with Microsoft 365 services such as Teams, SharePoint, Exchange, and Microsoft Entra. You do not need prior experience administering Microsoft 365 Copilot or agents, as the book introduces the core concepts from the ground up.

This book is designed as an AB-900 exam study guide, so it is useful to read each chapter alongside the AB-900 Skills Measured and use the review questions, exam tips, flashcards, and mock exam content to check your understanding as you progress.

Download the color images

We also provide a PDF file that has color images of the screenshots/diagrams used in this book. You can download it here:`https://packt.link/gbp/9781807306519`.

Conventions used

`CodeInText`: Indicates code words in text, database table names, folder names, filenames, file extensions, pathnames, dummy URLs, user input, and Twitter handles. For example: "For example, instead of users signing in as `user@tenantname.onmicrosoft.com`, a custom domain enables sign-in and email addresses such as `user@contoso.com`."

Bold: Indicates a new term, an important word, or words that you see on the screen. For instance, words in menus or dialog boxes appear in the text like this. For example: "The **Microsoft Teams admin center** provides the administrative control surface for Microsoft Teams."

> **Note**
>
> Warnings or important notes appear like this.

> **Tip**
>
> Tips and tricks appear like this.

Get in touch

Feedback from our readers is always welcome.

General feedback: If you have questions about any aspect of this book or have any general feedback, please email us at `customercare@packt.com` and mention the book's title in the subject of your message.

Errata: Although we have taken every care to ensure the accuracy of our content, mistakes do happen. If you have found a mistake in this book, we would be grateful if you reported this to us. Please visit `http://www.packt.com/submit-errata`, click **Submit Errata**, and fill in the form.

Piracy: If you come across any illegal copies of our works in any form on the internet, we would be grateful if you would provide us with the location address or website name. Please contact us at `copyright@packt.com` with a link to the material.

If you are interested in becoming an author: If there is a topic that you have expertise in and you are interested in either writing or contributing to a book, please visit `http://authors.packt.com/`.

Free benefits with your book

This book comes with free benefits to support your learning. Activate them now for instant access (see the "*How to Unlock*" section for instructions).

Here's a quick overview of what you can instantly unlock with your purchase:

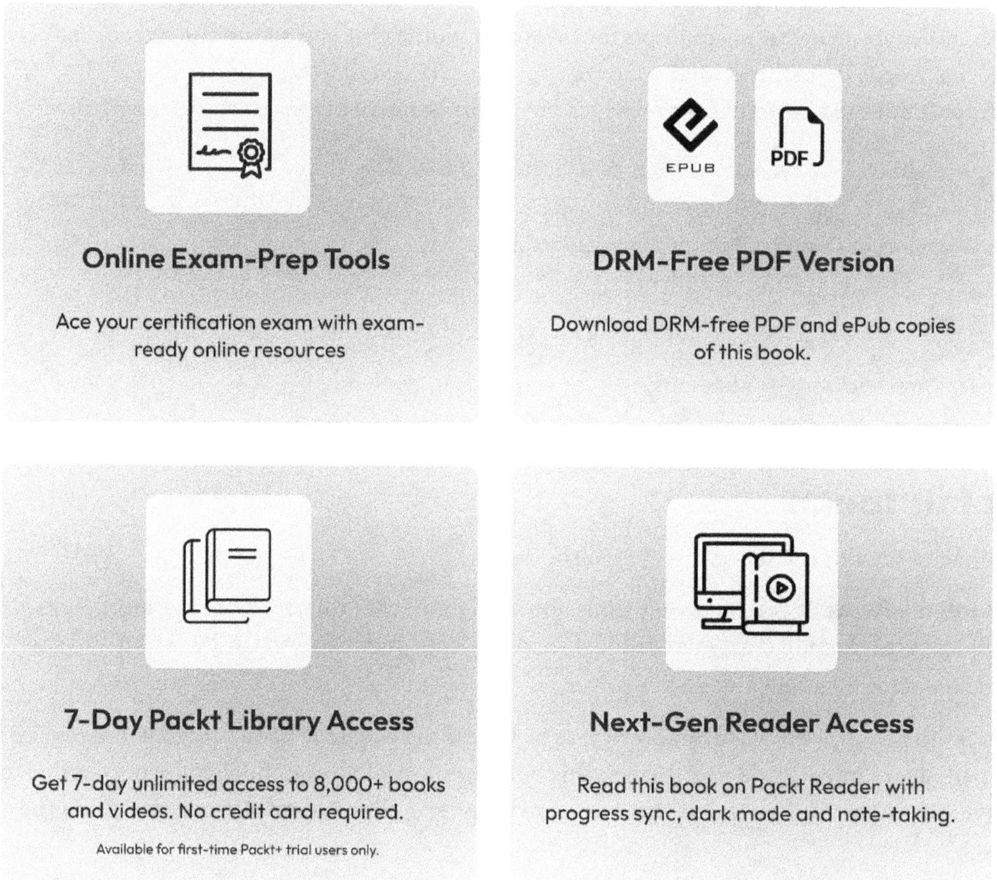

How to Unlock

Scan the QR code (or go to `packtpub.com/unlock`). Search for this book by name, confirm the edition, and then follow the steps on the page.

UNLOCK NOW

Note: Keep your invoice handy. Purchases made directly from Packt don't require one.

Join Packt | Future of Work Collective on Discord

Read, learn, and grow together with fellow readers and professionals.

- Discuss ideas and ask questions
- Share insights and resources
- Prepare for certifications
- Connect with experts and peers
- Learn, build, and innovate together

Scan the QR code or visit the link below to join the community.

`https://packt.link/Sqllw`

Exploring Copilot, AI Agents, Microsoft 365, Azure, and the future of work.

Share your thoughts

Once you've read *Microsoft 365 Copilot and Agent Administration Fundamentals*, we'd love to hear your thoughts! Scan the QR code below to go straight to the Amazon review page for this book and share your feedback.

`https://packt.link/r/1807306518`

Your review is important to us and the tech community and will help us make sure we're delivering excellent quality content.

1

Identifying the Core Features and Objects of Microsoft 365 Services

Microsoft 365 includes a range of services that help people communicate, collaborate, and get work done.

Behind these services are key settings and administrative objects that determine *who* can use them and *how* they behave. Understanding these basics is important, whether you are new to Microsoft 365 or supporting others who use it.

In this chapter, we will explore the core features and objects that shape how Microsoft 365 works. Rather than focusing on technical configuration steps, the goal is to build a clear understanding of how access is granted and how the main services are structured across a tenant.

This content primarily focuses on the **Identify the core features and objects of Microsoft 365 services** module from the *Skills Measured* section of the **AB-900** exam.

By the end of this chapter, you will be able to answer questions on the following topics:

- Explain how licensing affects access to Microsoft 365 features
- Explore organization configuration in the Microsoft 365 admin center
- Identify configuration objects in the Exchange Online admin center
- Identify configuration objects in the SharePoint admin center
- Identify SharePoint site roles and permissions
- Identify configuration objects in the Teams admin center

Together, these topics help you understand how **Microsoft 365** is organized and how access to its services is managed. We begin with **licensing** because it determines which features and services a user can use before anything else is configured.

Note

Free Benefits with Your Book

Your purchase includes a free PDF copy of this book along with access to an online cert prep platform designed to help you ace your **AB-900** certification. Check the *Free Benefits with Your Book* section in the *Preface* to unlock them instantly and maximize your learning experience.

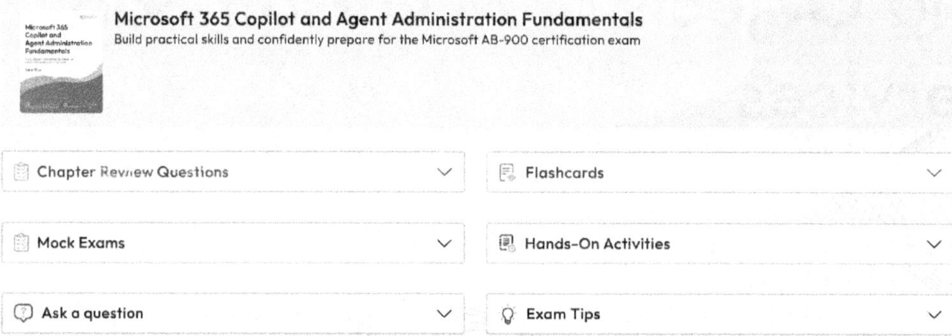

Dashboard interface of the online practice resources

Here's what you'll find on the online platform:

- 3 Mock Exams (40 questions each)
- 50 Flashcards
- 30 Exam Tips
- Hands-on Activities
- 100 Chapter Review Questions

Note

Important information regarding Microsoft Portal experiences and UI elements

Microsoft frequently updates portal experiences and UI elements. As a result, some screenshots, navigation paths, or interface details shown in this book may differ slightly from your individual tenant's environment at the time of reading.

Explaining how licensing affects access to Microsoft 365 features

Licensing in Microsoft 365 determines *which services* a user can access in a Microsoft 365 tenant; Microsoft sometimes refers to these services as **workloads**.

A user account can exist *without* a license, but access to services such as **Exchange Online**, **SharePoint Online**, **Microsoft Teams**, and so on, as well as advanced features in services such as **Entra ID**, begins only after *license assignment.*

The following methodology and hierarchy are adopted within a tenant:

- License assignment
- Services accessed and features enabled
- The organization can use those features

A license grants entitlement to use a service and access features; it *does not* configure how services or features are administered.

Identifying user-based and group-based license assignment

Licenses can be assigned directly to individual users or assigned to groups.

A *direct user assignment* gives one user entitlement to the workloads included in the license. A *group-based assignment* gives entitlement to members of the assigned group.

When a user is added to a licensed group, they inherit the license automatically. When the user is removed from that group, the inherited license is removed. The user account remains in the tenant; only the license entitlement changes.

In the **Microsoft 365 admin center** experience, **license assignments** are reviewed from **Billing** | **Licenses** by selecting the product license. The assignment view can show both *direct user assignments* and *group-based assignments* together. *User entries* represent individual license assignments, while *group entries* represent licenses assigned through group membership.

Figure 1.1 shows **Microsoft 365 Copilot** license assignments in the Microsoft 365 admin center, where user and group assignment types appear in the same license view in the updated UI experience.

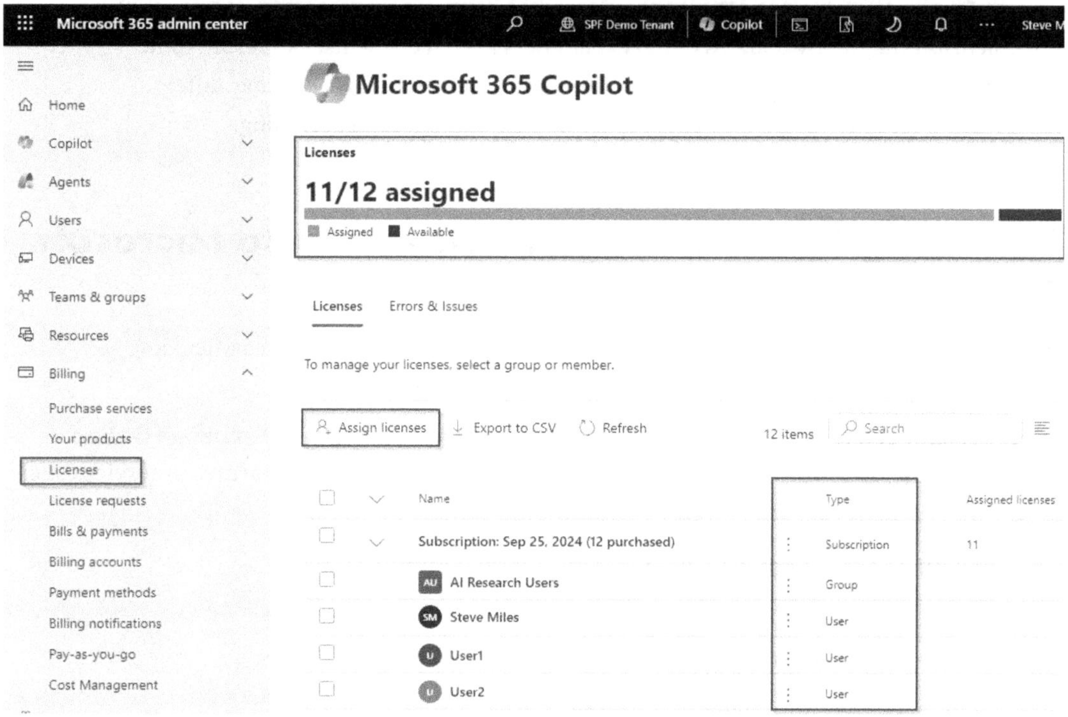

Figure 1.1: Direct license assignment in the Microsoft 365 admin center

Direct license assignment is typically used when managing a small number of users or when exceptions are required for specific individuals. It provides precise control but can become difficult to manage at scale.

Group-based licensing changes how licenses are applied, not what they contain. Entitlement still depends on the license's service plans. The difference lies in centralized management through group membership rather than individual assignment.

The following table provides a comparison of these license assignment types:

Direct assignment	Group-based assignment
Assigned to an individual user	Assigned to a group
Managed one user at a time	Managed by membership
Useful for special cases	Useful for standard roles
Becomes harder to manage at scale	Works better as the environment grows

Table 1.1: License assignment types

While the assignment method determines how a license is applied, it does not change what the license includes. Whether assigned directly to a **user** or through a **group**, access still depends on the components inside the license itself. To understand what services a user can actually use, we now need to look at the service plans that make up each license.

Identifying license components that affect service access

Each **Microsoft 365 license** contains multiple **service plans**.

A **service plan** represents an individual component within a broader license. A service plan corresponds to a specific service or feature. For example, a license may include service plans for **Exchange Online**, **SharePoint Online**, and **Microsoft Teams**, or a feature capability in a service such as **Entra ID**.

The apps and services included in a license can be turned **on** or **off** for a user within the license assignment. Turning **on** a service *allows* the user to access it. Turning **off** a service *removes* user access to that service.

The following figure shows the **apps & services** enabled for **Steve Miles** within a **Microsoft 365 E5** license.

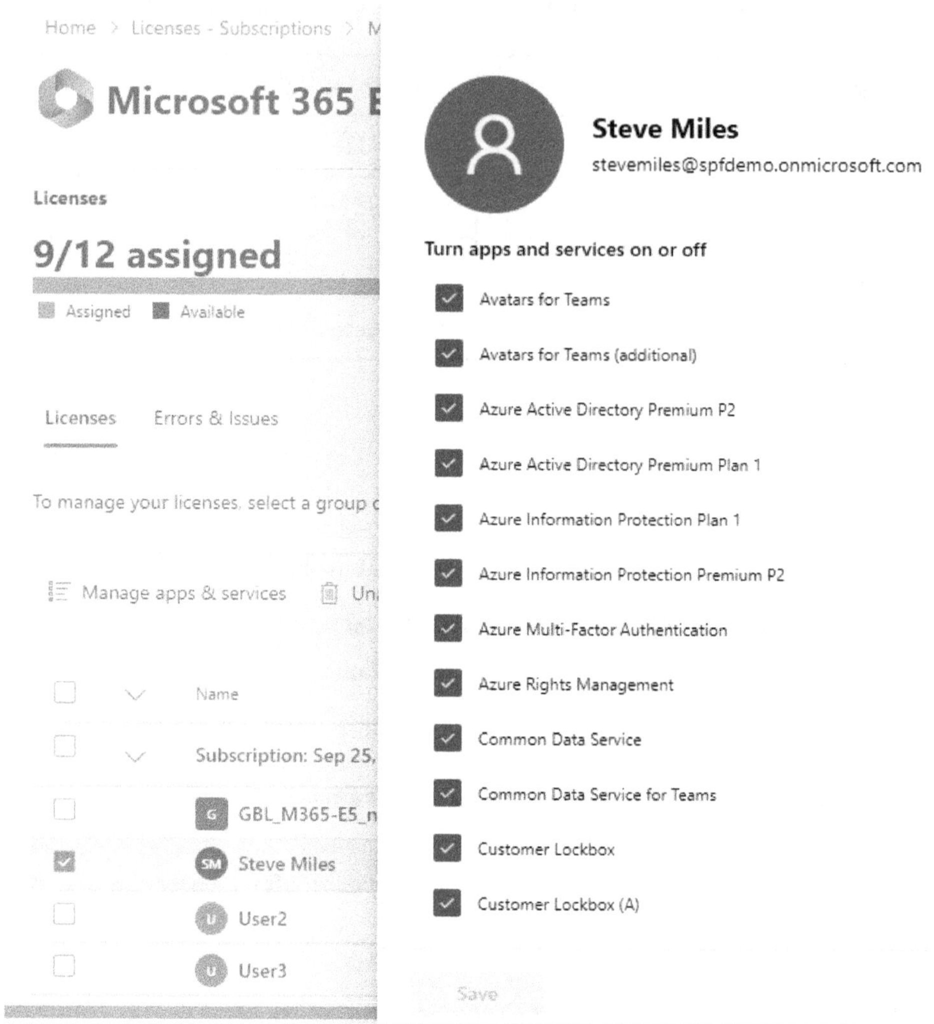

Figure 1.2: Apps and services enabled for a user within a Microsoft 365 E5 license

A service plan determines whether a user can access a service; it does not configure how that service operates. Administrative settings for mail flow, sharing policies, or meeting behavior are managed separately within their respective admin centers.

Exploring organization configuration in the Microsoft 365 admin center

The **Microsoft 365 admin center** provides centralized access to organization-level configuration settings.

Through this portal, administrators manage users, domains, licenses, billing, service health, Copilot, and agent-related administration across the tenant.

Understanding how these configurations relate to the tenant model is essential before exploring individual workload admin centers and service-specific portals.

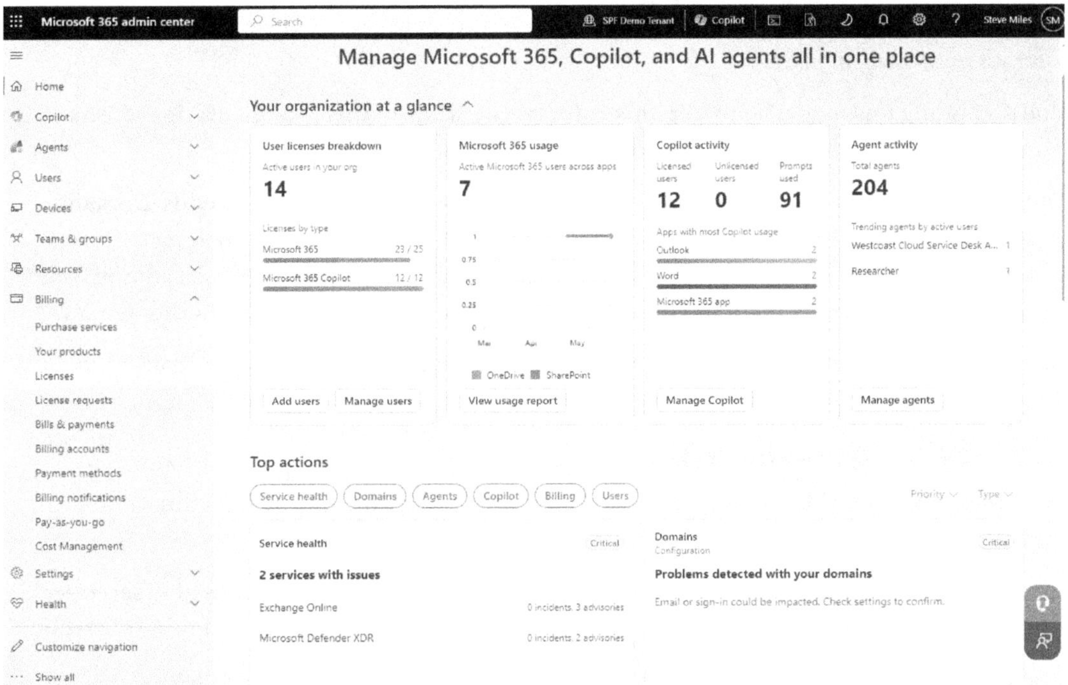

Figure 1.3: Microsoft 365 admin center dashboard

A **Microsoft 365 tenant** represents a *dedicated instance* of **Microsoft 365 services** for an organization. It is the organization's *private space* in **Microsoft 365**.

The **Microsoft 365 tenant** defines the *boundary* of your organization. Everything inside that tenant belongs to your organization, including users, groups, domains, licenses, services, Copilot settings, and agent-related administration.

All configuration settings, licensing decisions, and service controls operate inside this boundary. Each tenant is *logically isolated* from other tenants, meaning configuration changes apply only within that organization's environment.

Identifying the Microsoft 365 tenant model

The **Microsoft 365 tenant** functions as the **organizational container** for identity and service configuration. It contains user accounts, security groups, domains, and workload services such as **Exchange Online**, **SharePoint Online**, and **Microsoft Teams**. When administrators configure settings in the **Microsoft 365 admin center**, those changes are made within the scope of the **tenant**.

Tenant-level settings apply broadly across the organization unless explicitly scoped otherwise. For example, enabling or restricting a feature at the tenant level may influence *all users, all sites,* or *all mailboxes.*

Understanding this model helps administrators recognize whether a configuration affects a single user account, a specific workload, or the entire organization.

The tenant boundary defines where Microsoft 365 administration starts and ends. Domains, Microsoft 365 subscriptions, licenses, users, groups, and workload services belong to that tenant, and administrative roles only grant control within that environment. An administrator assigned a role in one tenant does not automatically receive permissions in another tenant.

Once this boundary is understood, it becomes easier to evaluate how identity namespaces and domain configuration influence service access within the tenant.

Identifying domain types

Domains define how identities and services are presented within and outside the organization.

A **domain** forms part of a *user's sign-in name* and *email address* and determines how services such as Exchange Online route mail.

Domains exist inside the Microsoft 365 tenant and are managed at the tenant level.

There are two primary domain types that administrators must understand:

- The default tenant domain
- Custom domains added by the organization

Each serves a distinct purpose. The **default domain** is created automatically during tenant provisioning, while **custom domains** allow the organization to align Microsoft 365 services with its public identity.

Figure 1.4 shows the **Domains** page in the **Microsoft 365 admin center**, where both *default* and *custom domains* are listed and managed.

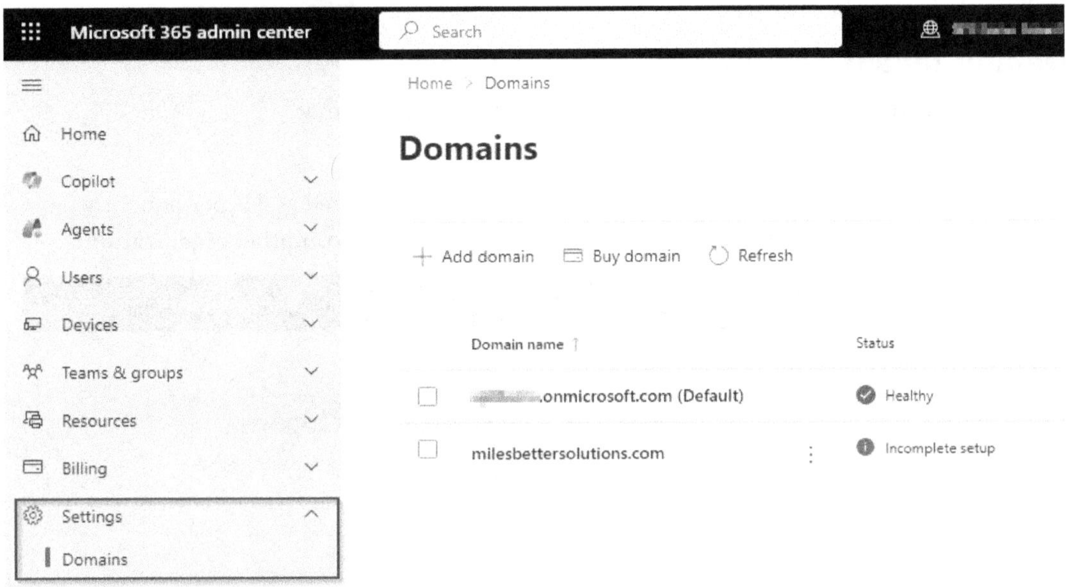

Figure 1.4: Domains page in the Microsoft 365 admin center showing default and custom domains

Understanding the differences between these domain types is essential before configuring identity or service routing.

Default Domain	**Custom Domain**
Created automatically when the tenant is set up	Added by the organization
Stays with the tenant; cannot be removed	Can be added or removed
Uses the onmicrosoft.com name (for example, *contoso.onmicrosoft.com*)	Uses your company's domain name (for example, *contoso.com*)
Always available, ready to use	Must be verified before use

Table 1.2: Default versus Custom Domains

The comparison highlights how default and custom domains differ in purpose and setup. Domain configuration in every Microsoft 365 tenant begins with the default tenant domain and its role within the organization.

Default tenant domain

Every **Microsoft 365 tenant** includes a **default domain** in the format `tenantname.onmicrosoft.com`.

This domain is created automatically when the tenant is provisioned and is permanently associated with that tenant. It cannot be removed or transferred to another organization.

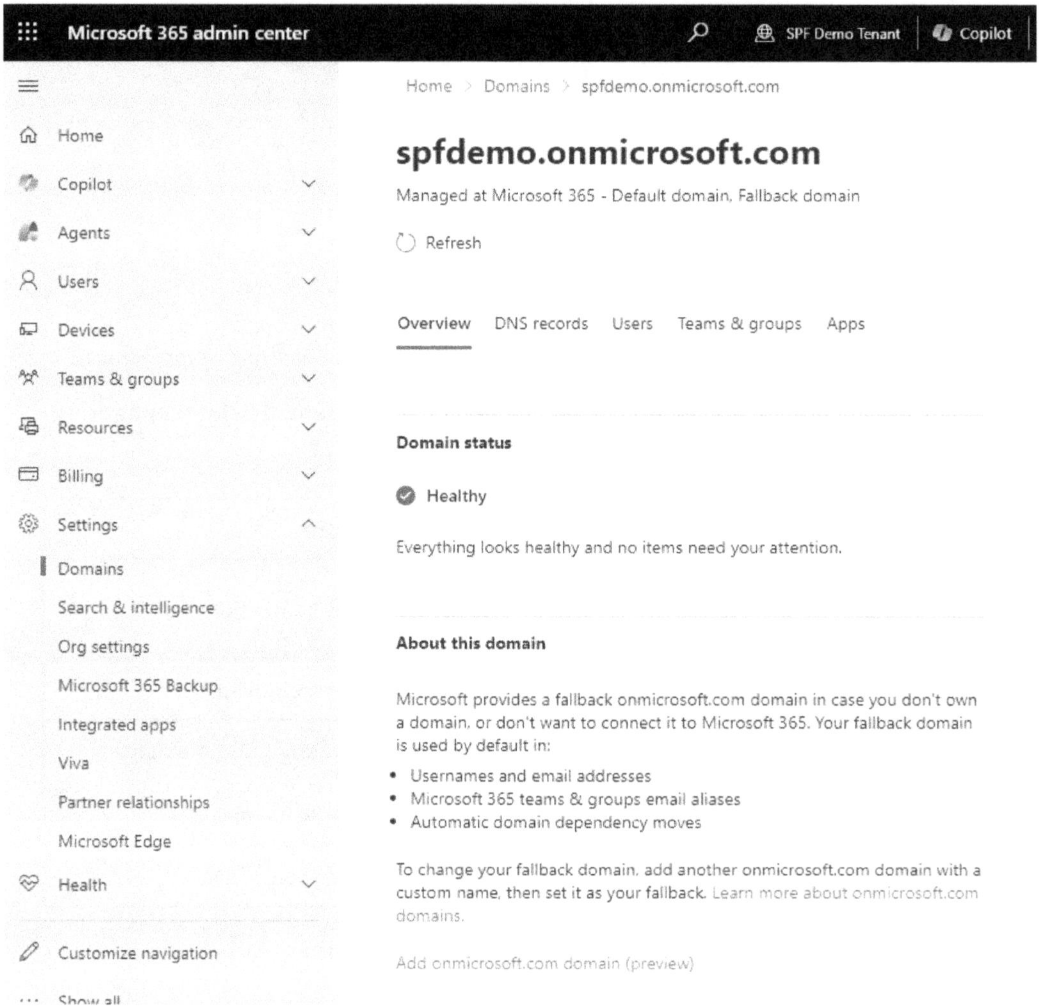

Figure 1.5: Default tenant domain in M365 admin center

The default domain enables administrators to begin creating user accounts and configuring services immediately. User accounts created during initial setup typically use this default namespace. Even when custom domains are later added, the default domain remains available for identity and administrative purposes.

The default domain also ensures continuity. Because it is system-generated and tied directly to the tenant, it provides a fallback identity namespace that remains functional regardless of changes to custom domain configuration. While organizations commonly prefer to use custom domains for email and sign-in names, the default tenant domain remains an integral part of the tenant's identity structure.

Custom domains, verification, and DNS records

Custom domains allows an organization to align Microsoft 365 services with its public identity.

For example, instead of users signing in as `user@tenantname.onmicrosoft.com`, a custom domain enables sign-in and email addresses such as `user@contoso.com`. This alignment is essential for branding, trust, and external communication.

Before a custom domain can be used, **ownership** must be **verified**.

Domain verification confirms that the organization controls the public DNS namespace. This prevents unauthorized use of a domain within Microsoft 365. Verification typically involves adding a temporary DNS record to the domain registrar, which Microsoft checks to confirm ownership.

Domain verification confirms that your organization owns the **domain name** (*the namespace*), but it does not enable service (workload) functionality. In exam questions, this is referred to as domain verification.

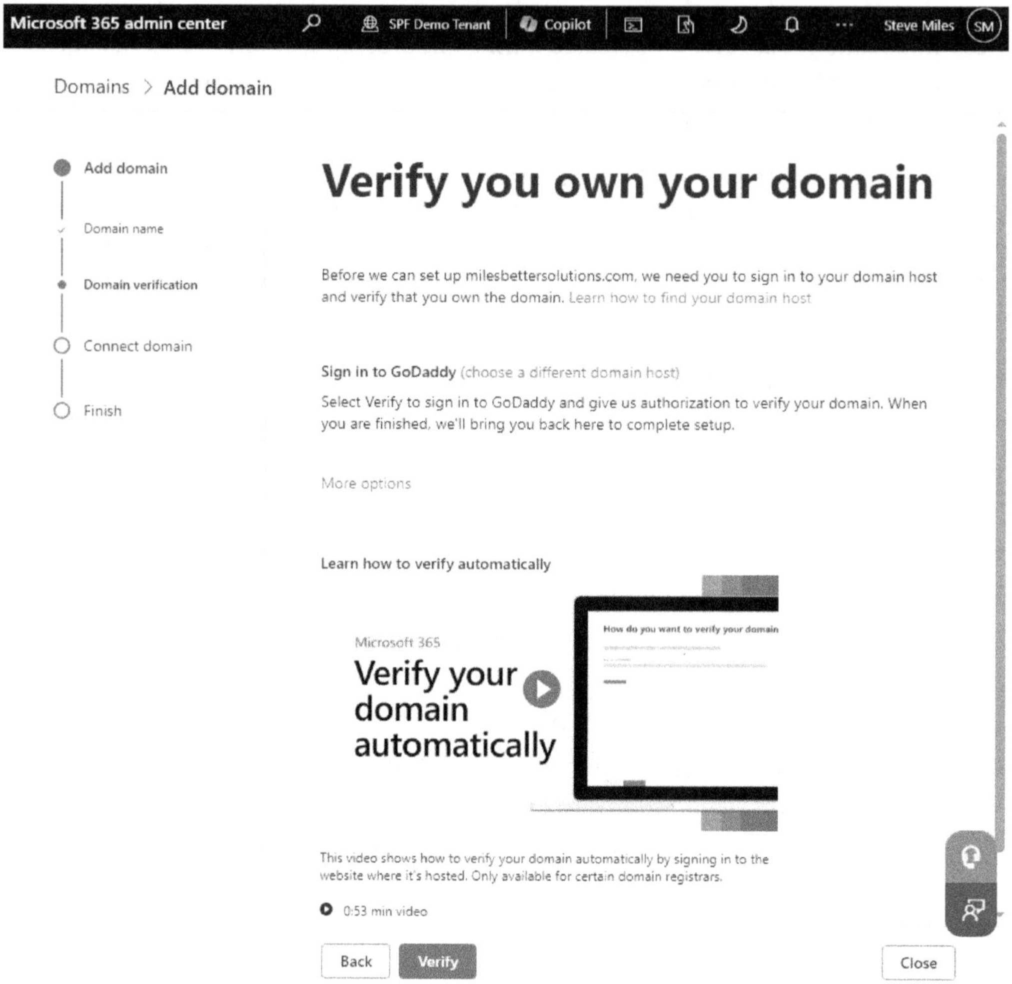

Figure 1.6: Domain verification

After verification, **DNS records** must be configured to support services. For example, Exchange Online requires an **MX record** to route email to Microsoft 365.

Additional records may be required to support identity validation or other services. Without proper DNS configuration, services may not function correctly even though the domain is verified.

Once verified and configured, a custom domain can be set as the primary domain for user sign-in and email addresses. Users, groups, and mail-enabled objects can then use this domain as part of their identity. However, all domains—default and custom—remain associated with the same Microsoft 365 tenant and are governed within that administrative boundary.

With domain verification and configuration in place, the focus now shifts to the default tenant domain and how it is used across Microsoft 365 services.

Identifying organization-wide settings

The Microsoft 365 admin center includes organization-wide settings that apply across the Microsoft 365 tenant.

These settings define how the organization is represented and how services behave at a broad level. Unlike workload-specific configuration performed in Exchange, SharePoint, or Teams admin centers, organization-wide settings affect the tenant as a whole.

Because these settings apply broadly, administrators must understand their scope before making changes. A tenant-wide configuration can influence user experience, collaboration boundaries, and external interaction across multiple services simultaneously.

Organization profile settings

Organization profile settings include tenant-level information such as the organization name, address, contact details, and other identifying attributes.

These values define how the tenant is represented within Microsoft 365 services and administrative interfaces.

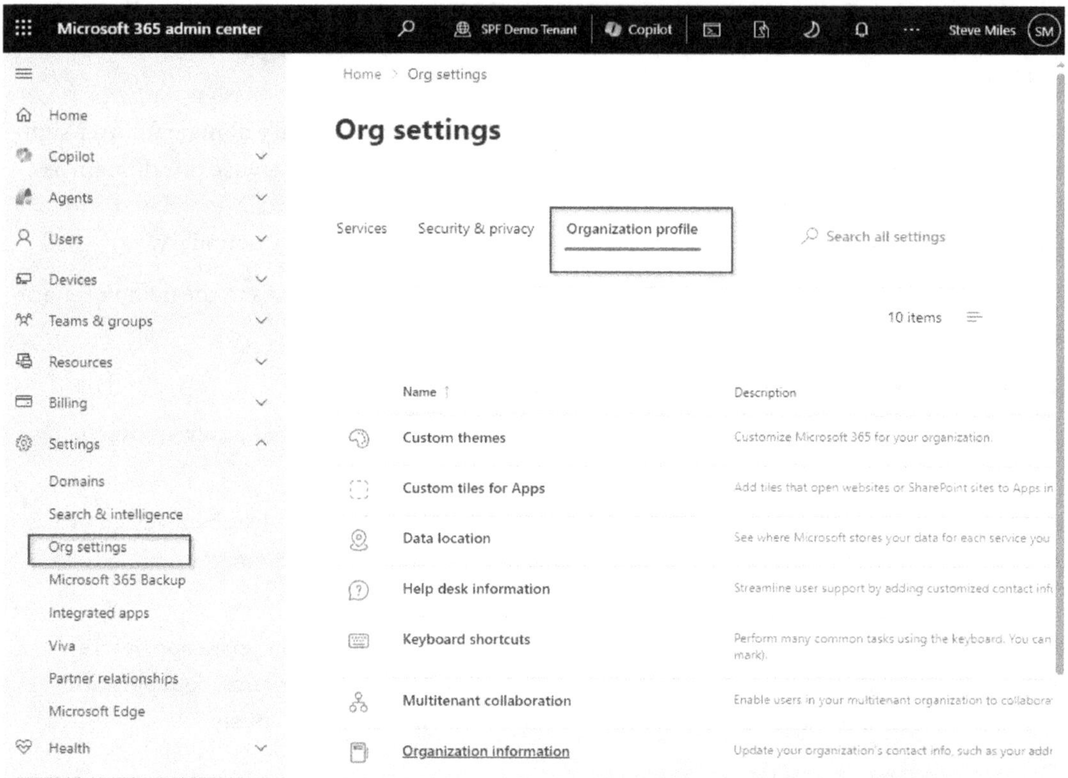

Figure 1.7: Organization profile settings

Although organization profile settings do not control service functionality, they establish the organization identity context of the tenant. This information may appear in service communications, directory views, or administrative reports. These settings apply consistently across the tenant rather than being scoped to a specific workload or user account.

Tenant-wide access and sharing settings

Tenant-wide access and sharing settings control broad collaboration behaviors across Microsoft 365 services.

Examples include policies that influence external sharing and guest access. These configurations determine whether users can collaborate with external identities and how broadly content may be shared.

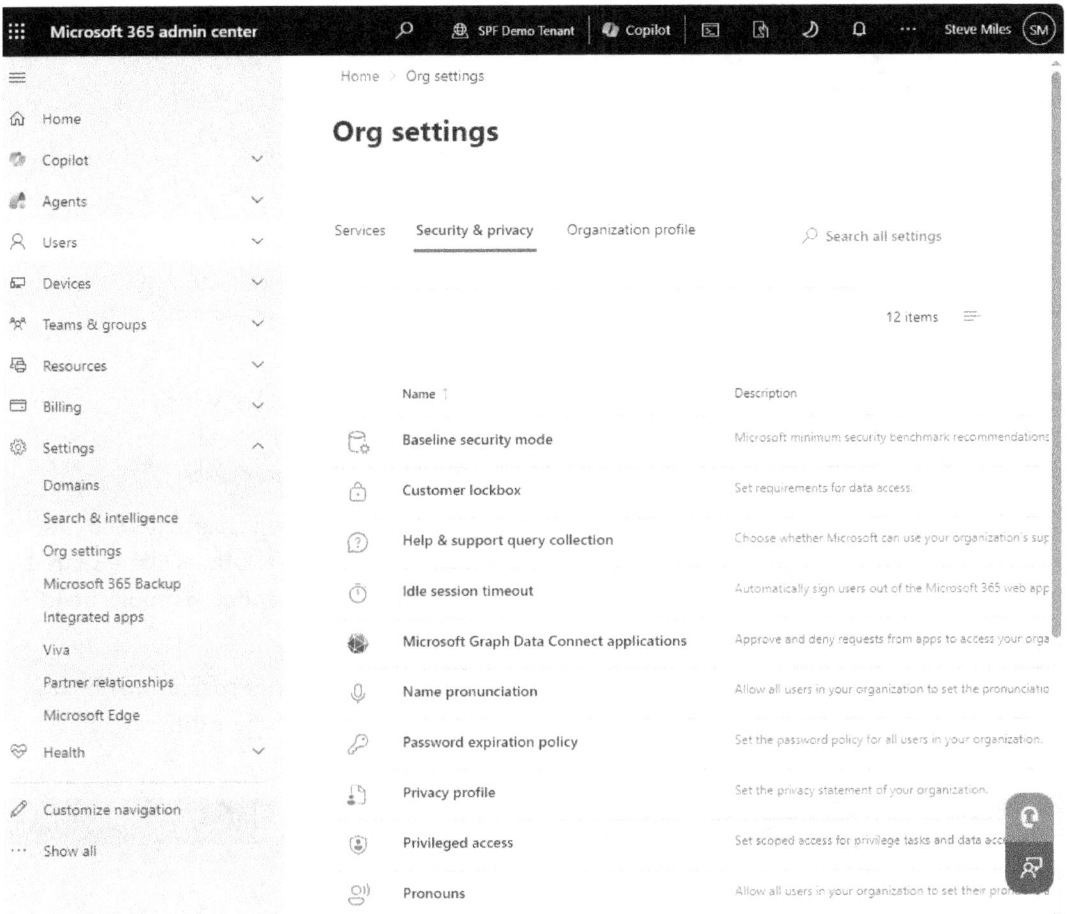

Figure 1.8: Tenant-wide security and privacy settings

Because these settings operate at the tenant level, they affect all relevant users and services rather than a single user, SharePoint site, mailbox, or team. Adjusting tenant-wide controls influences collaboration patterns across the organization. Administrators must recognize that these configurations define the outer boundary of collaboration within the tenant, not just isolated service behavior.

With tenant-wide configuration in place, we now move into configuring specific objects within services, starting with Exchange Online.

Identifying configuration objects in the Exchange Online admin center

The Exchange Online admin center is used to manage mail-enabled objects within Microsoft 365.

These objects define how email is stored, accessed, and distributed across the organization. Unlike tenant-wide configuration performed in the Microsoft 365 admin center, Exchange administration focuses on creating and managing specific mail-related objects inside the tenant.

The Exchange Online admin center is also used to configure mail flow rules, which control how messages are evaluated and handled as they pass through Exchange Online. License assignment and custom domain setup remain Microsoft 365 admin center tasks.

In Exchange Online, you work with different object types. Each object type has a defined purpose and behavior. Some objects are tied to individual user identities. Others allow shared access by multiple users. Some represent non-person resources such as rooms or equipment. Others distribute messages to multiple recipients without storing mail.

The Exchange Online admin center organizes these objects into categories such as mailboxes and groups. Understanding this layout helps administrators recognize where different object types are created and managed.

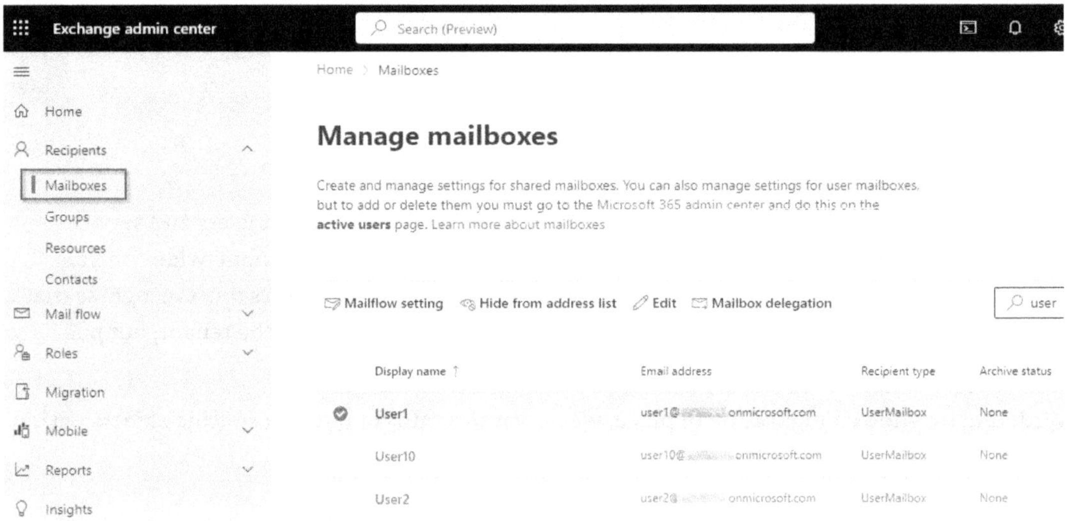

Figure 1.9: Mailbox management in Exchange admin center

Selecting the correct object type is essential because each behaves differently within the Exchange service. A mailbox stores messages and calendar data. A distribution object forwards messages without storing them. A resource object manages scheduling rather than personal correspondence. Although these objects are managed in the same administrative interface, their operational roles are distinct.

Understanding the Exchange object model allows administrators to interpret requirements accurately and choose the appropriate object type before configuration begins. In the following sections, we will examine the primary mailbox and group objects available in Exchange Online and clarify when each should be used.

Exploring mailbox types

Mailbox types define how email data is stored and accessed within Exchange Online. A mailbox is not simply an email address; it is a storage object with defined access and behavioral characteristics.

Selecting the correct mailbox type depends on whether the requirement involves an individual user, collaborative access by multiple users, or the management of a non-person resource such as a room or a piece of equipment.

In Exchange Online, different mailbox types exist because business needs differ. An individual employee requires a personal mailbox tied to their identity. A department may require a shared address accessed by several users. A meeting room requires scheduling capability rather than personal correspondence. Although these objects are all categorized as mailboxes, they are designed for distinct operational purposes.

When evaluating a scenario, administrators must determine whether the mailbox represents a person, a shared function, or a resource. The mailbox type selected affects licensing requirements, access control, and how messages and calendar data are handled. Understanding this distinction ensures that the appropriate mailbox object is chosen before configuration begins.

Let's explore the primary mailbox types available in Exchange Online and clarify when each should be used.

User mailboxes

A **user mailbox** is the standard mailbox type associated with an individual user account in Microsoft 365.

It stores the user's email messages, calendar entries, contacts, tasks, and other mailbox data within Exchange Online. The mailbox is tied directly to a single identity in Microsoft Entra ID and represents that individual's primary email presence within the organization.

A user mailbox is appropriate when the requirement involves a specific person who needs a personal email address and private mailbox storage. The mailbox is accessed by signing in with the associated user account credentials. All messages sent to that address are delivered to the mailbox storage assigned to that identity.

Unlike other mailbox types, a user mailbox is designed for individual ownership. Access permissions are not shared by default. Although additional access can be delegated, the mailbox fundamentally represents one licensed user and one identity.

A user mailbox requires a Microsoft 365 license that includes Exchange Online. Without a valid license assignment, the mailbox cannot be created or activated. The license provides entitlement to the Exchange Online service, and the mailbox becomes operational once licensing is in place.

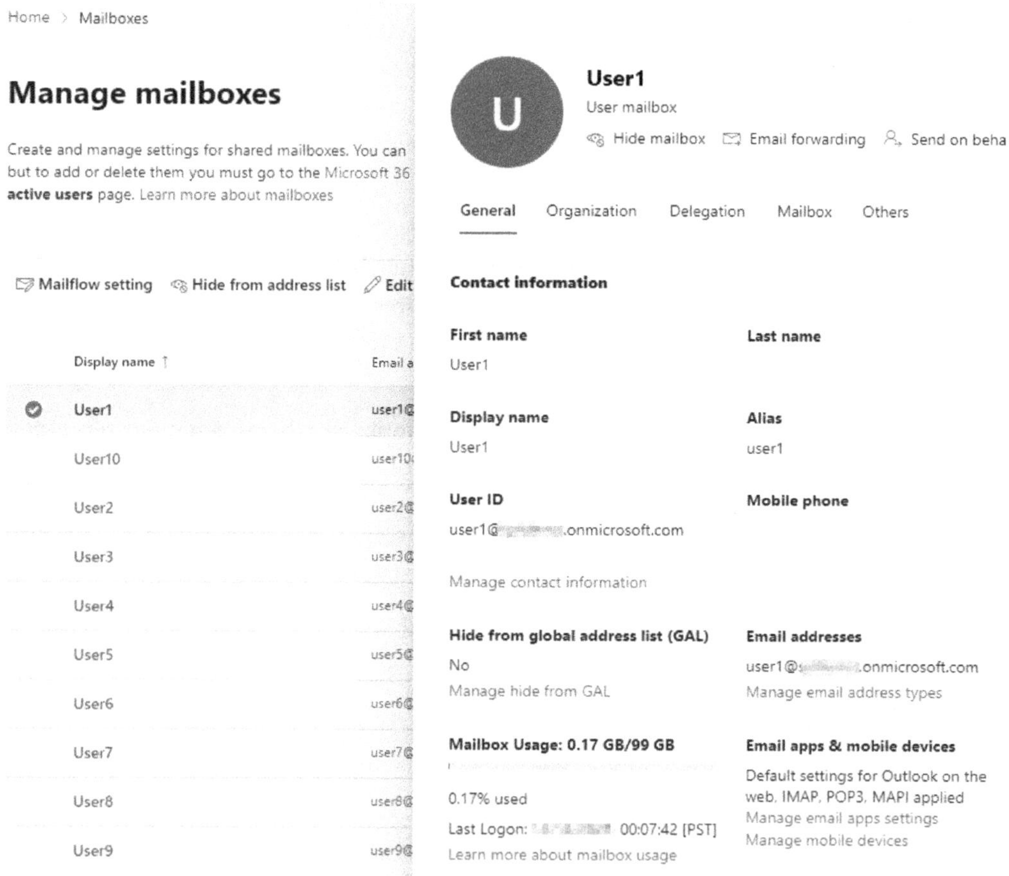

Figure 1.10: A user mailbox linked to a single Microsoft 365 user identity

A user mailbox supports full email functionality, including sending, and receiving messages, managing a personal calendar, and maintaining individual mailbox settings. Because it is identity-based, its access, and functionality depend on the user's assigned license and permissions.

When a scenario describes an individual employee who requires a personal email account and private mailbox storage, a user mailbox is the appropriate object to configure.

Shared mailboxes

A **shared mailbox** is a mailbox designed to allow multiple users to access and manage the same email address and mailbox content.

Unlike a user mailbox, it does not represent an individual identity. Instead, it represents a functional or departmental address that multiple users can access based on granted permissions.

A shared mailbox is appropriate when the requirement involves collaborative access to a common inbox.

For example, a department such as `sales@contoso.com` or `support@contoso.com` may need several employees to read and respond to incoming messages from the same address. The shared mailbox centralizes these messages so that all authorized users can view and manage them.

Access to a shared mailbox is granted to existing user accounts. Users sign in with their own credentials and are then permitted to open the shared mailbox in addition to their personal mailbox. The shared mailbox itself does not function as an independent sign-in identity in the same way as a licensed user mailbox.

A shared mailbox stores email messages and calendar data, similar to a user mailbox. However, it is intended for collective use rather than individual ownership. Because it represents a shared function rather than a person, responsibility for managing messages may be distributed among multiple authorized users.

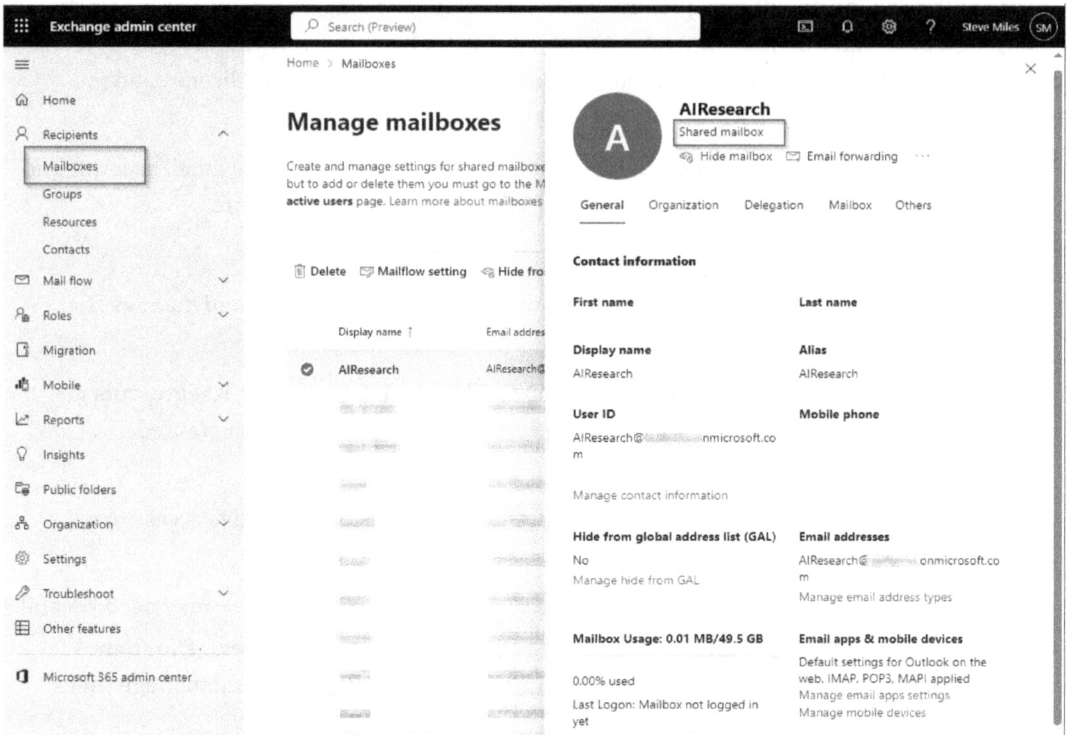

Figure 1.11: Shared mailbox object view in the Exchange admin center

This image should display the shared mailbox object view, clearly indicating the mailbox type and showing the permissions area. It should not show step-by-step configuration. The purpose is to visually reinforce that the mailbox type is defined as "Shared" and that access is permission-based.

When a scenario describes multiple users who must access and respond from the same email address, a shared mailbox is the appropriate object to configure.

Resource mailboxes

A **resource mailbox** represents a non-person entity, such as a meeting room or a piece of equipment.

Unlike user or shared mailboxes, a resource mailbox is not associated with an individual or a functional team inbox. Instead, it is used to manage scheduling availability for physical or shared assets within the organization.

Resource mailboxes are appropriate when the requirement involves reserving a room, booking equipment, or managing availability for a shared resource. Examples include conference rooms, training spaces, vehicles, or specialized equipment that must be scheduled through calendar requests.

A resource mailbox stores calendar data rather than functioning as a traditional personal inbox. When users send meeting requests to the resource mailbox, Exchange Online can automatically accept or decline the request based on availability. This automation allows administrators to manage resource scheduling centrally without requiring a person to monitor the mailbox manually.

Resource mailboxes are categorized as either room mailboxes or equipment mailboxes. Both types function similarly but represent different resource purposes. The mailbox type determines how the resource is presented within scheduling tools.

Figure 1.12: Resource mailbox management in the Exchange admin center

When a scenario describes the need to manage availability for a meeting space or shared asset rather than storing personal or collaborative email, a resource mailbox is the appropriate object to configure.

Comparison

To reinforce the distinctions between mailbox types, the following comparison summarizes their primary purpose and behavioral differences within Exchange Online:

Mailbox Type	Represents	Stores Email	Used For	How Accessed
User Mailbox	One person	Yes	A person's email and calendar	The person signs in to their own account
Shared Mailbox	A team or shared address	Yes	A shared inbox for a group	Access is given to selected users
Resource Mailbox	A room or piece of equipment	Primarily calendar and booking data; not used as a personal or shared inbox	Booking rooms or equipment	Reserved through meeting requests

Table 1.3: Mailbox type comparison

This comparison highlights that although all three are categorized as mailboxes within the Exchange Online admin center, their purpose and access model differ significantly. A user mailbox is identity-based and individually owned. A shared mailbox enables collaborative access to a common inbox. A resource mailbox supports scheduling for non-person entities rather than personal correspondence.

Understanding these distinctions ensures that administrators select the correct mailbox object based on whether the requirement involves individual ownership, shared access, or resource scheduling. With mailbox types clearly defined, the next step is to examine objects that distribute messages without storing them.

Identifying distribution lists

A **distribution list** is a mail-enabled object used to send email to multiple recipients at the same time.

Unlike mailbox objects, a distribution list does not store messages. Instead, it forwards incoming messages to its members based on group membership. The distribution list functions as a delivery mechanism rather than a storage location.

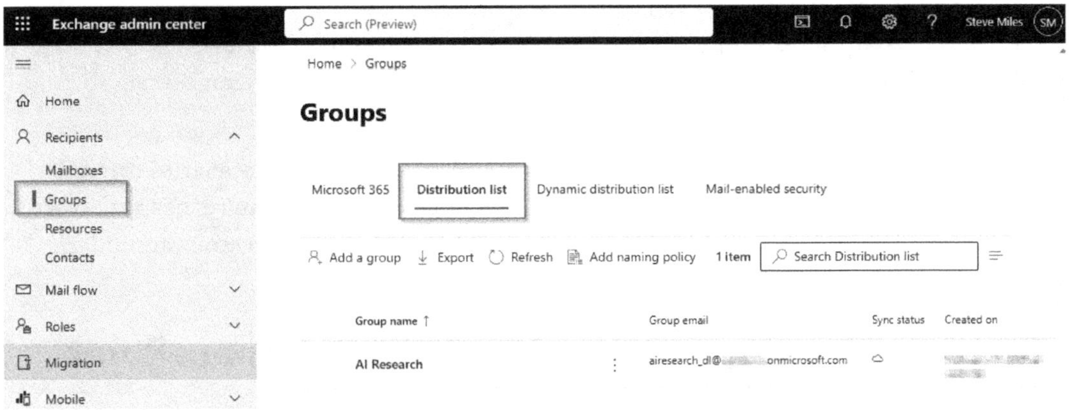

Figure 1.13: Distribution list view in the Exchange admin center

A distribution list is appropriate when the requirement involves sending the same message to multiple recipients without creating a shared inbox. For example, an announcement sent to all members of a department or project team can be delivered through a distribution list. When an email is sent to the list address, Exchange Online delivers a copy of that message to each member's individual mailbox.

Because a distribution list does not have its own mailbox, it cannot be used to store or manage messages centrally. There is no shared inbox to monitor, and users do not sign in to access a distribution list. Its purpose is message distribution, not collaboration through a common mailbox.

This distinction is important when comparing distribution lists to shared mailboxes. A shared mailbox stores messages in one location and allows multiple users to access that mailbox. A distribution list does not store messages; it simply routes them to members. Selecting the correct object depends on whether the requirement involves centralized message storage or simple message delivery to multiple recipients.

A distribution list also differs from Microsoft 365 groups. While both can send emails to multiple members, Microsoft 365 groups include additional collaboration features such as shared mailboxes, calendars, and SharePoint integration. A distribution list is limited to message distribution within Exchange Online.

Understanding that a distribution list distributes messages without storing them ensures administrators choose this object only when centralized mailbox access is not required.

In summary of this section, selecting the appropriate object in the Exchange Online admin center depends on whether the requirement involves storing mail for an individual, enabling collaborative access to a shared inbox, managing a schedulable resource, or distributing messages to multiple recipients without storing them. User mailboxes represent individual identities. Shared mailboxes support team-based access to a common address. Resource mailboxes manage room or equipment availability. Distribution lists deliver messages to multiple members without maintaining centralized mailbox storage.

Understanding how these objects differ ensures administrators interpret scenarios correctly and configure the appropriate object type within Exchange Online. With the Exchange object model defined, the next section examines how SharePoint objects differ in structure and purpose within Microsoft 365.

Identifying configuration objects in the SharePoint admin center

SharePoint in Microsoft 365 provides the organization's content layer.

It defines how files, collaboration spaces, and structured information are arranged across the tenant. When candidates are asked to identify appropriate objects within the SharePoint admin surface, the task is to select the correct content container for a business purpose.

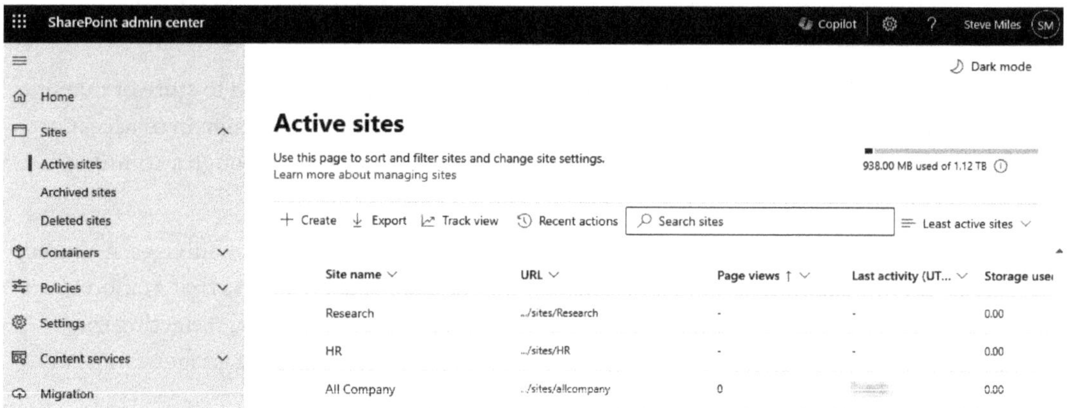

Figure 1.14: Sites management in SharePoint admin center

Each SharePoint object represents a boundary of ownership, collaboration scope, and information exposure. The object selected determines how content is organized and governed within the tenant. Choosing the correct object is therefore a structural decision about how information is arranged and controlled.

This section establishes the hierarchy of content containers available in SharePoint. Understanding it means recognizing which structural layer is being referenced and matching that requirement to the correct object type.

Identifying SharePoint site types

At the **site level**, SharePoint provides two primary site models, **Team site** and **Communication site**, each aligned to a distinct organizational purpose.

You should be able to distinguish between sites designed for *collaborative group work* and sites designed for *structured information publishing*.

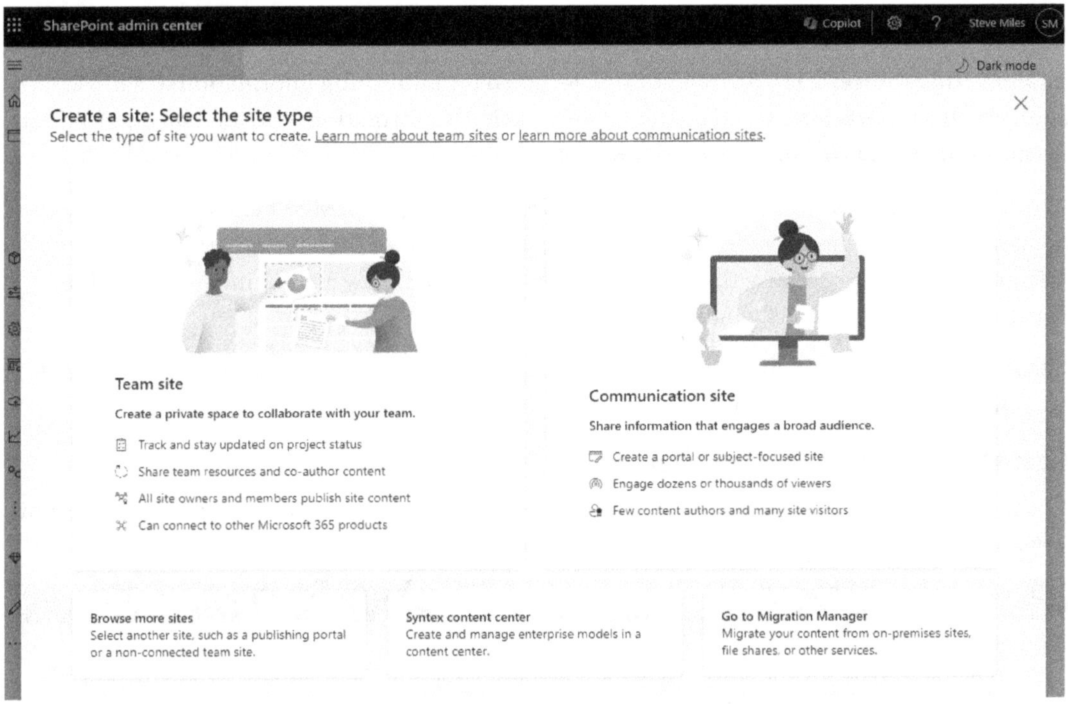

Figure 1.15: SharePoint site types

The selected site type defines the purpose of the site and its intended usage pattern:

- **Team site**: Designed for collaboration, shared authorship, and connected to a Microsoft 365 group, which controls site membership
- **Communication site**: Designed for broadcasting information to a wider audience, controlled publishing, and not connected to a Microsoft 365 group

The characteristics of each site type are examined in the sections that follow.

Team site

A **Team site** is designed to support active collaboration among a defined group of users. It provides a shared workspace where members contribute content, co-author documents, and work collectively toward a common objective.

Team sites are connected to a Microsoft 365 group. The group manages membership, meaning users added to the group automatically receive access to the SharePoint site. This connection enables integration with other Microsoft 365 collaborative services.

Because Team sites are group-connected, they are suited to scenarios requiring ongoing collaboration and shared ownership. The structure assumes active participation rather than one-way publishing.

Communication site

A **Communication site** is a SharePoint site designed for publishing information to a broad audience. It supports structured content delivery where information is created by a limited set of contributors and consumed by many readers.

Communication sites are not connected to a Microsoft 365 group. Membership and access are defined directly within the site through site permissions rather than directly through a Microsoft 365 group. Because they are not group-connected, they are not inherently tied to collaborative Microsoft 365 workloads.

Communication sites are suited to scenarios focused on information distribution and formal content presentation rather than shared authorship.

Identifying document libraries

Within a SharePoint site, files are stored in **document libraries**. Libraries exist inside sites and serve as the primary location for documents and other files.

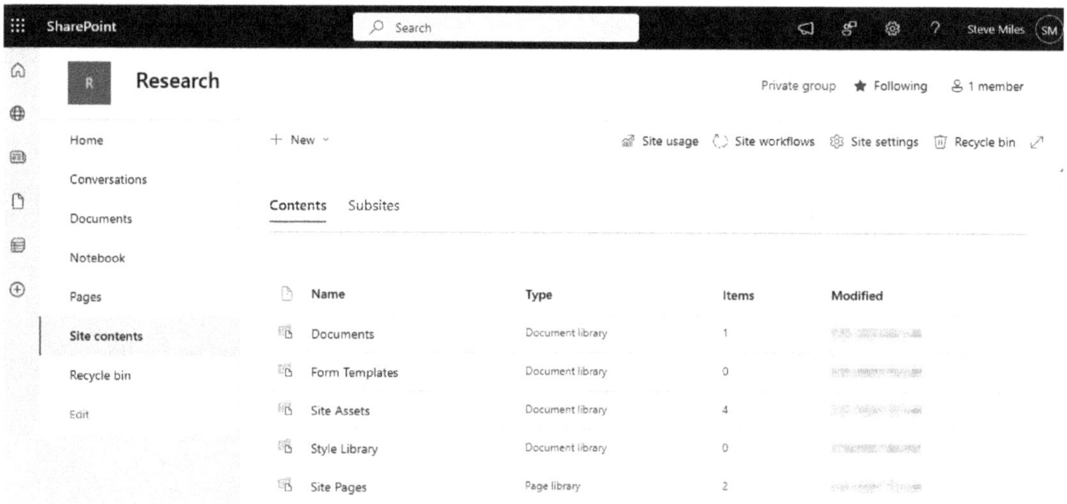

Figure 1.16: SharePoint site document libraries

A document library is designed to organize and manage files within a site. Libraries can contain documents and folders, and they support organization using metadata, such as categories or tags. Document libraries are different from SharePoint lists, which are used to manage structured data rather than files.

Understanding document libraries means recognizing that they define how files are grouped and organized within a site.

Identifying folders within libraries

Within a document library, **folders** are used to organize files into logical groupings, similar to folders in a file system.

Folders are not separate SharePoint sites or independent storage locations. They exist within the library and are part of its overall structure.

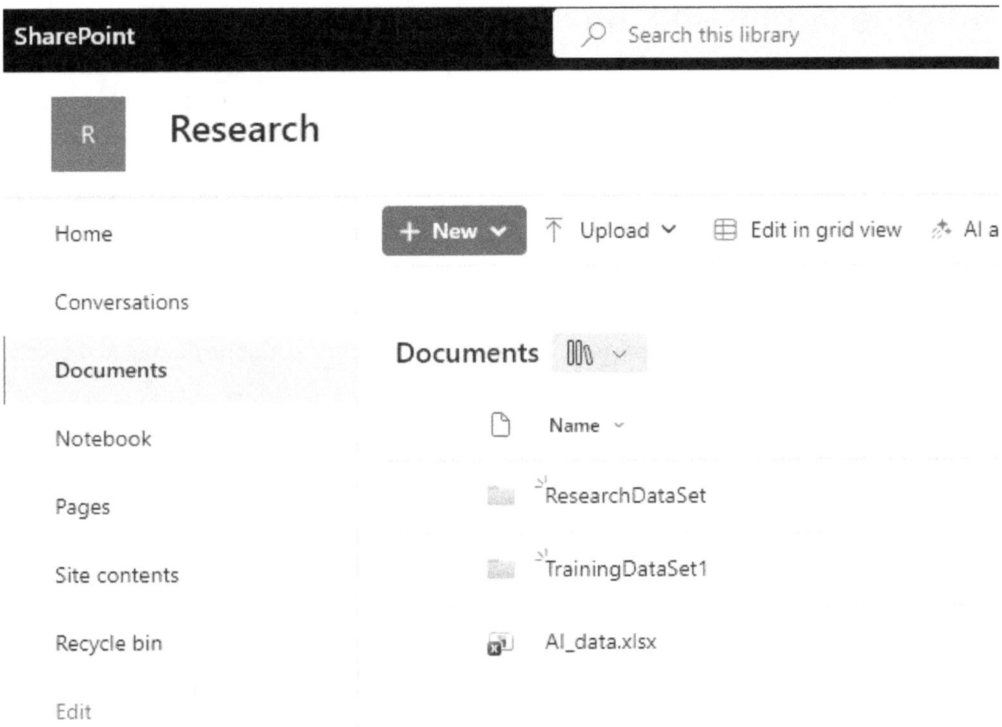

Figure 1.17: SharePoint document library folders

Folders are an organizational tool within a library, not a separate collaboration space. By default, folders follow the same permissions as the library in which they are created. This means that anyone who can view the library can also access its folders unless permissions are intentionally changed.

Document libraries and folders organize content, but access is controlled through roles and permissions, which you will see next.

Identifying SharePoint site roles and permissions

SharePoint uses **roles** and **permissions** to control who can access a site and what they are allowed to do within it, such as viewing content, editing documents, or managing the site.

Access can be inherited from a higher level or defined specifically for a site, library, folder, or item. This approach allows organizations to support collaboration while maintaining appropriate control.

Understanding how roles, inheritance, and scope fit together helps ensure that people have the right level of access where it is needed.

Identifying permission inheritance

In SharePoint, **permissions** can be **inherited** from a **parent site**. This means that access granted at a higher level automatically applies to the sites, libraries, and folders beneath it. By default, lower levels follow the permissions of the level above them.

Inheritance helps keep access consistent across a site. When permissions are managed at the site level, those same permissions apply throughout the structure unless they are intentionally changed. This reduces the need to manage access separately for every library or folder.

Inheritance can be stopped at a specific level. When this happens, that site, library, or folder receives unique permissions. Once permissions are unique, access must be managed directly at that level rather than flowing from the parent.

Inherited permissions

Inherited permissions mean that a site, library, or folder receives its access settings from the level above. When permissions are inherited, the same users and groups who have access at the parent level automatically have access at the lower level.

This approach keeps access consistent and easier to manage across the site. For example, changes made at the parent level, such as adding or removing users, automatically apply to all levels that inherit from it. This helps avoid differences in access across the site structure.

Inherited permissions are the default behavior in SharePoint. As long as inheritance is not stopped, lower levels continue to follow the permissions of their parent.

Breaking inheritance

Breaking inheritance means that a site, library, or folder no longer receives its permissions from the level above it. Instead of following the parent's permissions, it begins to use its own separate set of permissions.

When inheritance is broken, the existing permissions are copied from the parent at that moment. From that point forward, changes made at the parent level no longer affect that site, library, or folder. Access must then be managed directly at that level. Breaking inheritance provides flexibility when a specific area requires different access from the rest of the site. However, it also increases administrative effort because permissions must be maintained separately.

Identifying default SharePoint roles

SharePoint uses a set of **default permission groups** to control what users can do within a site. These groups combine common permission levels and simplify access management, making it easier to assign the right type of access without configuring individual settings.

The three primary default groups in SharePoint are **Owners**, **Members**, and **Visitors**. Each group represents a different level of responsibility and access within the site. Owners manage the site and its permissions, Members contribute and edit content, and Visitors can view content without making changes.

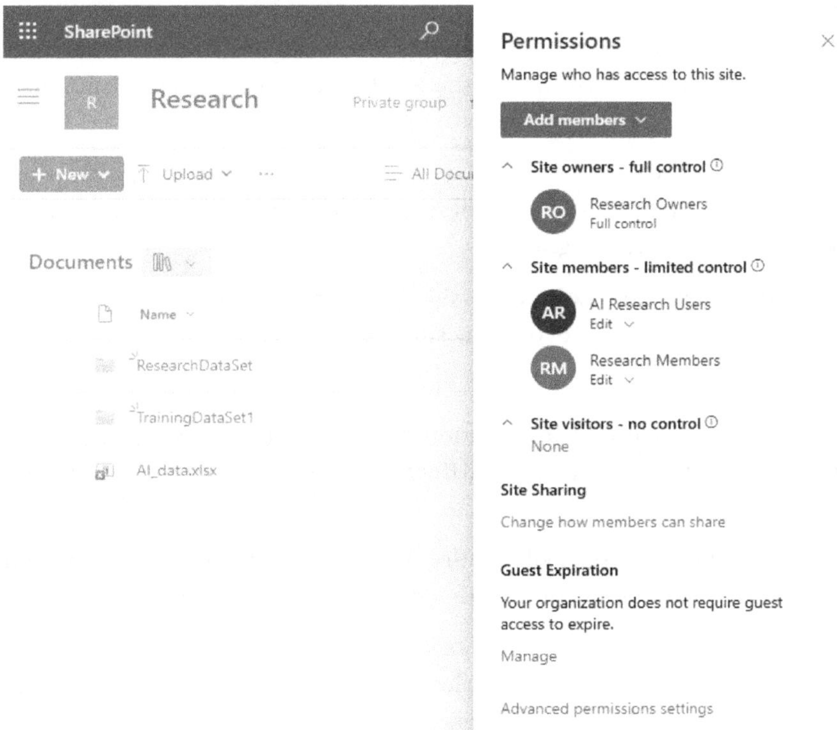

Figure 1.18: SharePoint site permissions

These groups provide a simple structure for managing access. By assigning users to the appropriate group, organizations can control who manages the site, who contributes to it, and who only needs read-only access.

Owners

Owners are responsible for managing a SharePoint site and its access settings. They have full control over the site, including the ability to manage users, change permissions, and modify site content.

Because Owners have the highest level of access, they can make structural changes to the site, manage document libraries, and control membership within the site's permission groups. This level of access is typically assigned to individuals who are accountable for the site's content and overall management.

The Owners group maps to the **Full control** permission level, which provides complete administrative access within the site.

Members

Members are users who contribute to a SharePoint site's content. They can create, edit, and delete documents and other content within the site, but they do not have full administrative control.

Members work with the site's content on a day-to-day basis, collaborating with others and updating information as needed. They cannot manage site-wide permissions or structural settings unless additional access is granted.

The Members group maps to the **Edit** permission level, which allows users to modify content while limiting administrative control over the site itself.

Visitors

Visitors are users who need to view information on a SharePoint site without making changes. They can open documents, read content, and download files, but they cannot edit or delete items within the site.

This level of access is typically assigned to individuals who need visibility into information but are not responsible for maintaining or updating it. Visitors cannot manage permissions or modify the structure of the site.

The Visitors group maps to the **Read** permission level, which allows users to view content while preventing changes to documents or site settings.

Identifying permission scope levels

Permissions in SharePoint can be applied at different levels within a site. Access can be set for the entire site or for specific document libraries, folders, or individual items.

By default, permissions set at a higher level apply to the levels beneath it. This means that site-level permissions flow down to libraries, folders, and items unless inheritance is stopped.

When permissions are defined at a lower level, inheritance is stopped at that point, and unique permissions are created. From then on, access at that level is managed independently of its parent.

Site-level permissions

Site-level permissions apply to the entire SharePoint site. Access assigned at this level applies to all document libraries, folders, and items within the site unless inheritance is stopped at a lower level.

This level of permission is typically used when the same group of users needs access across the whole site. Managing permissions here provides a consistent and centralized way to control who can view, edit, or manage content.

Because site-level permissions sit at the top of the structure, changes made here automatically apply to lower levels that continue to inherit from the site.

Library-level permissions

Library-level permissions apply to a specific document library within a SharePoint site. By default, a library follows the permissions set at the site level. If inheritance is stopped, the library can use its own unique set of permissions.

This allows access to be adjusted for that library without affecting the rest of the site. For example, a library containing sensitive documents may require more restricted access than other areas of the site.

When a library has unique permissions, access is managed independently from the site, while other libraries continue to follow the site-level permissions unless those are changed.

Folder-level permissions

Folder-level permissions apply to a specific folder within a document library. By default, a folder follows the permissions set at the library level. If inheritance is stopped, the folder can use its own unique set of permissions. This allows access to be adjusted for a particular group of documents without changing access for the entire library. For example, a folder containing confidential files may require more restricted access than other folders in the same library.

When a folder has unique permissions, access is managed independently at that level, while the rest of the library continues to follow its existing permission settings unless they are changed.

Item-level permissions

Item-level permissions apply to an individual document or list item within a library. By default, an item follows the permissions set at the folder or library level. If inheritance is stopped, the item can use its own unique set of permissions.

This allows access to be controlled for a single file without changing access for the rest of the folder or library. For example, a specific document may need to be restricted to a small group of users while other documents remain accessible.

When an item has unique permissions, access is managed independently at that level, while other items continue to follow their existing permission settings unless those settings are changed.

Identifying configuration objects in the Teams admin center

The **Microsoft Teams admin center** provides the administrative control surface for Microsoft Teams. It is used to manage the settings and objects that define how users communicate, collaborate, and participate in meetings across the organization.

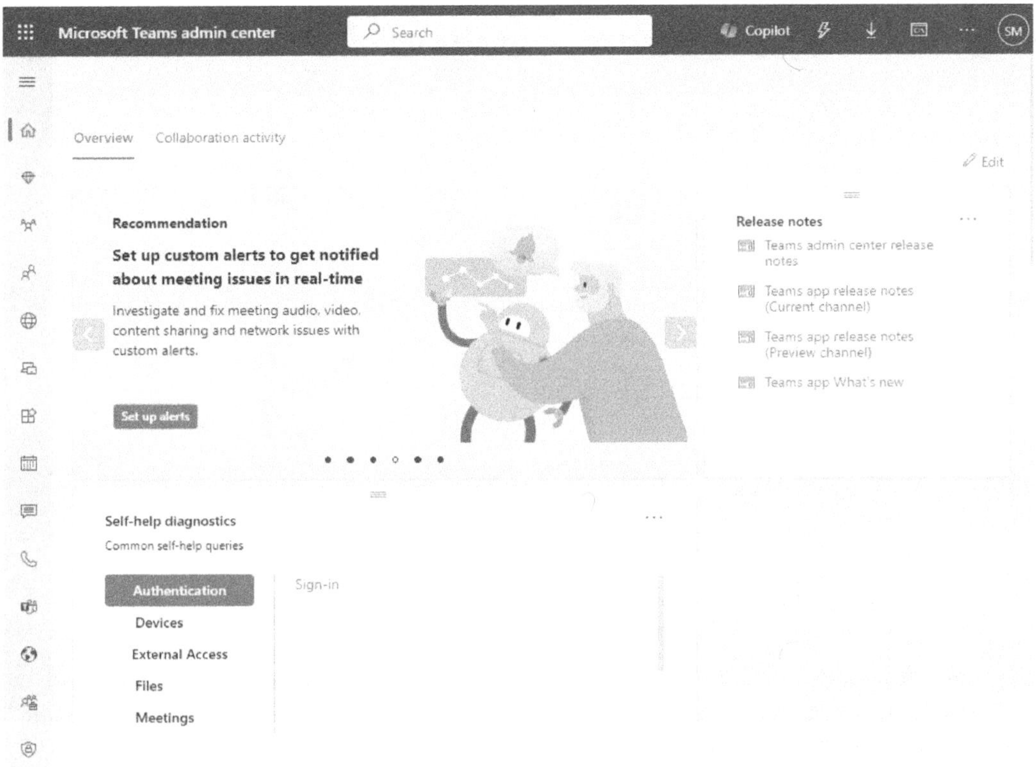

Figure 1.19: Teams Admin Center

Within the Teams admin center, different administrative objects control different aspects of the service. Some objects apply to the entire organization, while others apply to specific users or groups. Selecting the correct object ensures that changes affect the intended scope and workload.

Understanding these objects and how they relate to one another helps ensure that Teams is configured in a way that supports collaboration while maintaining appropriate control and consistency.

Identifying teams

A **team** is the primary collaboration unit in Microsoft Teams. It brings together people, conversations, files, meetings, and apps into a shared workspace focused on a common purpose.

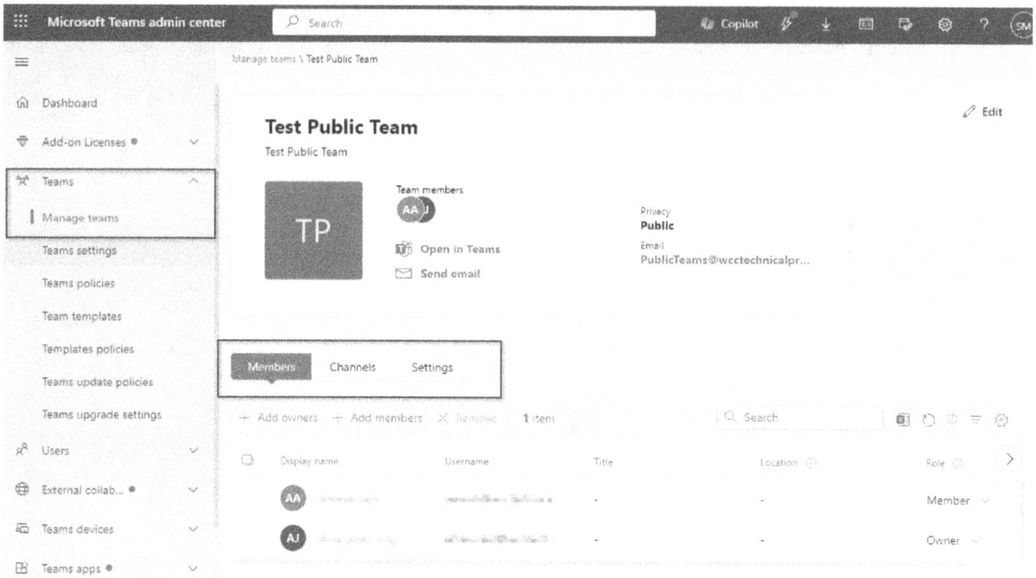

Figure 1.20: Teams Admin Center manages teams

Each team contains one or more channels, which organize discussions and content around specific topics or workstreams. Channels sit within a team and structure collaboration inside that broader space.

Every team is backed by a Microsoft 365 group, which manages membership. Users added to the group automatically receive access to the team and its associated resources, including shared files and conversations.

Because a team controls its membership, it defines who can participate in chats, access files, join meetings, and use apps within that workspace. A team, therefore, acts as both a collaboration container and a membership boundary.

Identifying channels

Channels exist within a team and serve as the primary way conversations and content are organized in Microsoft Teams. While a team brings together a group of people, channels divide that collaboration into focused areas such as projects, departments, or topics. Conversations, shared files, and related activities take place inside channels rather than at the team level itself.

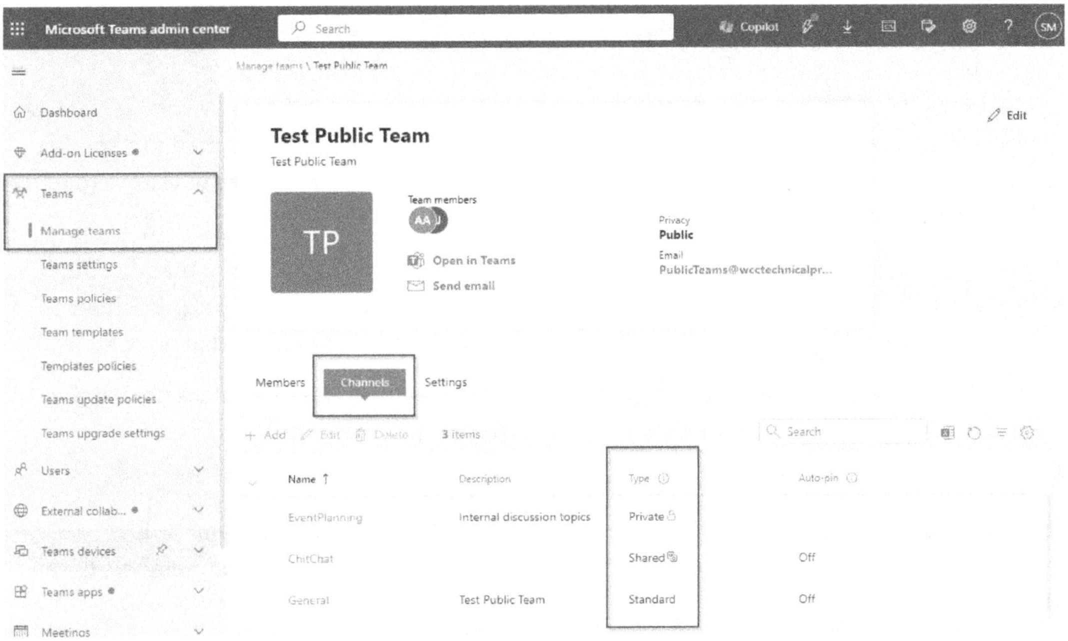

Figure 1.21: Teams Channels

Because channels structure how members interact, the type of channel determines who can access its conversations and files. Microsoft Teams includes three primary channel types:

- Standard channels
- Private channels
- Shared channels

Each channel type defines a different membership and access model. Understanding these differences ensures that collaboration is organized appropriately and that the right users have access to the right discussions. The characteristics of each channel type are explained in the sections that follow.

Standard channels

Standard channels are the default channel type within a team. They are accessible to all members of the team and are used for collaboration that involves the full group.

Access to a standard channel is determined by team membership. Any user who belongs to the team can view conversations, share files, and participate in discussions within that channel. There is no separate membership list for a standard channel.

Standard channels are typically used for topics, projects, or areas of work that are relevant to everyone in the team rather than to a limited subset of members.

Private channels

Private channels are used when collaboration within a team needs to be limited to a smaller group of members. Access to a private channel is restricted to team members who are explicitly added to that private channel.

A private channel has its own membership list, separate from the overall team membership. Only users included in that list can view conversations, access shared files, and participate in discussions within the channel. Other team members cannot see the channel or its content.

Private channels are typically used for sensitive topics or focused work that does not involve the entire team, while still remaining part of the broader team structure.

Shared channels

Shared channels enable collaboration beyond the boundaries of a single team. Unlike standard or private channels, a shared channel can include users who are not members of the parent team.

A shared channel has its own membership list. It can include users from other teams within the organization and, where shared channel and Microsoft Entra B2B direct connect settings permit, users from external organizations without adding them to the full team. These users can participate in conversations and access files within the shared channel without being added to the full team.

Shared channels are typically used when collaboration is required across teams or organizational boundaries, while keeping access limited to a specific channel rather than expanding membership to the entire team.

Identifying Teams policy types

Policies in Microsoft Teams control how features behave for users. They define what users can do within meetings, messaging, and apps and allow different settings to be applied to different groups of users.

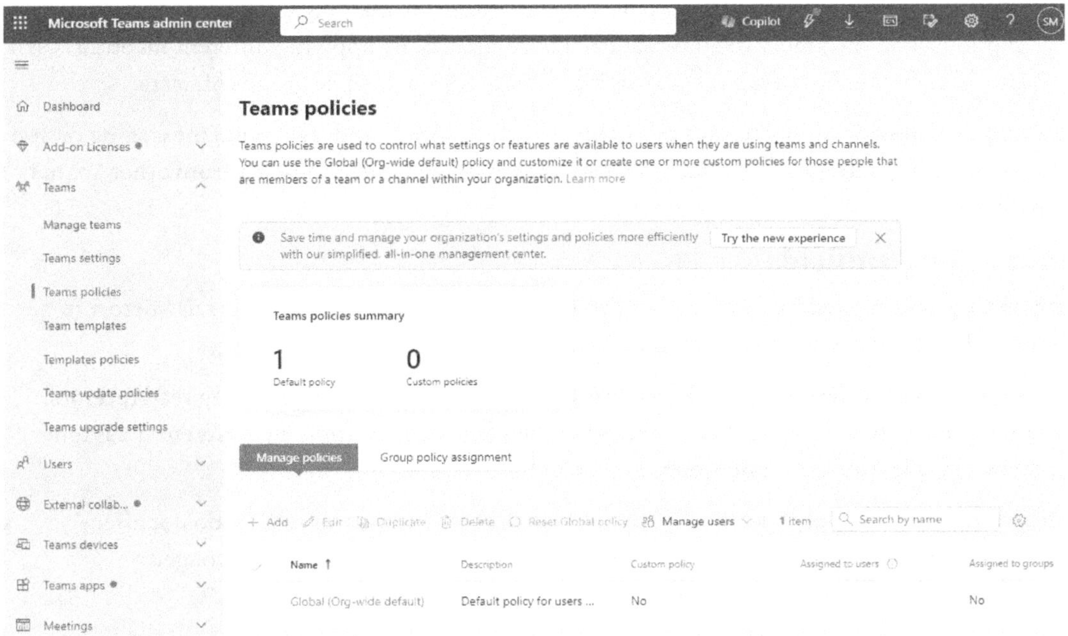

Figure 1.22: Teams policies

There are several policy types in Teams, and each governs a specific area of functionality. The primary policy types include:

- Meeting policies
- Messaging policies
- App permission policies

Meeting policies control how meetings function, including available features and participant capabilities. Messaging policies define how chat and channel messaging behave. App permission policies determine which apps users are allowed to access within Teams.

Each policy type focuses on a distinct feature area. Understanding these differences ensures that the correct policy object is used when managing user behavior. The characteristics of each policy type are explained in the sections that follow.

Meeting policies

Meeting policies define how meetings function for users in Microsoft Teams. They control the features available during meetings and determine how participants can interact.

These policies govern settings such as meeting recording, in-meeting chat, content sharing, live captions, and the ability to allow external participants. By applying different meeting policies, organizations can tailor the meeting experience for specific groups of users.

Meeting policies apply only to meeting behavior. They do not control general messaging or app access, ensuring that meeting-related features are managed independently from other Teams capabilities.

Messaging policies

Messaging policies define how chat and channel messaging behave for users in Microsoft Teams. They control what users can do when sending and managing messages.

These policies govern settings such as editing or deleting sent messages, using read receipts, sending priority messages, and enabling other chat features. By applying different messaging policies, organizations can tailor how users communicate within Teams.

Messaging policies apply specifically to chat and channel interactions. They do not affect meeting functionality or app access, ensuring that messaging behavior is managed independently from other Teams features.

App permission policies

App permission policies control which apps users are allowed to access within Microsoft Teams. They determine whether Microsoft, third-party, or custom apps are available to specific users or groups.

By applying different app permission policies, organizations can permit or restrict access based on business requirements and ensure that users only see approved apps within Teams.

App permission policies focus solely on app availability. They do not affect meeting behavior or messaging features, keeping app access governance separate from other Teams capabilities.

Summary

In this chapter, you examined the core administrative objects used to manage collaboration in Microsoft Teams. You began with teams, the primary collaboration unit, and saw how they bring together people, conversations, files, meetings, and apps within a shared workspace backed by a Microsoft 365 group.

You then explored channels and how they organize collaboration inside a team. Standard channels support collaboration across the full team, private channels restrict access to a subset of members, and shared channels enable collaboration across teams or organizational boundaries. Each channel type defines a distinct membership and access model.

Finally, you reviewed Teams policy types and how they control user behavior. Meeting policies govern meeting functionality, messaging policies define chat behavior, and app permission policies determine which apps users can access. These policies allow organizations to shape the Teams experience while maintaining appropriate control.

Together, teams, channels, and **policies** form the foundation of administration in the Teams admin center. Understanding how these objects relate to one another ensures that collaboration is structured effectively and governed appropriately across the organization.

Core Microsoft 365 objects reference

The following table lists the primary administrative objects introduced in this chapter, explains what each object represents, and provides links to the corresponding Microsoft documentation for further reference.

Object	What it represents	Learn more
Users	Individual accounts with identity, access, and permissions	Microsoft Entra ID user management — `https://learn.microsoft.com/en-us/entra/fundamentals/how-to-create-delete-users`
Licenses	Define which Microsoft 365 services and features a user can access	Assign licenses to users —`https://learn.microsoft.com/en-us/microsoft-365/admin/manage/assign-licenses-to-users`
Tenant	The organization's dedicated Microsoft 365 environment and administrative boundary	What is a Microsoft 365 tenant — `https://learn.microsoft.com/en-us/microsoft-365/enterprise/tenant-roadmap-microsoft-365`
Domains	Custom sign-in and email domains associated with the organization	Add a custom domain — `https://learn.microsoft.com/en-us/microsoft-365/admin/setup/add-domain`

Object	What it represents	Learn more
Mailboxes	Email storage for messages, calendars, contacts, and scheduling	Manage user mailboxes — `https://learn.microsoft.com/en-us/exchange/recipients-in-exchange-online/manage-user-mailboxes`
Files and Documents	Stored business content with permissions, sharing, and versioning	OneDrive overview — `https://learn.microsoft.com/en-us/sharepoint/onedrive-overview`
SharePoint Sites	Collaboration spaces and document libraries for teams and publishing	Introduction to SharePoint — `https://learn.microsoft.com/en-us/sharepoint/introduction`
Teams and Channels	Collaboration hubs for chat, meetings, files, and conversations	Teams and channels overview — `https://learn.microsoft.com/en-us/microsoftteams/teams-channels-overview`
Groups	Collections of users used for collaboration, access, and permissions	Microsoft 365 groups — `https://learn.microsoft.com/en-us/microsoft-365/admin/create-groups/office-365-groups`
Policies	Rules controlling access, security, compliance, and user behavior	Microsoft 365 compliance policies — `https://learn.microsoft.com/en-us/microsoft-365-apps/security/compliance-overview`

Table 1.4: Core Microsoft 365 objects reference

These references help reinforce the object model introduced in this chapter and provide a useful point of return when reviewing how Microsoft 365 services are structured across the tenant.

Key terms and acronyms

This quick reference helps readers who are new to Microsoft 365 understand the common terms used throughout this chapter. It is designed for first-time familiarity, helping build recognition of the words and concepts that appear across licensing, identity, Exchange, SharePoint, and Teams administration.

Term	Meaning
Public Cloud	Computing services such as identity, email, storage, and applications are delivered through shared online platforms rather than relying only on an organization's local infrastructure.
M365	Short form for Microsoft 365, the cloud platform that includes identity, email, collaboration, and productivity services.
Tenant	The organization's dedicated Microsoft 365 environment where users, groups, domains, and services exist.
Service Plan	An individual service or feature inside a Microsoft 365 license, such as Exchange Online or Microsoft Teams.
Default Domain	The automatically created tenant domain that uses the onmicrosoft.com namespace and always remains with the tenant.
Custom Domain	The organization's own domain name, such as contoso.com, is added for user sign-in and email addresses.
DNS	Domain Name System, used to verify ownership of a custom domain and support service routing such as email delivery.
MX record	A Mail Exchange record is used to route email to Exchange Online so messages are delivered correctly.
User Mailbox	A personal mailbox linked to one licensed user for email, calendar, contacts, and individual mailbox storage.
Shared Mailbox	A mailbox used by multiple users to manage a shared address such as support@ or sales@ without each user needing a separate mailbox for that function.

Term	Meaning
Resource Mailbox	A mailbox used for booking meeting rooms or equipment rather than for personal email communication.
Distribution List	A mail-enabled object used to send one email to multiple recipients without storing messages in a shared mailbox.
Document Library	The main file storage area inside a SharePoint site where documents, folders, and business content are organized.
Permission Inheritance	The process where permissions flow from a parent site to libraries, folders, and items unless inheritance is intentionally broken.
Owners	Users with full control of a SharePoint site, including permissions, membership, and overall site management.
Members	Users who can create, edit, and manage content within a SharePoint site but do not control site permissions.
Visitors	Users with read-only access can view content but cannot make changes to documents or site settings.
Standard Channel	The default Teams channel that all members of the team can access and use for general collaboration.
Private Channel	A Teams channel restricted to only selected members within the team for focused or sensitive collaboration.
Shared Channel	A Teams channel that can include users outside the parent team without adding them to the full team membership.

Table 1.5: Key terms and acronyms

These key terms provide a practical reference point as you move through Microsoft 365 administration. Understanding how these terms relate to one another makes it easier to recognize where configuration happens, how access is controlled, and which administrative object should be used for a specific requirement.

For new readers, this creates the foundation needed to follow later chapters with confidence. For exam preparation, it also reinforces the terminology that frequently appears in scenario-based questions, where selecting the correct answer often depends on recognizing the purpose of an object rather than simply memorizing its name.

Exam readiness drill – chapter review questions

Apart from mastering key concepts, strong test-taking skills under time pressure are essential for acing your certification exam. That's why developing these abilities early in your learning journey is critical.

Exam readiness drills, using the free online practice resources provided with this book, helps you progressively improve your time management and test-taking skills while reinforcing the key concepts you've learned.

HOW TO GET STARTED

1. Open the link or scan the QR code at the bottom of this page
2. If you have unlocked the practice resources already, log in to your registered account. If you haven't, follow the instructions in the *Free Benefits with Your Book* section in this book's *Preface* and come back to this page.
3. Once you log in, click the START button to start this chapter's quiz
4. We recommend attempting a quiz multiple times until you're able to answer most of the questions correctly and well within the time limit
5. You can use the following practice template to help you plan your attempts:

Working On Accuracy		
Attempt	**Target**	**Time Limit**
Attempt 1	40% or more	Till the timer runs out
Attempt 2	60% or more	Till the timer runs out
Attempt 3	75% or more	Till the timer runs out
Working On Timing		
Attempt 4	75% or more	1 minute before time limit
Attempt 5	75% or more	2 minutes before time limit
Attempt 6	75% or more	3 minutes before time limit

The above drill is just an example. Design your drills based on your own goals and make the most out of the online quizzes accompanying this book.

Link to this chapter's quiz

You need to unlock the online practice resources to access the link below. Check the *Free Benefits with Your Book* section in the *Preface* for detailed instructions on how to do this. You only need to unlock the resources once.

Open Quiz `https://packt.link/ckQrf` or scan the QR code

2

Understanding Microsoft 365 Security Principles

In the previous chapter, we explored how Microsoft 365 services are *structured*, how identities and workloads are organized within a tenant, and how access is granted through licensing and administrative objects; this chapter builds on that foundation by shifting to the controls that protect identities, access paths, and data.

Security in Microsoft 365 begins with a few core ideas that shape how identity, access, and threat protection work together. It introduces Zero Trust as the model for evaluating access, explains the roles of authentication and authorization within that model, and shows how Microsoft 365 detects and responds to threats across modern cloud environments.

This chapter primarily supports the **Understand the Microsoft 365 security principles** module from the AB-900 Skills Measured outline.

By the end of this chapter, you will be able to confidently answer questions on the following topics:

- Explaining Zero Trust Principles
- Understanding Authentication Methods
- Understanding Authorization in Microsoft 365
- Understanding Threat Protection and Intelligence
- Understanding Microsoft Defender XDR Capabilities

Understanding these principles gives readers the foundation needed to make sense of how Microsoft 365 protects identities, controls access, and responds to threats in modern cloud environments.

Microsoft 365 security capabilities are built on a common security model. Before examining authentication methods, authorization decisions, or threat protection technologies, it is important to understand the philosophy that governs how access is evaluated and enforced.

That philosophy is reflected in the Zero Trust security model. The following sections explain why traditional perimeter-based thinking became less effective and how Microsoft 365 applies Zero Trust principles in practice.

> Note
>
> **Important information regarding Microsoft Portal experiences and UI elements**
>
> Microsoft frequently updates portal experiences and UI elements. As a result, some screenshots, navigation paths, or interface details shown in this book may differ slightly from your individual tenant's environment at the time of reading.

Explaining Zero Trust principles

Cloud services and remote access have changed how organizations approach security. Employees now access applications and data from many locations and devices, while services communicate across cloud platforms and internet-connected systems.

Traditional enterprise security models assumed that systems operating inside a corporate network could generally be trusted. Firewalls and network gateways were used to keep attackers outside the perimeter, and activity inside the network was often treated as safe.

As organizations adopted cloud services and hybrid work, this assumption became less reliable. Users, devices, and applications now operate far beyond the traditional network boundary, making location alone a weak indicator of whether access should be trusted.

To deal with that shift, organizations increasingly adopted a security model known as **Zero Trust**. Instead of assuming activity inside a network can be trusted, **Zero Trust** *verifies identities* before access is granted, *limits permissions* to only what is necessary, and continuously *monitors activity* for signs that an account or device may have been compromised.

Traditional perimeter-based security

Historically, enterprise security models relied heavily on network boundaries to control access. Corporate networks were separated from the internet by firewalls and gateway devices that blocked unauthorized connections.

Because this network perimeter served as the primary security boundary, systems inside the network were often treated as trusted by default. Employees typically connected from corporate devices within office environments, and once inside the network, they could often access multiple internal systems.

The model worked well when applications and data were hosted inside corporate data centers. However, as organizations adopted cloud services and hybrid work, the network boundary became less meaningful. Users now often access systems from home networks, personal devices, and cloud platforms, making network location alone a weak indicator of whether access should be trusted.

The Zero Trust security model

The **Zero Trust** model addresses the limitations of *perimeter-based security* by removing the assumption that internal activity is automatically trustworthy.

Instead of relying on network boundaries, every attempt to access a system, application, or data must be evaluated before access is granted.

Figure 2.1 illustrates how the traditional perimeter-based security model differs from the Zero Trust approach.

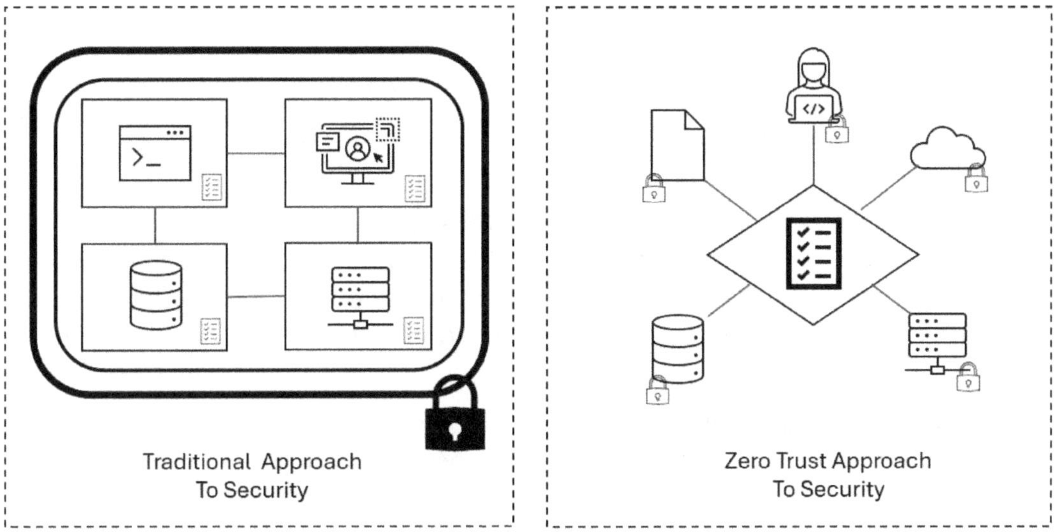

Figure 2.1: Traditional perimeter security compared with the Zero Trust security model

When a user, application, or service requests access to a resource, centralized security policy controls examine details about that request. This may include the identity of the user, the device being used, the location of the request, and any indicators that the activity may present a security risk.

By verifying each request using this information, Zero Trust helps organizations reduce the risk that compromised credentials or devices could be used to gain unauthorized access.

Core principles of Zero Trust

The **Zero Trust** security model is built on *three principles* that guide how organizations control access and protect resources.

Instead of assuming that activity inside a network can be trusted, Zero Trust treats every request for access as potentially risky and evaluates it using identity and contextual signals.

Figure 2.2 illustrates the three core principles that guide the Zero Trust security model.

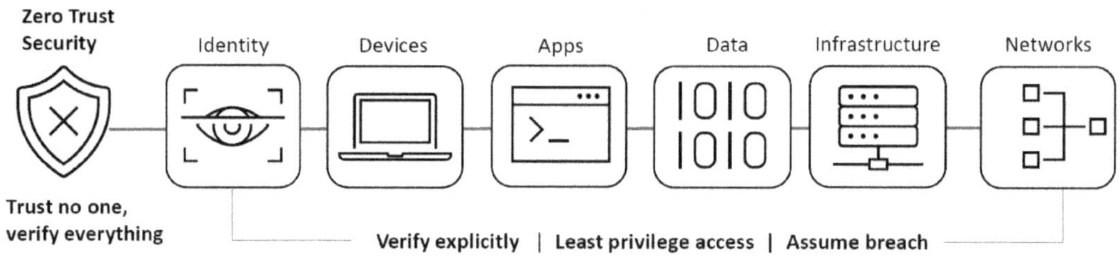

Figure 2.2: The three core principles of the Zero Trust security model

These principles shape how organizations evaluate access, limit permissions, and monitor activity across users, devices, and services.

First, Zero Trust requires organizations to **verify explicitly**. Access requests are examined using signals such as the user's identity, device health, location, and behavioral indicators, with Conditional Access policies evaluating these signals before granting access. Rather than relying on network location alone, security decisions are based on multiple signals that help determine whether the request is legitimate.

Second, it applies **least-privilege access**. Users, applications, and services receive only the permissions required to perform their tasks. Limiting permissions in this way reduces the potential damage that could occur if an identity or device becomes compromised.

Third, it **assumes breach**. Security strategies recognize that attackers may eventually gain access to part of an environment. As a result, organizations focus not only on preventing attacks but also on detecting suspicious behavior and limiting how far a compromise can spread.

Together, these principles encourage continuous verification, tightly controlled permissions, and faster detection of abnormal activity.

Zero Trust in Microsoft 365

In Microsoft 365, **Zero Trust** is implemented as an architectural approach across identities, endpoints, applications, data, infrastructure, and networks.

Identity verification is handled through **Microsoft Entra**, which authenticates users, devices, and applications before allowing access to services.

Microsoft Defender provides threat detection by analyzing activity across identities, endpoints, email systems, and cloud applications. By correlating signals from these different sources, Defender helps security teams identify suspicious behavior and potential attacks.

Microsoft Purview focuses on protecting data. It helps organizations classify sensitive information and apply policies that prevent that data from being exposed or accessed inappropriately.

Together, these platforms support the Zero Trust model by verifying identities, limiting permissions, and monitoring activity across the Microsoft 365 environment.

Because every access request must be verified in a Zero Trust architecture, identity verification becomes one of the most critical security controls in modern cloud environments.

Understanding authentication methods

Before a system can determine what a user or service is allowed to access, it must first confirm the identity of the user, device, or service making the request. This process is known as authentication.

Authentication is fundamental to security because modern cloud environments include many different types of interactions. Users sign in to applications, devices connect to organizational resources, and automated services communicate with cloud platforms. Each of these activities requires a reliable way to confirm that the identity requesting access is genuine.

In Microsoft environments, authentication occurs whenever an identity attempts to access a service. Whether a user signs in to Microsoft 365, an application connects to an API, or a device attempts to access a protected resource, authentication ensures that the identity involved can be trusted.

Understanding identities

To understand authentication, it helps to start with identity.

An identity represents a digital account that can request access to a system, application, or resource.

In practice, identities represent people, devices, applications, or automated services that interact with technology systems. Each identity includes information that allows systems to recognize and verify who or what is requesting access.

Identity providers (**IDPs**) store these identities and the information associated with them. When a sign-in attempt occurs, the authentication system locates the identity in the IDP and verifies that the request is legitimate.

Types of identities

Modern cloud environments support several different identity types. Some identities represent people signing in to use applications and services, while others represent devices, applications, or background services interacting with systems without direct user involvement. These are described as follows:

- **User identities** represent people who sign in to access applications and services. These identities typically include usernames and authentication credentials used during the sign-in process.
- **Device identities** represent managed or registered devices that connect to organizational services. By recognizing a device as a trusted identity, systems can evaluate whether the device meets security requirements before allowing access.
- **Application identities** represent software applications that request access to services or data. Applications often authenticate when communicating with APIs or integrating with other systems.
- **Service identities** represent background services or automated processes that run tasks without direct user interaction.

Defining identities for users, devices, applications, and automated services allows organizations to control how each type interacts with systems and resources.

The purpose of authentication

Authentication *verifies* an identity during the sign-in process. When a user or system attempts to access a resource, the authentication process requires evidence that the identity is genuine.

This evidence may involve entering a **password** or **PIN**, approving a request through an **authentication application**, using a **hardware security key**, or confirming identity through **biometric methods** such as a **fingerprint** or **facial recognition**.

By confirming identity before access is granted, authentication helps prevent unauthorized users from entering systems using stolen or guessed credentials.

Authentication versus authorization

Authentication and **authorization** work together to *control access* to systems and data, but they serve different purposes.

Authentication (*also referred to as AuthN*) confirms identity; it verifies that the person, device, or service requesting access is genuinely who or what it claims to be.

Authorization (*also referred to as AuthZ*) determines what that verified identity is allowed to do.

Once authentication confirms the identity, authorization uses permissions and policies to determine which resources the identity can access, meaning authentication always occurs before authorization in the access process.

Figure 2.3 illustrates the difference between authentication and authorization in the access process.

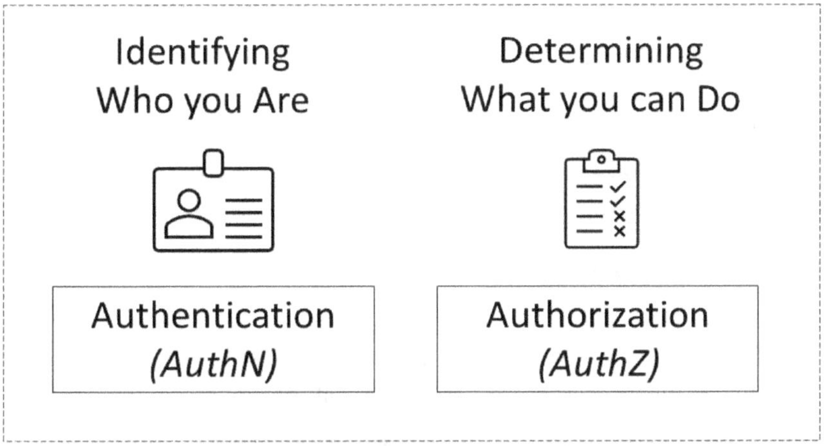

Figure 2.3: Authentication and authorization in the access process

A simple way to understand the relationship between the two processes is to imagine entering a secured building. Showing your identification badge at the entrance confirms who you are. That step represents authentication. Once inside the building, the rooms you are allowed to enter depend on your role or responsibilities. That decision represents authorization.

Authentication confirms identity, while authorization determines access. If identity cannot be verified, access is denied. If identity is verified but permissions are insufficient, access is still denied.

Because access decisions depend on knowing the identity of the requester, authentication always occurs before authorization in the access process.

Authentication methods

Authentication methods determine how users, devices, and applications prove their identity during the sign-in process. Different methods provide varying levels of assurance depending on the type of credential used.

Some methods rely on knowledge-based credentials such as passwords or PINs, while others use device-based verification or biometrics such as security keys, mobile authentication applications, or fingerprint recognition.

Organizations often support multiple authentication methods so users can access services securely while still maintaining a simple and practical sign-in experience.

Multi-factor authentication

Multi-factor authentication (**MFA**) adds an additional layer of verification during sign-in. Instead of relying on a single credential such as a password, the user must provide another form of proof.

For example, a user may enter a password and then approve the sign-in request using a mobile authentication application. Even if a password is stolen, access would still require the second verification factor.

Because many attacks attempt to steal passwords through phishing or credential theft, requiring multiple authentication factors greatly reduces the risk of unauthorized access.

Authentication factors

Multi-factor authentication strengthens sign-in security by combining different categories of identity verification. Instead of relying on a single credential such as a password, the system requires more than one form of proof that the user is legitimate.

These verification methods are usually grouped into **three types**.

The first is **something you know**, which includes information known only by the user, such as passwords or PIN codes. Another is **something you have**, which involves a device that confirms the sign-in attempt, such as a mobile phone, an authentication application, or a hardware security key. The third type is **something you are**, which relies on biometric characteristics such as fingerprints or facial recognition.

Figure 2.4 shows the three common categories of authentication factors used in multi-factor authentication.

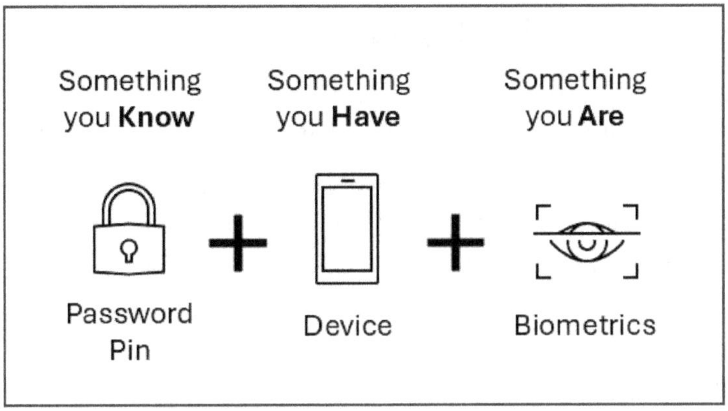

Figure 2.4: Authentication factor categories

Each factor category provides a different way to verify the identity of the user attempting to sign in. By combining factors from multiple categories, authentication systems create additional layers of protection that make unauthorized access more difficult.

For example, even if an attacker discovers a password, access can still be prevented if the attacker does not possess the registered device or cannot complete the biometric verification. This layered approach is what makes multi-factor authentication significantly more secure than relying on a single credential alone.

Passwordless authentication

Passwordless authentication removes the need for users to enter passwords during sign-in. Instead, identity is verified through secure device-based authentication, biometric methods, or authentication applications.

Passwords have historically been a common target for attackers because they can be stolen, guessed, or reused across services. Removing passwords from the sign-in process reduces the risks associated with compromised credentials.

Passwordless authentication also improves usability by allowing users to sign in quickly using trusted devices or biometric verification while still maintaining strong security controls.

Verifying identity, however, is only the first step in controlling access to systems and data.

Understanding authorization

After authentication confirms the identity of a user, device, or application, the system must decide what that identity is allowed to do. This step is known as authorization.

Authorization controls access to resources by using the permissions assigned to an authenticated identity. These permissions determine whether the identity can read data, modify information, run applications, or perform administrative tasks.

In cloud environments where thousands of users and services interact with systems, authorization helps ensure that access to resources remains controlled and aligned with organizational roles and responsibilities.

The purpose of authorization

Authorization makes sure an identity can access only the resources it actually needs for its role. Even when authentication confirms that an identity is valid, the system must still evaluate whether the identity should be allowed to perform a specific task.

For example, an employee may successfully sign in to a system, but that does not automatically grant access to financial records, administrative settings, or sensitive customer data. Authorization rules determine which resources a user can access.

By restricting access to only the resources that are necessary, authorization helps organizations protect sensitive information and reduce the potential impact of compromised accounts.

Role-based access control

Role-based access control (**RBAC**) is a common approach used to manage permissions in modern systems. Instead of assigning permissions individually to each user, administrators define roles that represent sets of permissions.

Each role defines the actions that users assigned to that role are allowed to perform. Users are then assigned to roles that match their job responsibilities.

For example, an administrator role might allow a user to configure system settings, while a reader role might allow a user to view information without making changes.

Figure 2.5 illustrates how roles are assigned to users.

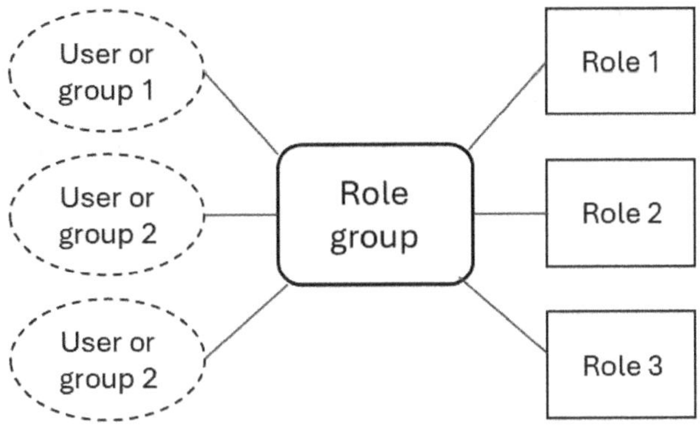

Figure 2.5: Role-based access control

In this model, roles act as containers for permissions that define administrative actions a user can perform within a system, while groups are commonly used to assign access to shared resources such as sites, files, or applications. Instead of assigning permissions individually to every user, administrators assign users to roles that already contain the appropriate permissions.

This approach simplifies access management because changes can be made at the role level rather than updating permissions for each individual user. When responsibilities change, administrators can simply adjust the user's assigned role to update the permissions they receive.

Benefits of role-based access control

RBAC provides several advantages when managing access in large environments.

One benefit is consistency. Permissions can be applied across users who perform similar tasks. Instead of configuring access for every individual user, administrators assign users to roles that already contain the appropriate permissions.

RBAC also supports the principle of least-privilege access. Organizations can design roles that grant only the permissions required for specific responsibilities, reducing the risk of excessive access.

Another advantage is simplified administration. When responsibilities change, administrators can update a user's role assignment rather than modifying permissions individually.

Managing permissions with groups

Groups provide another way to manage access to resources. A group represents a collection of identities that share common permissions or responsibilities.

Administrators can assign permissions to a group and then add users as members. When users join the group, they automatically inherit the permissions assigned to it.

For example, a finance team group might be granted access to financial reporting systems. Any employee added to that group would automatically receive the required permissions.

Using groups simplifies permission management and helps ensure that access policies are applied consistently across teams and departments.

Even with strong authentication and carefully managed permissions, organizations must assume that attackers will attempt to bypass security controls.

Understanding threat protection and intelligence

In modern environments, users, devices, and services interact constantly across cloud platforms and internet-connected systems.

While these technologies enable collaboration and productivity, they also give attackers more opportunities to target identities, systems, and data.

Security, therefore, has to go beyond verifying identity and controlling access. Activity across the environment must also be continuously monitored so that suspicious behavior can be detected and investigated quickly.

Threat protection focuses on identifying and responding to malicious activity, while threat intelligence helps organizations understand how attackers operate and how threats evolve. Together, these capabilities help organizations recognize attacks earlier and respond more effectively.

The modern threat landscape

The modern threat landscape reflects the growing complexity of digital environments. Cloud services, mobile devices, and remote access have expanded how users interact with systems and data.

Attackers increasingly target identities rather than network infrastructure because stolen credentials can provide direct access to applications and sensitive information. If attackers obtain valid credentials, they may appear to systems as legitimate users.

Because of this shift, organizations must monitor activity patterns and behavioral signals instead of relying only on traditional network defenses.

Common attack techniques

Attackers use a variety of techniques to gain unauthorized access to systems and data. One of the most common methods is phishing, where attackers send messages designed to trick users into revealing sensitive information such as passwords or authentication codes.

Another common technique is malware, which places malicious software on a device. Malware can steal data, monitor activity, or allow attackers to gain remote access to systems.

Attackers also attempt credential theft by capturing usernames and passwords through phishing, keylogging, or other attack methods. Once attackers obtain valid credentials, they may try to sign in to services while appearing to be legitimate users.

Understanding these techniques helps organizations recognize warning signs of potential attacks and build defenses that prevent or detect them.

Threat detection and intelligence

Threat detection involves monitoring activity across users, devices, and applications to identify behavior that may indicate a potential attack.

Security systems collect telemetry, which refers to the activity signals produced by systems during normal operation. These signals may include sign-in attempts, device activity, network connections, or interactions between applications.

Threat intelligence supports detection by providing information about known attacker techniques, malicious infrastructure, and emerging threats that help security systems recognize suspicious activity more quickly.

By combining internal activity monitoring with external intelligence sources, organizations can recognize suspicious patterns more quickly.

Security alerts and investigation

When security systems detect activity that may indicate a potential threat, they generate alerts to notify security teams.

Alerts highlight unusual behavior, such as suspicious sign-in attempts, unexpected device activity, or abnormal access patterns. Security analysts review these alerts to determine whether the activity represents legitimate behavior or a possible attack.

Investigating alerts often requires examining related events across multiple systems to understand how the activity occurred and whether further action is needed to protect the environment.

Understanding Microsoft Defender XDR capabilities

Modern cyber-attacks rarely affect a single system. Attackers often move across identities, email systems, devices, and applications as an attack unfolds. Because this activity spans multiple platforms, security teams need tools that can analyze signals from different systems and show how events may be connected.

Microsoft Defender XDR provides a unified security platform designed to detect, investigate, and respond to threats across Microsoft environments.

For exam scenarios that ask where to review security incidents, alerts, or the impact of phishing activity across Microsoft 365, that review is performed in the Microsoft Defender portal.

By collecting and analyzing security signals from multiple services, the platform helps organizations see the broader context of potential attacks and respond more effectively.

For endpoint-specific scenarios, such as investigating incidents or alerts from Windows devices, Microsoft Defender for Endpoint is the Defender service used to protect and monitor those devices.

Defender XDR brings signals together from several Microsoft security services, giving analysts a broader view of how an attack is unfolding. These services include Microsoft Defender for Identity, Microsoft Defender for Endpoint, Microsoft Defender for Office 365, and Microsoft Defender for Cloud Apps.

Rather than analyzing each security event separately, Defender XDR examines activity across the environment to identify how events are connected. This broader view helps security teams understand how attacks develop and move across systems.

By bringing together security data from different services, Defender XDR allows analysts to investigate threats through a unified security platform instead of switching between separate tools.

Security signals and telemetry

Security systems continuously generate activity signals during normal operation. These signals, often referred to as telemetry, provide insight into how users, devices, and applications interact with services.

For example, telemetry may include sign-in attempts, device activity, email interactions, and application access events. Individually, these signals may appear harmless. However, when analyzed together, they can reveal patterns that indicate suspicious behavior.

Microsoft Defender XDR collects security telemetry from multiple Microsoft services and correlates those signals to identify behavior that may indicate a coordinated attack.

Alert correlation and incidents

Security alerts often represent individual indicators within a larger attack. For example, a suspicious sign-in attempt, a malicious email attachment, and unusual device behavior may all be connected events within the same incident.

Microsoft Defender XDR correlates related alerts and groups them into incidents. An incident represents the overall attack scenario rather than separate isolated events.

By grouping related activity together, security analysts can more easily understand the scope of an attack and identify how different activities are connected.

Investigation and response capabilities

Once an incident is identified, security teams begin examining the activity to understand what occurred and how the attack developed.

Defender XDR provides investigation tools that allow analysts to review alerts, examine related activity, and trace how an attack moved through the environment. During this process, analysts review identity activity, device behavior, email interactions, and application access to reconstruct the sequence of events.

The platform also supports response actions that help organizations contain threats. These actions may include blocking malicious activity, isolating compromised devices, disabling compromised user accounts, or requiring a credential reset where appropriate.

By combining detection, investigation, and response capabilities, Microsoft Defender XDR enables organizations to identify and respond to complex attacks across Microsoft cloud environments.

Summary

Today's cloud environments require security strategies that verify identities, control access to resources, and detect threats across distributed systems.

As organizations adopt cloud services, mobile devices, and remote work, traditional security models based on network boundaries are no longer sufficient to protect systems and data.

The Zero Trust model addresses these challenges by removing assumptions of trust within a network. Instead of relying on location-based security, every access request must be verified using identity and contextual signals. By continuously validating access and limiting permissions, organizations reduce the likelihood that attackers can move freely within their environments.

Authentication plays a critical role in this model by verifying the identity of users, devices, and services during the sign-in process. Modern authentication methods, including multi-factor authentication and passwordless sign-in, strengthen security by reducing the risks associated with compromised credentials.

Once authentication confirms an identity, authorization determines what that identity is permitted to access. Techniques such as role-based access control and group-based permission management help organizations assign appropriate access rights while maintaining the principle of least-privilege access.

In addition to verifying identities and controlling access, organizations must monitor activity across their environments to detect potential threats. Threat protection and threat intelligence help security teams identify suspicious behavior, understand attacker techniques, and respond quickly to potential incidents.

Microsoft Defender XDR supports this process by analyzing security signals across identities, devices, email systems, and cloud applications. By correlating related alerts into incidents and providing investigation tools, the platform helps security teams detect and respond to attacks that span multiple services.

Together, these capabilities explain how Microsoft 365 approaches security across identity, access, and threat detection. By combining Zero Trust principles, strong authentication, controlled authorization, and integrated threat detection, Microsoft 365 helps organizations protect identities, systems, and data across modern cloud environments.

The next chapter, *Identify Core Security Features of Microsoft 365 Services*, moves deeper into identity as the control plane for Microsoft 365 security. It focuses on how Microsoft Entra verifies identities, evaluates access decisions through Conditional Access, and provides visibility into authentication activity through sign-in logs and Identity Secure Score.

Microsoft 365 security principles reference

The following table lists the primary security concepts introduced in this chapter, explains what each topic covers, and provides links to the corresponding Microsoft documentation for further reference. These references help reinforce the security model introduced in this chapter and provide a useful point of return when reviewing how Microsoft 365 protects identities, controls access, and detects threats across modern cloud environments.

Topic	What it Covers	Learn More
Zero Trust Principles	Explains the Zero Trust model, its purpose, and its three core principles: verify explicitly, least privilege, and assume breach	`https://learn.microsoft.com/en-us/security/zero-trust/zero-trust-overview`
Authentication Methods	Identity verification methods including passwords, MFA, passwordless authentication, and sign-in verification flows	`https://learn.microsoft.com/en-us/entra/identity/authentication/concept-authentication-methods`
Multi-Factor Authentication (MFA)	How MFA works and why multiple verification factors reduce the risk of unauthorized access	`https://learn.microsoft.com/en-us/entra/identity/authentication/concept-mfa-howitworks`
Passwordless Authentication	Modern authentication without passwords using biometrics, trusted devices, FIDO2 keys, and Microsoft Authenticator	`https://learn.microsoft.com/en-us/entra/identity/authentication/concept-authentication-passwordless`
Authentication vs Authorization	The difference between verifying identity (AuthN) and determining permissions (AuthZ)	`https://learn.microsoft.com/en-us/entra/identity-platform/authentication-vs-authorization`
Authorization in Microsoft 365	How access decisions are made after authentication and how permissions are applied to resources	`https://learn.microsoft.com/en-us/entra/identity-platform/permissions-consent-overview`

Topic	What it Covers	Learn More
Role-Based Access Control (RBAC)	Managing permissions by assigning users to roles rather than assigning permissions individually	`https://learn.microsoft.com/en-us/azure/role-based-access-control/overview`
Threat Protection and Intelligence	Monitoring, detecting, and responding to threats while understanding attacker techniques and behaviors	`https://learn.microsoft.com/en-us/defender-xdr/defender-threat-intelligence`
Microsoft Defender XDR	Unified detection, investigation, and response across identities, endpoints, email, and cloud applications	`https://learn.microsoft.com/en-us/defender-xdr/microsoft-365-defender`
Security Alerts, Incidents, and Investigation	How alerts are generated, correlated into incidents, and investigated by security teams	`https://learn.microsoft.com/en-us/microsoft-365/security/defender/incident-response-overview`
Security Signals and Telemetry	How activity data is collected and analyzed to detect suspicious behavior across the environment	`https://learn.microsoft.com/en-us/defender-xdr/advanced-hunting-overview`

Table 2.1: Microsoft 365 security principles reference

These references provide a practical way to revisit the security concepts introduced in this chapter and connect them to Microsoft's official guidance. They are especially useful when reviewing how Zero Trust, authentication, authorization, and threat detection work together across Microsoft 365 services.

Key terms and acronyms

This quick reference introduces the common security terms used throughout this chapter and helps new readers become familiar with the language of Microsoft 365 security. It focuses on the words and concepts that appear across Zero Trust, authentication, authorization, threat protection, and Microsoft Defender XDR so that the security model is easier to understand from the start.

Term	Meaning
Zero Trust	A security model that assumes no user, device, or service should be trusted automatically. Every access request must be verified before access is granted.
Authentication	The process of verifying that a user, device, application, or service is genuinely who or what it claims to be.
Authorization	The process of determining what an authenticated identity is allowed to access or do after sign-in is verified.
Identity	A digital account representing a user, device, application, or service that can request access to a resource.
Identity Provider (IdP)	The system that stores identities and verifies sign-in requests during authentication.
MFA	Multi-Factor Authentication, which requires more than one form of verification during sign-in to reduce the risk of unauthorized access.
Passwordless Authentication	A sign-in method that removes passwords and uses trusted devices, biometrics, or authentication apps instead.
AuthN	Short form for authentication, used when referring to identity verification during sign-in.
AuthZ	Short form for authorization, used when referring to permissions and access decisions after authentication.
RBAC	Role-Based Access Control, a method of managing permissions by assigning users to roles instead of assigning permissions individually.
Least Privilege	A security principle where users and services receive only the minimum access required to perform their tasks.
Assume Breach	A Zero Trust principle that assumes attackers may already have some access, so organizations focus on detection, containment, and limiting movement.

Term	Meaning
Threat Protection	The process of identifying, detecting, and responding to suspicious or malicious activity across systems and users.
Threat Intelligence	Information about attacker techniques, malicious behavior, and emerging threats used to improve detection and response.
Telemetry	Activity signals generated by users, devices, applications, and services that security systems analyze for suspicious behavior.
Security Alert	A notification generated when suspicious activity is detected that may indicate a potential threat.
Incident	A collection of related security alerts grouped together to represent the full attack scenario rather than isolated events.
Microsoft Defender XDR	Microsoft's unified security platform for detecting, investigating, and responding to threats across identities, devices, email, and applications.

Table 2.2: Key terms and acronyms

These terms provide a useful reference point as you move through Microsoft 365 security concepts. Understanding what each term represents makes it easier to recognize how identities are verified, how access decisions are made, and how threats are detected and investigated across modern cloud environments.

For exam preparation, this also helps reinforce the terminology that appears in scenario-based questions, where selecting the correct answer often depends on recognizing the purpose of a security control or platform rather than recalling a definition word for word.

Exam readiness drill – chapter review questions

Apart from mastering key concepts, strong test-taking skills under time pressure are essential for acing your certification exam. That's why developing these abilities early in your learning journey is critical.

Exam readiness drills, using the free online practice resources provided with this book, helps you progressively improve your time management and test-taking skills while reinforcing the key concepts you've learned.

HOW TO GET STARTED

1. Open the link or scan the QR code at the bottom of this page
2. If you have unlocked the practice resources already, log in to your registered account. If you haven't, follow the instructions in the *Free Benefits with Your Book* section in this book's *Preface* and come back to this page.
3. Once you log in, click the START button to start this chapter's quiz
4. We recommend attempting a quiz multiple times until you're able to answer most of the questions correctly and well within the time limit
5. You can use the following practice template to help you plan your attempts:

Working On Accuracy		
Attempt	**Target**	**Time Limit**
Attempt 1	40% or more	Till the timer runs out
Attempt 2	60% or more	Till the timer runs out
Attempt 3	75% or more	Till the timer runs out
Working On Timing		
Attempt 4	75% or more	1 minute before time limit
Attempt 5	75% or more	2 minutes before time limit
Attempt 6	75% or more	3 minutes before time limit

The above drill is just an example. Design your drills based on your own goals and make the most out of the online quizzes accompanying this book.

Link to this chapter's quiz

You need to unlock the online practice resources to access the link below. Check the *Free Benefits with Your Book* section in the *Preface* for detailed instructions on how to do this. You only need to unlock the resources once.

Open Quiz `https://packt.link/D5hXf` or scan the QR code

3

Identifying Core Security Features of Microsoft 365 Services

This chapter builds on your understanding of Zero Trust principles, authentication and authorization, and Microsoft Defender XDR's threat protection, and moves into how these concepts are applied through the core identity features of Microsoft 365 services.

In Microsoft 365, **identity** manages how people and applications interact with services across the environment.

Users sign in to access resources, applications connect to services, and administrators manage access and security settings. All of this is coordinated through a central identity system. Core identity features define how identities are managed, how access is controlled, and how activity is monitored across the environment.

These capabilities work together to secure Microsoft 365 services in a way that is easy to understand, without requiring deep technical knowledge.

This chapter aligns with the **Identify the core features and objects of Microsoft 365 services** area of the **AB-900** exam.

The following identity capabilities show how Microsoft 365 secures access across the environment:

- Understanding features and capabilities of Microsoft Entra
- Understanding conditional access and policies
- Identifying the appropriate security object to use in an organization (users and groups)

- Understanding the purpose and benefits of **single sign-on** (**SSO**)
- Understanding app registrations and enterprise applications
- Identifying the role of **Privileged Identity Management** (**PIM**) in an organization
- Interpreting Identity Secure Score in Microsoft Entra ID
- Using tools to review audit logs for user and admin activity
- Identifying the appropriate tools to troubleshoot common sign-in issues (MFA, Conditional Access, and risky sign-ins)

These capabilities define how Microsoft 365 verifies identity, evaluates access decisions, and provides visibility into authentication activity.

> Note
>
> **Important information regarding Microsoft Portal experiences and UI elements**
>
> Microsoft frequently updates portal experiences and UI elements. As a result, some screenshots, navigation paths, or interface details shown in this book may differ slightly from your individual tenant's environment at the time of reading.

Understanding features and capabilities of Microsoft Entra

Access to Microsoft 365 services begins with identity verification. Every sign-in request is evaluated to confirm who the user is and what they are allowed to access.

In Microsoft environments, **Microsoft Entra** acts as the **identity provider** (**IDP**). Instead of each service managing its own access control, Microsoft 365 services rely on Entra to handle authentication and authorization consistently across the environment.

These capabilities are managed through the **Microsoft Entra admin center** `https://entra.microsoft.com/`, where identity objects, access controls, governance, and security insights are centralized.

Figure 3.1 highlights where identity is managed in Microsoft Entra and how key components are organized in one place.

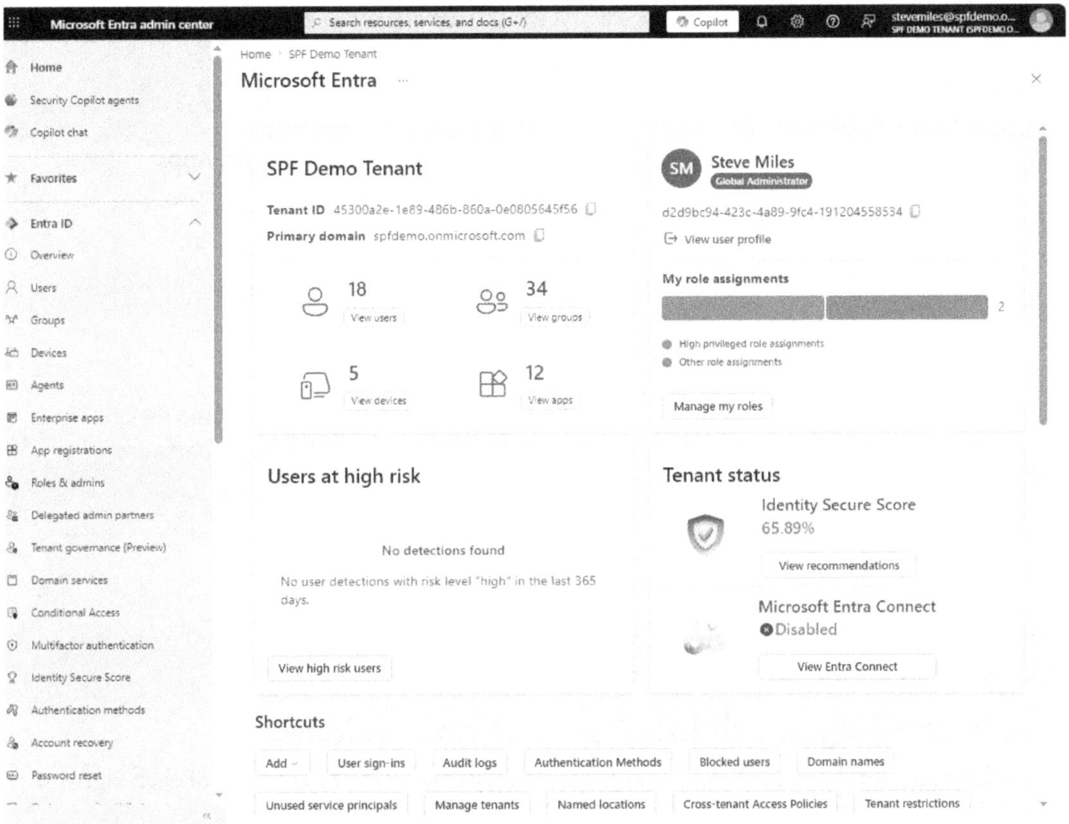

Figure 3.1: Microsoft Entra admin center overview

The platform organizes key identity components in one place:

- **Users and groups** define who can access services
- **Applications** represent services that identities interact with
- **Roles** control administrative permissions
- **Identity Secure Score** reflects the security posture

Microsoft Entra acts as the central identity system. It stores users, groups, and application identities, and uses this information during sign-in to decide what access should be allowed.

When a user attempts to access a service, the request is redirected to Entra. The platform validates the **identity** (*authentication*) and determines what access is **allowed** (*authorization*) based on permissions, group membership, and assigned roles.

Because access is controlled through identity, Microsoft Entra becomes a key security point. If an identity is compromised, it can affect multiple connected services.

Figure 3.2 shows how identities connect across the environment.

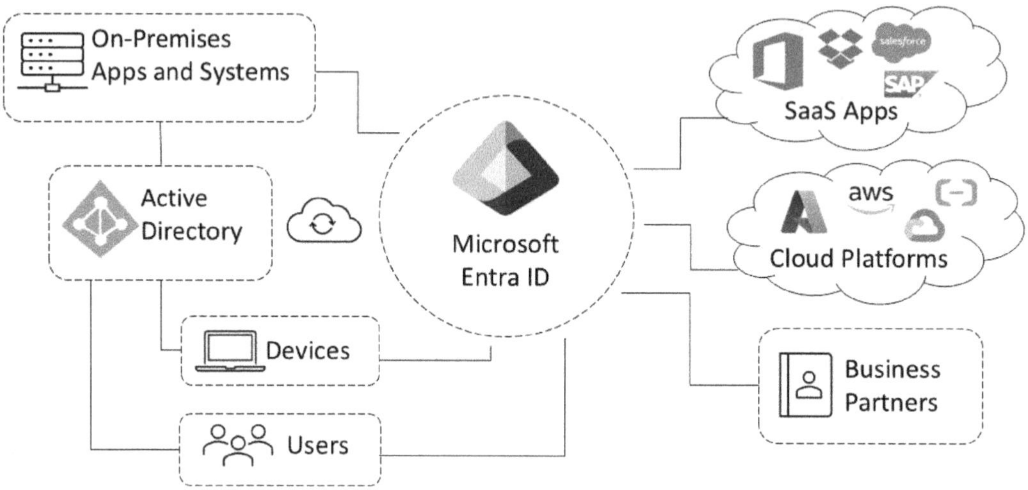

Figure 3.2: Microsoft Entra identity provider connections

Identities extend across Microsoft 365 services, cloud applications, and external platforms, enabling consistent access control across the environment.

Understanding conditional access and policies

Conditional Access controls how access is granted by evaluating the context of each sign-in.

Instead of relying only on a username and password, it considers signals such as location, device state, and sign-in risk to determine whether access should be allowed, require additional verification such as multifactor authentication, or be blocked.

These decisions are enforced through **Conditional Access policies**, which apply consistent access rules across Microsoft 365 services before a user reaches an application.

It does not replace authentication but adds an extra layer of decision-making before access is allowed.

Figure 3.3 illustrates the Conditional Access Overview in the Microsoft Entra admin center.

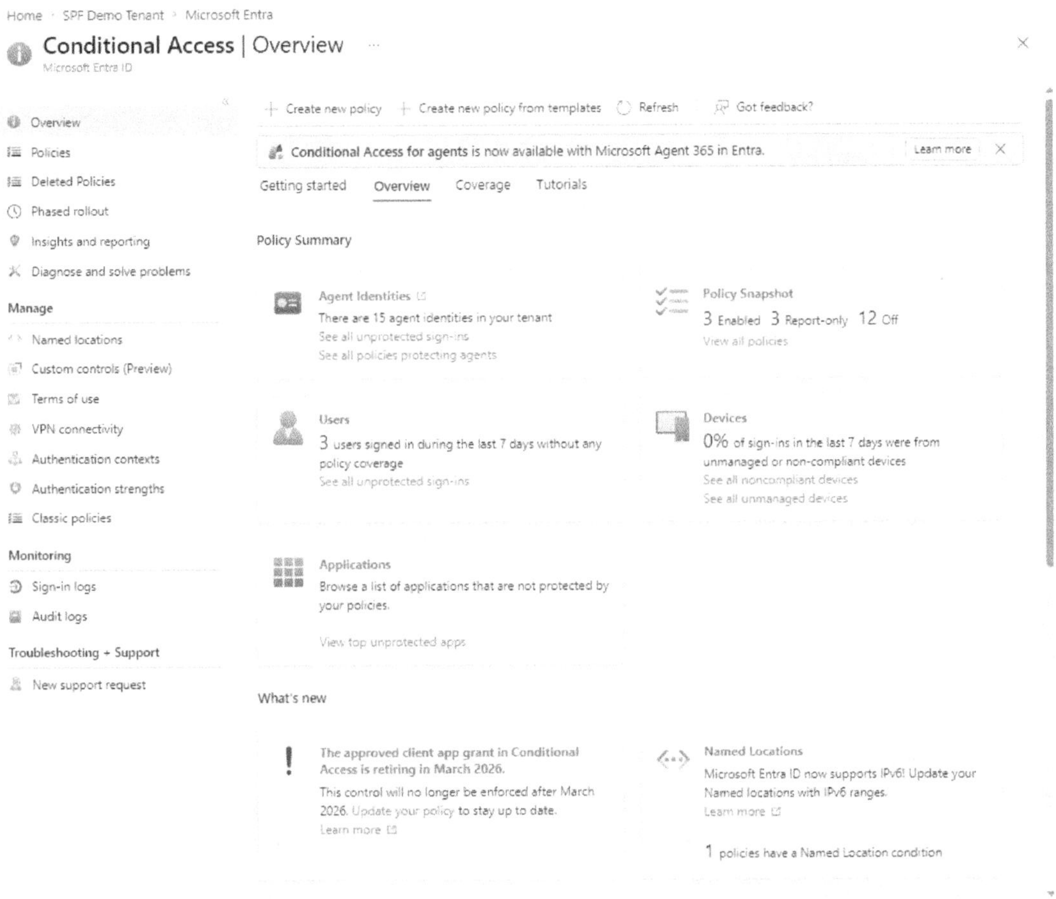

Figure 3.3: Conditional Access overview in Microsoft Entra

This view highlights how users, devices, applications, and policies are governed and where coverage gaps may exist. Administrators use it to create and manage access policies.

Figure 3.4 shows how Conditional Access evaluates authentication signals before granting access.

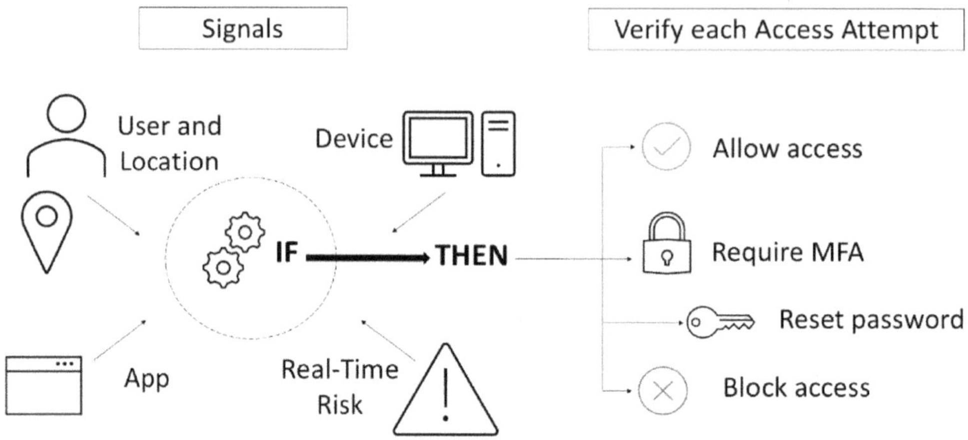

Figure 3.4: Conditional Access evaluating authentication signals before granting access

These decisions are defined within **Conditional Access** policies, which control how access is evaluated and enforced during sign-in.

Each policy defines three key elements:

- **Assignments**: who the policy applies to
- **Conditions**: the signals evaluated during sign-in
- **Access controls**: the result enforced, such as blocking access or granting access only after requirements such as MFA or device compliance are satisfied

Together, these elements define how access decisions are evaluated and enforced during sign-in. *Figure 3.5* shows how these elements are combined within a Conditional Access policy.

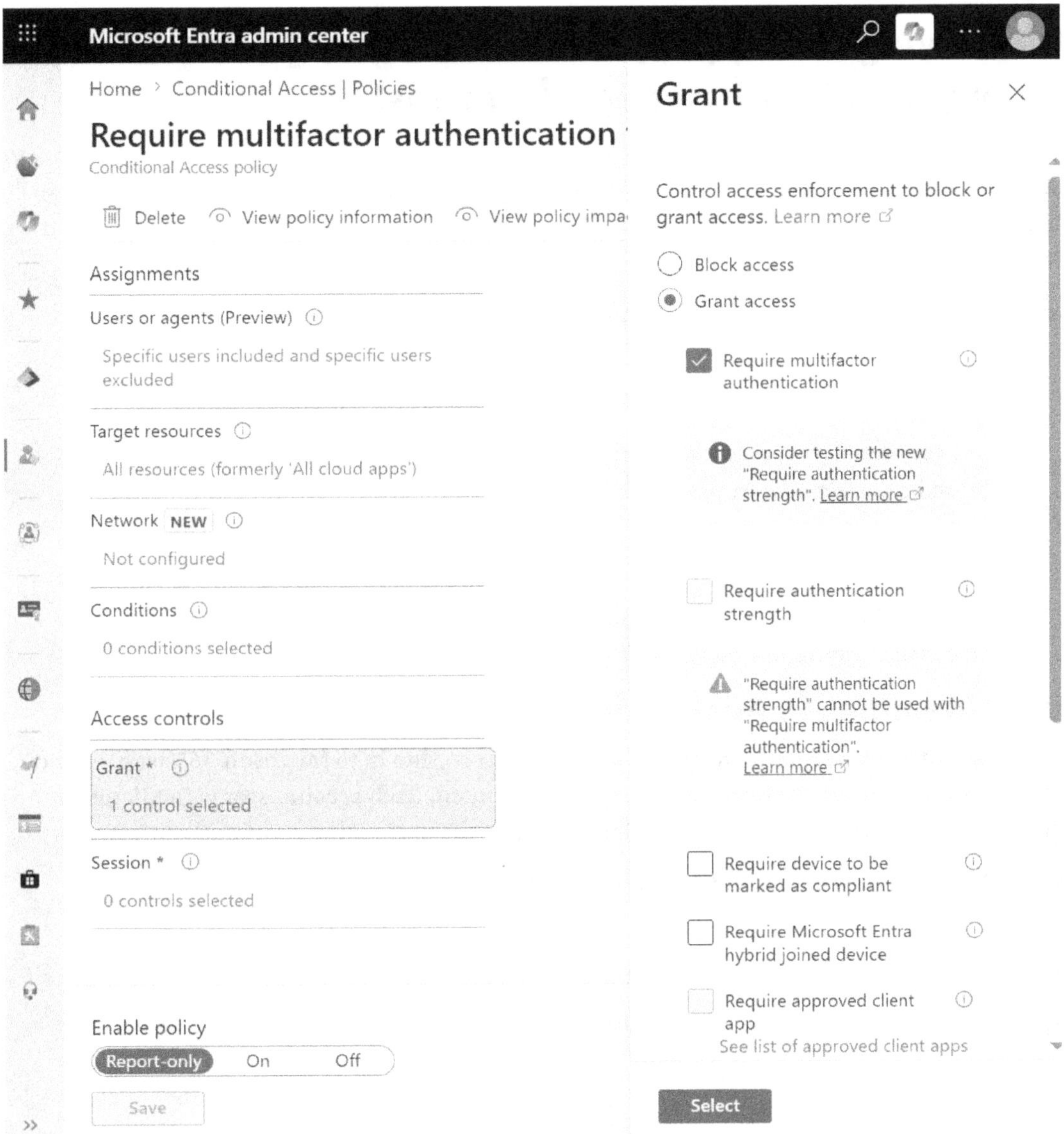

Figure 3.5: Conditional Access policy showing assignments, conditions, and access controls

Policies are evaluated at the point of authentication, ensuring access decisions are applied consistently across all services that rely on Microsoft Entra.

Identifying the appropriate security object to use in an organization (users and groups)

In **Microsoft 365 environments**, access to services and resources is managed through **identity objects** stored in Microsoft Entra. These objects represent the people and organizational structures that interact with applications, data, and administrative features across the cloud environment.

Identity objects provide the foundation for how access is assigned and managed across services.

Two of the most commonly used identity objects are users and groups:

- A **user identity** represents an individual account that can sign in and perform actions based on assigned permissions
- **Groups** organize multiple users into a single unit that can be used for access management

Together, users and groups provide a simple way to organize access so permissions can be managed consistently across the organization.

User identities in Microsoft Entra

A **user identity** represents an *individual account* that can sign in to Microsoft 365 services and access resources in the organization's cloud environment. Each account stored in Microsoft Entra contains the information required to recognize the user and support authentication.

Figure 3.6 shows how **user identities** are represented and managed in Microsoft Entra.

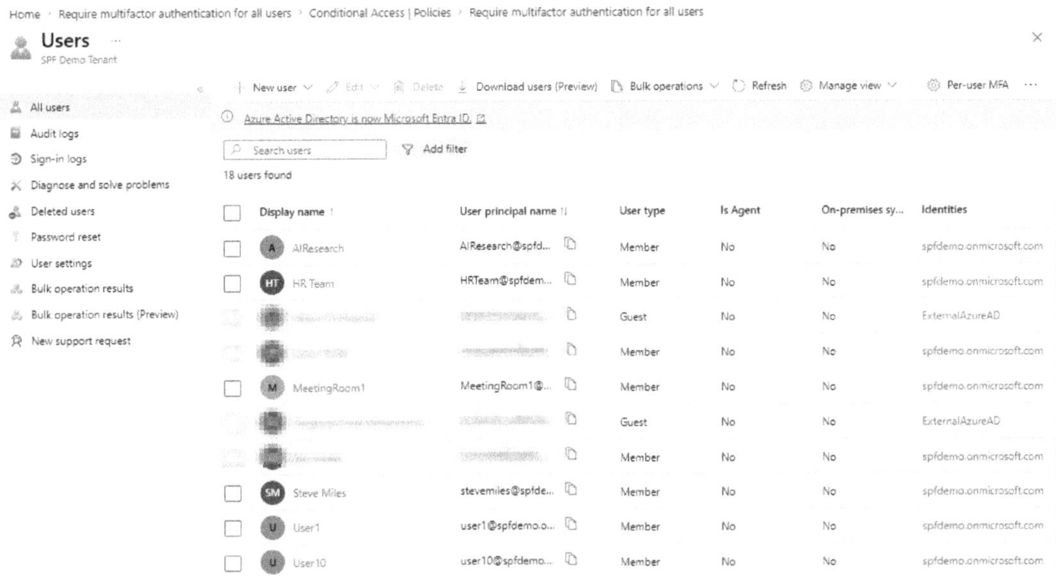

Figure 3.6: Users in Microsoft Entra showing identity accounts in the directory

The **Users** page lists the accounts that exist in the directory and provides key details such as **Display name**, **User principal name,** and **User type**. This view shows which identities are present in the environment and how they are configured.

When a user signs in, Microsoft Entra validates the credentials associated with the account. After successful authentication, the account is used to determine access across services.

Applications evaluate permissions assigned directly to the user or inherited through group membership and administrative roles to determine what actions are allowed.

User accounts form the foundation of access in Microsoft Entra, as every sign-in and access decision begins with an authenticated identity.

Groups as identity containers for managing access

While *user identities* represent individual accounts, **groups** provide a way to organize multiple users and manage access more efficiently.

A **group** acts as a *container* for users. Instead of assigning permissions to each individual, access is assigned once to the group, and all members inherit those permissions. This makes access management simpler and more consistent.

For example, if a team needs access to a SharePoint site or application, permissions can be assigned to a group rather than to each user. When someone joins or leaves the team, updating group membership automatically adjusts their access.

Figure 3.7 shows how **groups** are used to organize identities and manage access.

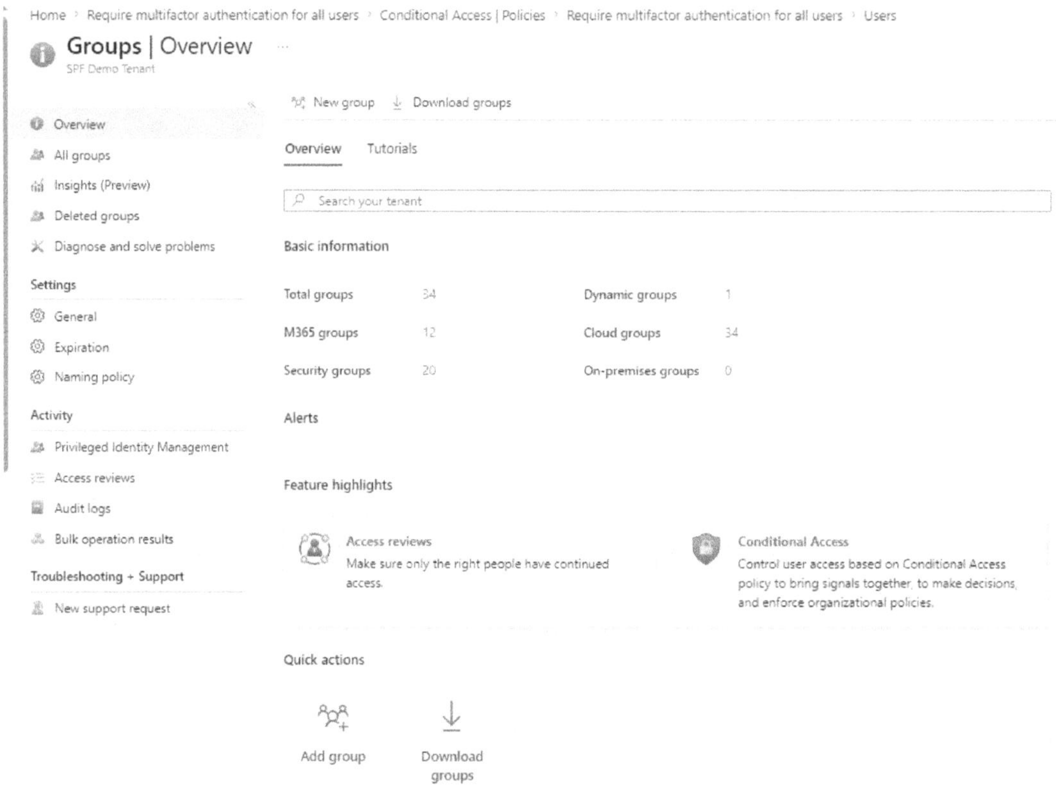

Figure 3.7: Groups in Microsoft Entra used for access management

This approach reduces administrative effort and ensures access is applied consistently across services.

Common group types used in Microsoft environments

Microsoft environments support different types of groups, each designed for a specific purpose:

- **Security groups**: Used to assign permissions to applications, resources, or roles

- **Microsoft 365 groups**: Used for collaboration, providing shared resources such as a mailbox, calendar, SharePoint site, and Microsoft Teams workspace
- **Distribution groups**: Used for email communication, allowing messages to be sent to multiple users through a single address

Each type supports a different need: *access control*, *collaboration*, or *communication*.

Using groups to simplify access management

Groups provide a scalable way to manage access as organizations grow. Instead of configuring permissions for each user, access is controlled through group membership.

Figure 3.8 illustrates how group membership is used to grant access to applications and resources.

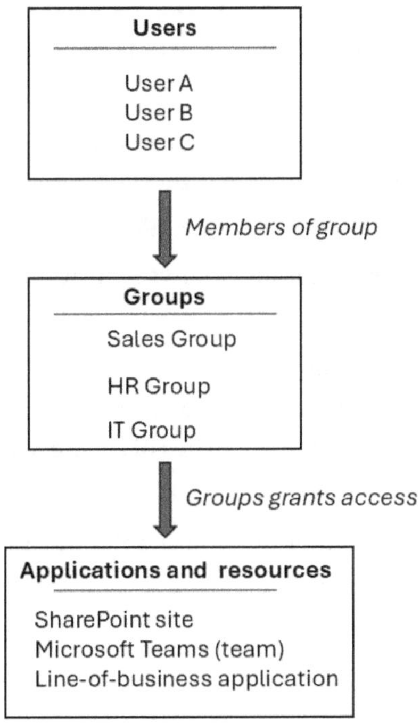

Figure 3.8: Users assigned to groups to grant access to applications and resources

When membership changes, access updates automatically. This allows organizations to manage permissions centrally without repeatedly configuring individual accounts.

Understanding the purpose and benefits of single sign-on (SSO)

In modern organizations, users need access to multiple applications throughout the day. Without a centralized identity system, each application requires separate authentication, increasing credential fatigue and creating a fragmented sign-in experience.

Single sign-on (**SSO**) solves this by allowing users to authenticate once and access multiple trusted applications without signing in again. This works because applications rely on a central identity provider rather than maintaining separate authentication systems.

In Microsoft environments, Microsoft Entra performs this role. When a user signs in, Entra verifies the identity and generates a **security token**, which is a digital representation of that identity. This token is then presented to other trusted applications as proof that the user has already authenticated.

Because these applications trust the same identity provider, they accept the token instead of prompting the user to sign in again. This allows the authentication session to be reused across Microsoft 365 services and integrated third-party applications.

This approach reduces repeated sign-ins and allows security controls to be applied consistently across connected services.

As a result, SSO becomes a core component of managing secure and seamless access across Microsoft environments. While SSO explains how users authenticate across services, applications and services must also have identities of their own to securely interact with resources.

Figure 3.9 illustrates how a single authentication enables access to multiple applications using a security token.

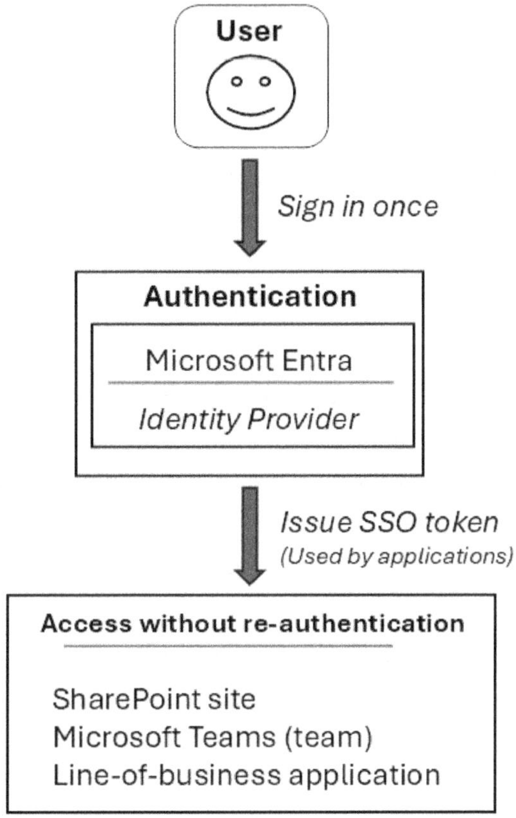

Figure 3.9: SSO token flow showing authentication through Microsoft Entra and access to multiple applications

The token remains valid for a defined period, allowing the user to move between applications without repeating the sign-in process. The user experience becomes seamless, while authentication remains centrally controlled.

Understanding App registrations and Enterprise applications

In addition to *users*, **applications** also require **identities** to interact securely with services in a cloud environment. When an application accesses data or communicates with Microsoft 365 services, the identity platform must recognize and authenticate that application.

In Microsoft environments, Microsoft Entra provides these identities. By assigning identities to applications, organizations can control how software accesses resources, enforce permissions, and monitor activity using the same identity-based model applied to users.

Microsoft Entra represents application identities using two related identity objects: **app registrations** and **enterprise** applications. Together, these define what an application is and how it operates within an organization.

App registrations

An **app registration** defines the identity of an application within Microsoft Entra. It acts as the blueprint for the application, containing the information required for authentication, such as identifiers and configuration settings.

Once registered, the application can authenticate with Microsoft Entra and receive tokens that allow it to request access to protected resources.

Enterprise applications (service principals)

An **enterprise application** represents an application within a specific Microsoft Entra tenant. Also known as a **service principal**, it acts as the control point for managing how the application interacts with users and resources in the organization.

Administrators use this object to assign users or groups, manage permissions, and control access.

Figure 3.10 shows how enterprise applications are represented and managed within a tenant.

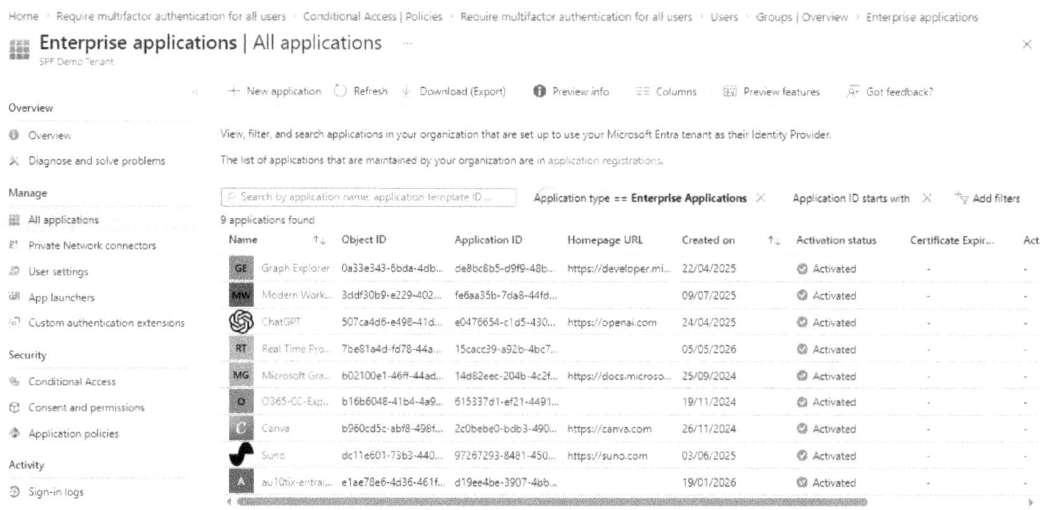

Figure 3.10: Enterprise applications in Microsoft Entra

The Enterprise applications page lists the applications available in the tenant and allows administrators to manage access to each one. From this view, administrators can determine which identities can access an application and how that access is controlled.

Because the service principal exists within the tenant, it defines how the application is used in the organization, including who can access it and what permissions are applied.

Relationship between an app registration and an enterprise application

App registrations and **enterprise applications** represent two parts of the same identity approach.

The app registration defines the application itself, while the enterprise application represents how that application is used within a specific tenant.

When an application is registered, Microsoft Entra creates a corresponding enterprise application in the tenant. This allows each organization to control access and permissions independently.

Figure 3.11 compares how app registrations define an application and how enterprise applications represent it within a tenant.

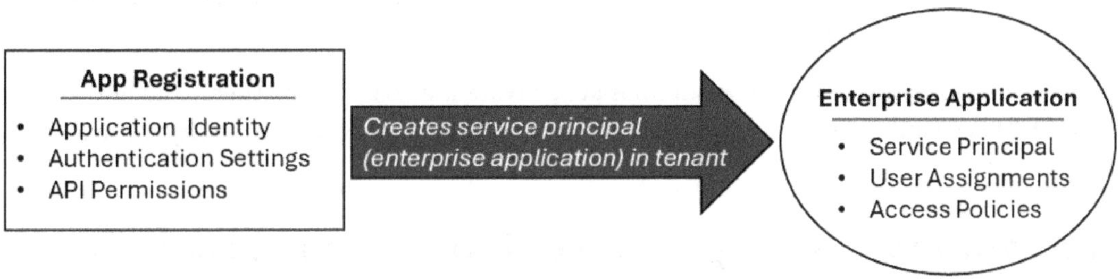

Figure 3.11: App registration and enterprise application relationship in Microsoft Entra

This relationship allows Microsoft Entra to separate the definition of an application from how it is used within an organization. A single app registration exists once, while each tenant maintains its own enterprise application to control access, permissions, and usage.

Identifying the role of Privileged Identity Management (PIM) in an organization

Privileged accounts have elevated permissions that allow them to manage systems, modify security settings, and control access to critical resources. Because these accounts can make significant changes, they present a higher security risk if misused or compromised.

In Microsoft environments, Microsoft Entra **Privileged Identity Management** (**PIM**) helps reduce this risk by controlling how and when administrative access is granted. Instead of assigning permanent permissions, PIM introduces controls that limit, approve, and monitor privileged access.

Just-in-time privileged access using Privileged Identity Management

PIM enables **just-in-time** (**JIT**) access by allowing users to activate privileged roles only when needed. Users are assigned as eligible rather than permanently active.

When access is required, the user requests **activation**. Additional verification steps, such as multifactor authentication or justification, may be required. Once approved, the role becomes active for a limited time. When the activation period expires, the permissions are no longer active.

This reduces the exposure of privileged permissions by ensuring they are only active when required.

Controlling and monitoring privileged role activation

PIM provides mechanisms to govern and track how privileged roles are used.

Activation requests can require multifactor authentication, justification, or approval from another administrator before access is granted.

Administrators can also monitor when roles are activated, who activated them, and how they are used. This visibility helps detect unusual activity and maintain accountability through audit records.

Interpreting Identity Secure Score in Microsoft Entra ID

After implementing identity security controls such as Conditional Access and Privileged Identity Management, organizations need a way to evaluate how effectively those protections are working.

Identity Secure Score provides this visibility by measuring how well recommended identity security practices have been implemented across the environment. Instead of focusing on a single configuration, it evaluates multiple controls and presents an overall view of the organization's identity security posture.

Each **recommendation** represents a specific security improvement, such as enabling multifactor authentication, protecting privileged roles, or blocking legacy authentication where appropriate. Every recommendation has a **point value**, and the overall **score increases** as these protections are implemented.

Exam scenarios may also refer to identity-focused factors such as the number of global administrators or accounts with passwords set to never expire; these affect Identity Secure Score, while SharePoint site permissions and user location do not.

Figure 3.12 shows how Identity Secure Score presents security posture and recommended improvements.

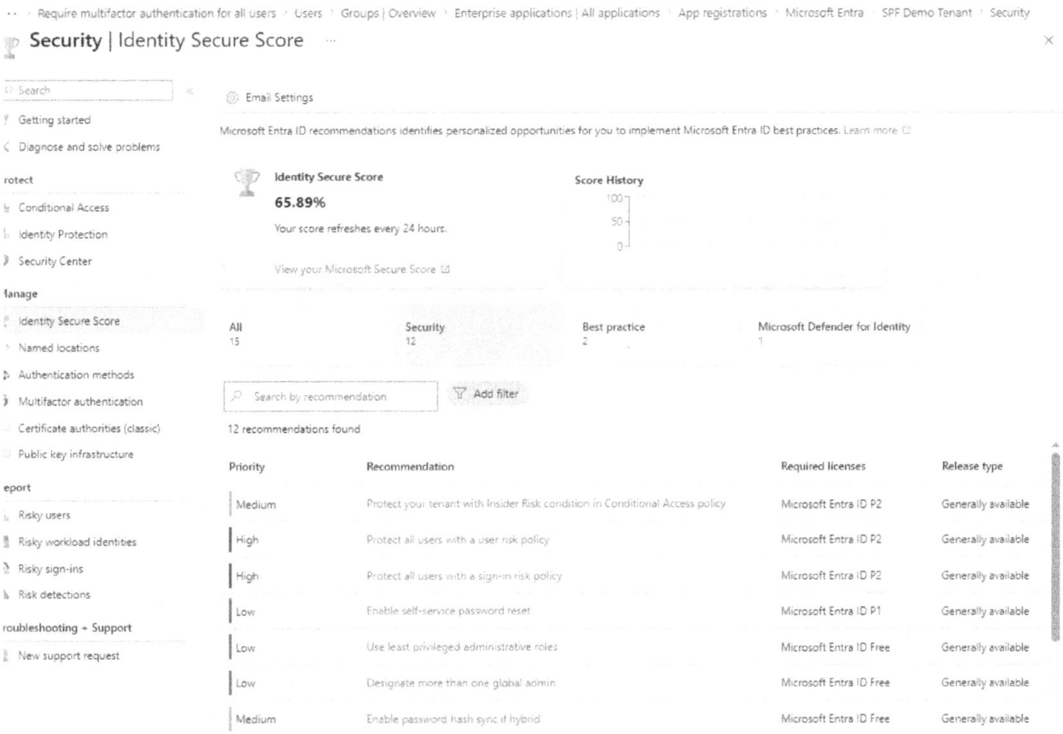

Figure 3.12: Identity Secure Score in Microsoft Entra showing security posture and recommended improvements

The view combines the current score with recommended actions, allowing administrators to identify gaps and prioritize the changes that will have the greatest impact on identity security.

Using Identity Secure Score to improve and monitor security posture

Identity Secure Score not only reflects the current state of identity protection but also provides a roadmap for improvement.

Administrators can review recommendations, understand their impact, and prioritize actions based on organizational requirements. As improvements are implemented, the score increases, providing a measurable indication of progress.

Because the score is continuously updated, it also helps organizations track changes over time and identify new recommendations as they become available. Regular review ensures that identity protections continue to evolve as the environment changes.

Using the appropriate tools to review audit logs for user and admin activity

After identity protections and access controls are implemented, organizations need visibility into authentication activity and administrative changes to ensure systems are operating as expected.

In Microsoft environments, Microsoft Entra provides this visibility through **sign-in logs** and **audit logs**.

These logs record how users sign in and what changes are made in the environment, helping administrators investigate issues such as failed sign-ins or unexpected configuration changes.

Microsoft Entra audit logs focus on identity and directory changes, while broader Microsoft 365 audit activity can be reviewed from Audit in the Microsoft Purview portal or the Microsoft Defender portal.

Reviewing sign-in logs in Microsoft Entra

Sign-in logs record authentication attempts made by users accessing applications and services connected to the identity platform.

Figure 3.13 shows how sign-in logs capture authentication activity and outcomes.

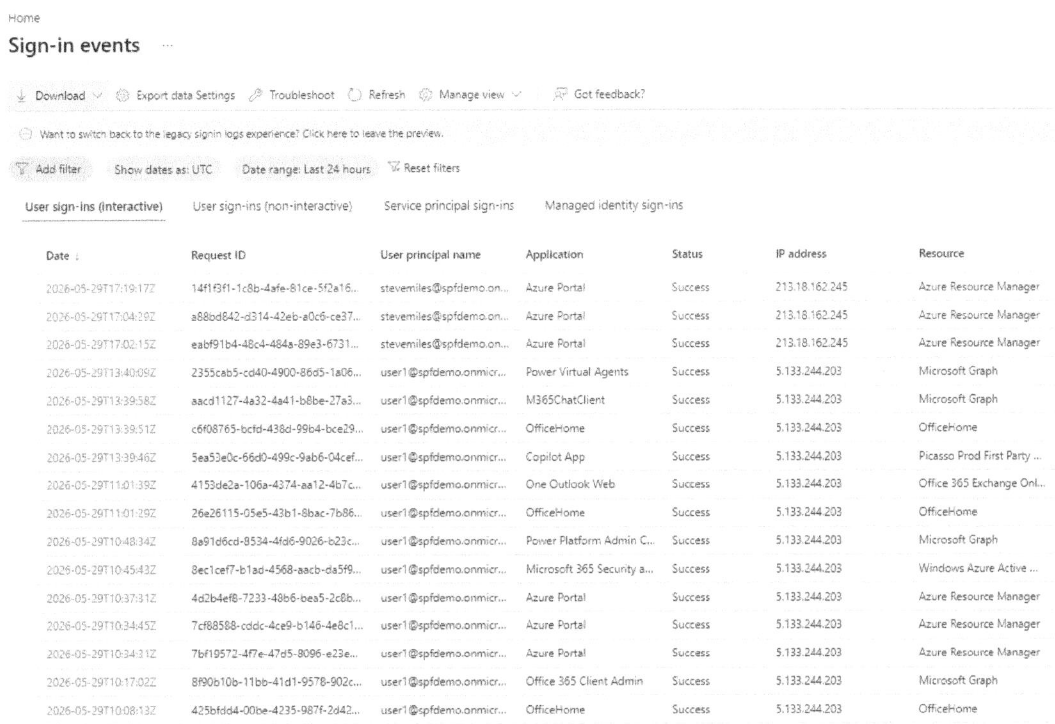

Figure 3.13: Sign-in logs in Microsoft Entra showing authentication activity and outcomes

Each entry represents a single authentication event and includes details such as the user, the application, the time of the attempt, and the outcome. This allows administrators to determine whether access was successful, required additional verification, or was blocked.

The logs also show how access decisions were applied, including whether controls such as Conditional Access influenced the outcome.

Reviewing audit logs for administrative and configuration activity

Audit logs capture changes made to the identity environment, including administrative and configuration actions.

Figure 3.14 shows how audit logs capture administrative and configuration activity.

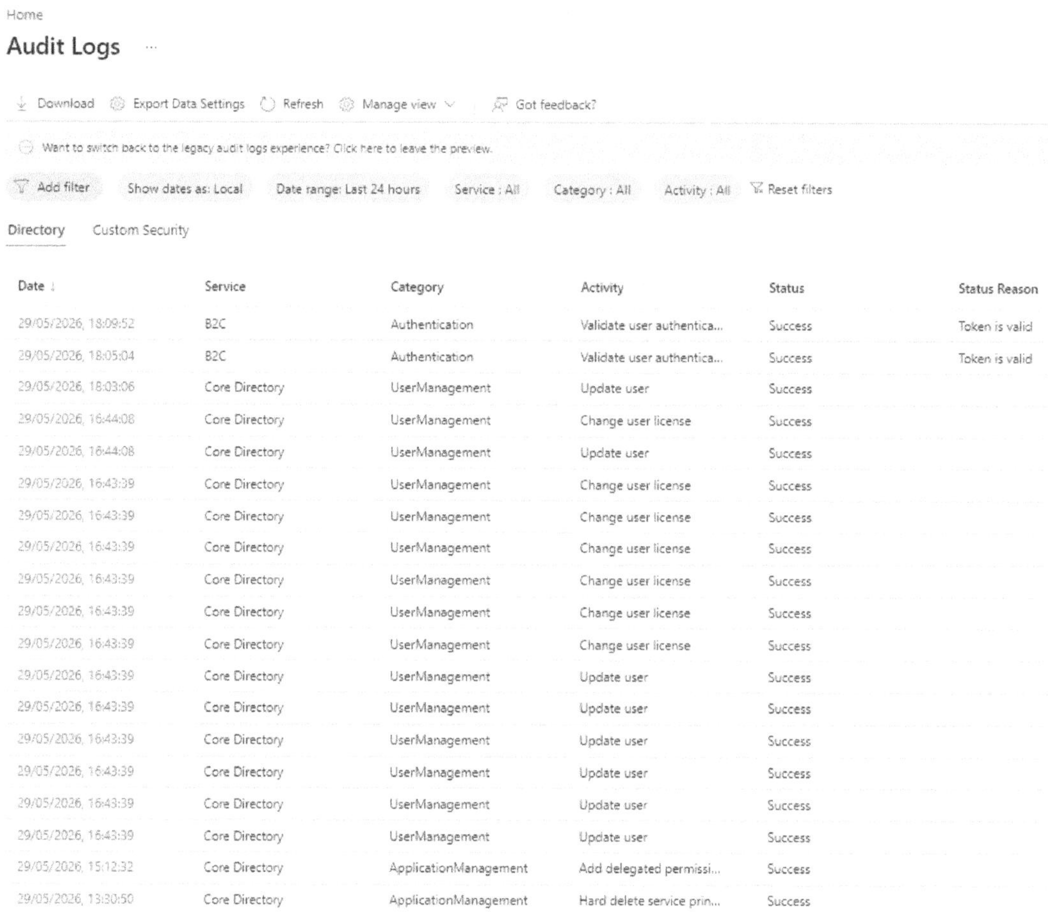

Figure 3.14: Audit logs in Microsoft Entra showing administrative and configuration activity

Each entry records the action performed, the account that performed it, and when the change occurred. This allows administrators to trace changes over time and investigate unexpected updates, such as modifications to user accounts, group memberships, or roles.

Identifying the appropriate tools to troubleshoot common sign-in issues (MFA, Conditional Access, and risky sign-ins)

Even in well-configured environments, users may experience sign-in issues when authentication requirements are not completed or when security controls block access.

Most sign-in problems fall into three categories:

- **Multifactor authentication (MFA)** has not completed
- Conditional Access requirements not met
- Risk-based blocking triggered by Identity Protection

Risky sign-ins and risky users are detected by Microsoft Entra ID Protection, which can trigger risk-based blocking or remediation during sign-in.

Identifying which condition caused the failure is key to resolving the issue.

In Microsoft environments, Microsoft Entra provides tools to review authentication activity and identify the cause of failed sign-in attempts.

Investigating sign-in issues using Microsoft Entra tools

The primary tool for troubleshooting sign-in issues is the sign-in log, which records authentication attempts and their outcomes.

Administrators can review each sign-in event to see when the attempt occurred, which application was accessed, and whether authentication was successful. The log also shows whether additional requirements were triggered, such as MFA, Conditional Access policies, or risk-based detections.

This allows administrators to determine why the sign-in failed.

Understanding sign-in results and resolving issues

Sign-in results show whether authentication was successful or blocked and indicate which security control affected the outcome.

If a sign-in fails, the log identifies the reason. For example:

- MFA required but not completed
- Conditional Access policy conditions not satisfied
- Sign-in flagged as risky and blocked

These results allow administrators to determine which control interrupted the sign-in and what action is required to resolve it. For example, completing MFA satisfies identity verification, meeting Conditional Access requirements satisfies policy conditions, and resolving risk signals addresses potential identity compromise.

Summary

This chapter explained how identity controls access to Microsoft 365 services.

Microsoft Entra provides the identity platform that supports authentication and access control across Microsoft 365.

This includes managing identity objects such as users and groups, enabling single sign-on, and allowing users to securely access multiple services, while applications authenticate through app registrations and enterprise applications.

The chapter also examined how Conditional Access policies evaluate sign-in conditions to enforce security requirements such as multifactor authentication. In addition, Privileged Identity Management helps organizations protect administrative roles by limiting when elevated permissions can be activated.

You also explored how Identity Secure Score helps organizations evaluate their identity security posture and identify improvements that strengthen protection against identity-based attacks. Finally, you learned how administrators use sign-in logs and audit logs to monitor authentication activity, investigate administrative changes, and troubleshoot sign-in issues.

Together, these capabilities show how Microsoft Entra controls access, applies security decisions, and provides visibility into identity activity across Microsoft 365.

In the next chapter, you will explore how Microsoft 365 protects and governs data using Microsoft Purview, focusing on how data is classified, labeled, protected, and retained, and how capabilities such as Data Loss Prevention, Insider Risk Management, and Data Security Posture Management for AI are used to manage and protect data across the environment.

Core Microsoft 365 objects reference

This quick reference summarizes the core Microsoft 365 identity objects used throughout this chapter. These objects represent the users, groups, applications, roles, policies, and logs that Microsoft 365 uses to control access, govern administrative activity, and record identity events.

Object	What it represents	Why it matters
User	An individual identity that can sign in to Microsoft 365 services.	Users are the starting point for authentication, access assignment, licensing, and activity tracking.
Group	A collection of users managed as a single unit.	Groups simplify access management by allowing permissions to be assigned once and inherited by members.

Object	What it represents	Why it matters
Security group	A group used mainly for assigning permissions to resources, applications, or roles.	Security groups are used when access control is the main requirement.
Microsoft 365 group	A collaboration group with shared resources such as a mailbox, calendar, SharePoint site, and Teams workspace.	Microsoft 365 groups are used when the group needs shared collaboration services, not only access control.
Distributio n group	A group used to send email to multiple recipients through one address.	Distribution groups support communication rather than resource permission assignment.
App registration	The identity definition for an application in Microsoft Entra.	App registrations define how an application authenticates and requests access to protected resources.
Enterprise application	The tenant-specific representation of an application, also known as a service principal.	Enterprise applications are used to manage how an application is assigned, accessed, and governed inside the organization.
Role	A collection of permissions assigned to users or groups for administrative tasks.	Roles define what administrators can manage across Microsoft 365 and Microsoft Entra.
Conditional Access policy	A policy that evaluates sign-in signals and applies access controls.	Conditional Access policies determine whether access is allowed, blocked, or requires extra verification such as MFA.
Privileged role assignment	An assignment that grants elevated administrative permissions, either permanently or through PIM activation.	Privileged role assignments must be controlled carefully because they allow high-impact administrative actions.

Object	What it represents	Why it matters
Sign-in log	A record of authentication attempts and access outcomes.	Sign-in logs help administrators troubleshoot MFA, Conditional Access, risky sign-ins, and failed access attempts.
Audit log	A record of administrative and configuration changes.	Audit logs help administrators review who changed users, groups, roles, policies, and other identity settings.

Table 3.1: Core Microsoft 365 identity objects

These objects form the identity foundation for Microsoft 365. They give readers a quick reference point before reviewing the chapter terminology and help connect Microsoft Entra, Conditional Access, app identities, privileged access, secure score, and troubleshooting back to the objects used across the environment.

Key terms and acronyms

This quick reference introduces the common identity and access terms used throughout this chapter and helps new readers become familiar with the language of Microsoft 365 identity security. It focuses on the words and concepts that appear across Microsoft Entra, Conditional Access, users and groups, single sign-on, application identities, privileged access, Identity Secure Score, and sign-in troubleshooting so that the identity model is easier to understand from the start.

Term	Meaning
Microsoft Entra	Microsoft's identity and access platform used to manage identities, authentication, authorization, access controls, and identity security across Microsoft 365 services.
Microsoft Entra ID	The identity service within Microsoft Entra that stores users, groups, applications, and roles, and helps control access to Microsoft cloud services.
Identity Provider (IdP)	A system that stores identities and verifies sign-in requests. In Microsoft 365, Microsoft Entra acts as the identity provider.

Term	Meaning
User Identity	An individual account that represents a person who can sign in to Microsoft 365 services and access resources based on assigned permissions.
Group	A collection of users used to manage access more efficiently. Permissions can be assigned to the group so members inherit the required access.
Security Group	A group type commonly used to assign permissions to applications, resources, or roles for multiple users at once.
Microsoft 365 Group	A collaboration-focused group that provides shared resources such as a mailbox, calendar, SharePoint site, and Microsoft Teams workspace.
Distribution Group	A group used for email communication, allowing messages to be sent to multiple users through a single email address.
Conditional Access	A Microsoft Entra capability that evaluates sign-in signals such as user, device, location, and risk before allowing, blocking, or requiring extra verification for access.
Conditional Access Policy	A policy that defines who it applies to, which conditions are evaluated, and what access control is enforced during sign-in.
Assignments	The part of a Conditional Access policy that defines which users, groups, or applications the policy applies to.
Conditions	The signals evaluated by a Conditional Access policy such as device state, location, application, or sign-in risk.
Access Controls	The actions enforced by a Conditional Access policy, such as allowing access, blocking access, or requiring multifactor authentication.
MFA	Multi-Factor Authentication, which requires more than one form of verification during sign-in before access is granted.
SSO	Single Sign-On, which allows users to authenticate once and access multiple trusted applications without signing in again each time.

Term	Meaning
Security Token	A digital representation of a verified identity issued by Microsoft Entra and used by trusted applications to confirm that the user has already authenticated.
App Registration	The identity definition or blueprint for an application in Microsoft Entra. It contains the configuration needed for the application to authenticate and request access to resources.
Enterprise Application	The representation of an application within a specific Microsoft Entra tenant. It is used to manage user assignment, permissions, and access for that organization.
Service Principal	The tenant-specific identity for an application. In Microsoft Entra, an enterprise application is also known as a service principal.
PIM	Privileged Identity Management, a Microsoft Entra capability used to control, approve, monitor, and limit privileged role access.
JIT Access	Just-in-time access, where privileged permissions are activated only when needed and for a limited time rather than being permanently assigned.
Eligible Role Assignment	A role assignment that allows a user to request activation of privileged access when needed instead of holding the role permanently.
Active Role Assignment	A role assignment where the privileged permissions are currently available for use.
Identity Secure Score	A Microsoft Entra measurement that shows how well recommended identity security practices have been implemented across the environment.
Recommendation	A suggested security improvement in Identity Secure Score, such as enabling MFA, protecting privileged roles, or reducing risky identity configurations.

Term	Meaning
Sign-in Logs	Logs that record authentication attempts, including the user, application, time, outcome, and whether controls such as MFA or Conditional Access affected the sign-in.
Audit Logs	Logs that record administrative and configuration changes in Microsoft Entra, such as updates to users, groups, roles, or settings.
Risky Sign-in	A sign-in attempt that has been flagged because the activity may indicate identity compromise or suspicious behavior.
Risky User	A user account flagged by Microsoft Entra because activity associated with the identity may indicate possible compromise.
Identity Protection	A Microsoft Entra capability that detects identity-based risks, such as risky users or risky sign-ins.
Sign-in Troubleshooting	The process of reviewing sign-in logs and related details to identify why access failed, such as incomplete MFA, unmet Conditional Access requirements, or risk-based blocking.

Table 3.2: Key terms and acronyms

These terms provide a useful reference point as you move through Microsoft 365 identity and access concepts. Understanding what each term represents makes it easier to recognize how Microsoft Entra manages identities, how Conditional Access evaluates sign-ins, how users and groups support access management, and how administrators review identity activity across the environment.

For exam preparation, this also helps reinforce the terminology that appears in scenario-based questions, where selecting the correct answer often depends on recognizing which identity object, access control, or troubleshooting tool should be used.

Exam readiness drill – chapter review questions

Apart from mastering key concepts, strong test-taking skills under time pressure are essential for acing your certification exam. That's why developing these abilities early in your learning journey is critical.

Exam readiness drills, using the free online practice resources provided with this book, help you progressively improve your time management and test-taking skills while reinforcing the key concepts you've learned.

HOW TO GET STARTED

1. Open the link or scan the QR code at the bottom of this page
2. If you have unlocked the practice resources already, log in to your registered account. If you haven't, follow the instructions in *Free Benefits with Your Book* section in this book's *Preface* and come back to this page.
3. Once you log in, click the START button to start this chapter's quiz
4. We recommend attempting a quiz multiple times till you're able to answer most of the questions correctly and well within the time limit.
5. You can use the following practice template to help you plan your attempts:

Working On Accuracy		
Attempt	**Target**	**Time Limit**
Attempt 1	40% or more	Till the timer runs out
Attempt 2	60% or more	Till the timer runs out
Attempt 3	75% or more	Till the timer runs out
Working On Timing		
Attempt 4	75% or more	1 minute before time limit
Attempt 5	75% or more	2 minutes before time limit
Attempt 6	75% or more	3 minutes before time limit

The above drill is just an example. Design your drills based on your own goals and make the most out of the online quizzes accompanying this book.

Link to this chapter's quiz

You need to unlock the online practice resources to access the link below. Check the *Free Benefits with Your Book* section in the *Preface* for detailed instructions on how to do this. You only need to unlock the resources once.

Open Quiz `https://packt.link/n3CS7` or scan the QR code

4

Understanding Microsoft Purview

In the previous chapter, we looked at how Microsoft 365 identity controls help decide who can access services, apps, and resources. This chapter builds on that foundation by shifting from identity to the data those users create, share, and store across Microsoft 365.

Every day, people create and share documents, send emails, chat with colleagues, and store files as part of their normal work. Most of this happens without much thought about where that information ends up or who can access it.

This chapter explains how **Microsoft Purview** manages and protects that data.

The content aligns with the **AB-900** exam *skills measured*, covering: **Understand features and capabilities of Microsoft Purview Information Protection**, **Microsoft Purview Data Loss Prevention (DLP)**, **Microsoft Purview Insider Risk Management**, **Microsoft Purview Communication Compliance**, **Microsoft Purview Data Security Posture Management (DSPM) for AI**, and **Microsoft Purview Data Lifecycle Management**.

This chapter covers the following areas:

- Understanding Microsoft Purview capabilities
- Understanding how Microsoft Purview identifies and classifies sensitive data
- Identifying the use cases for sensitivity labels in Microsoft Purview
- Understanding Microsoft Purview Data Loss Prevention (DLP)
- Understanding Microsoft Purview Insider Risk Management
- Understanding Microsoft Purview Communication Compliance
- Understanding Microsoft Purview Data Security Posture Management (DSPM) for AI
- Understanding Microsoft Purview data lifecycle and retention management

These capabilities collectively form the foundation of Microsoft Purview's approach to data governance and protection in Microsoft365.

Introduction to Microsoft Purview and data governance

Modern organizations generate and share large amounts of data through emails, documents, chat conversations, application logs, customer records, financial records, and employee information that move constantly between users, devices, and services.

Much of this data lives in cloud platforms such as **Microsoft 365**, while other data flows through external services, platforms, and hybrid environments. This creates opportunities for collaboration and insight, but it also introduces risk as data moves across services and users.

Sensitive data can be *shared* too broadly, *retained* longer than necessary, or *accessed* by the wrong individuals. Regulations also require control over how information is *stored*, *protected*, and *audited*. To address these challenges, organizations need a unified way to manage and protect data.

What is Microsoft Purview

Microsoft Purview is a cloud-based platform for **governing**, **protecting**, and **managing** data across Microsoft 365 and connected environments. It enables organizations to **locate** data, **control** how it is used, and apply **protection** based on **sensitivity** and **risk**.

As data expands across emails, documents, collaboration platforms, and business applications, maintaining consistent control becomes harder, especially at scale. Without a unified approach, data can be misclassified, overexposed, or retained longer than intended.

Figure 4.1 shows how **Microsoft Purview** integrates **governance**, **compliance**, and **security** within a **unified data protection** model.

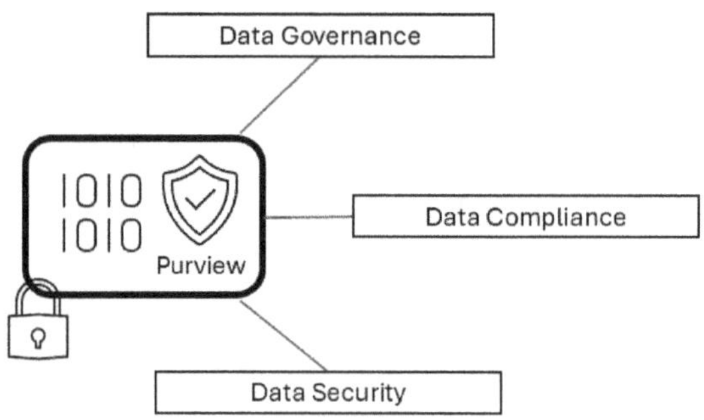

Figure 4.1: Microsoft Purview unified data protection model across governance, compliance, and security

Together, these capabilities operate as a connected system rather than separate functions, ensuring that data remains controlled, compliant, and protected throughout its lifecycle:

- **Data Governance** capabilities help organizations discover data, classify it (for example, sensitive or public), and understand how it is used across the business. It addresses challenges such as not knowing where data is located or being unable to find and understand it.
- **Data Compliance** capabilities are used by risk, legal, and compliance teams to monitor user activity, investigate policy violations, meet regulatory requirements, and provide retention rules (keep/delete data), legal hold, and audit readiness. Regulatory requirements are met because data handling is consistently enforced.
- **Data Security** teams use Data Security capabilities to protect sensitive information from unauthorized access, accidental exposure, and data leakage.

These areas create a continuous model where data is understood, governed, and protected across Microsoft 365.

Key Microsoft Purview capabilities

Microsoft Purview brings together capabilities to **identify** and **protect** critical data across Microsoft environments.

These capabilities cover **classification**, **protection**, **monitoring**, and **retention** across Microsoft 365, representing how information is handled throughout its lifecycle.

Figure 4.2 shows how Microsoft Purview applies **classification**, **protection**, **monitoring**, and **retention** as a *continuous data protection lifecycle.*

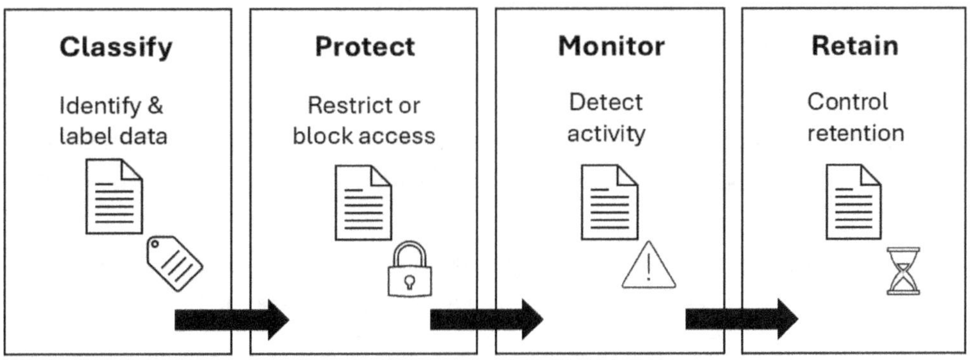

Figure 4.2: Microsoft Purview data protection lifecycle across classify, protect, monitor, and retain

The *lifecycle* begins with **classification**, where sensitive information is identified and labeled. **Protection** then enforces controls by restricting or blocking access to that data. **Monitoring** builds on this by detecting activity and identifying potential risks or policy violations. Finally,

retention governs how long the data is kept and when it is deleted, ensuring that information is managed appropriately throughout its lifecycle.

As organizations use AI productivity tools such as Microsoft 365 Copilot, these capabilities become increasingly important because AI systems rely on organizational data, which may include sensitive or regulated information.

Understanding data classification in Microsoft Purview

Before organizations can protect sensitive information, they first need to understand where that information exists. In large environments with thousands or millions of files, manually reviewing every document or message is not practical, so classification provides a way to automatically understand what data exists.

Data classification helps identify critical data and understand how it is shared. By detecting specific types of data within documents, emails, and other content, organizations can understand how widely it is distributed.

Classification capabilities in Microsoft Purview scan content across Microsoft 365 services such as Exchange, SharePoint, OneDrive, and Teams. These capabilities detect *sensitive information* such as financial data, personal identifiers, or confidential business content.

Data Explorer is the Microsoft Purview view used to see where classified and sensitive information, such as sensitive information types, exists across Microsoft 365 workloads.

Understanding where this data exists allows risk to be assessed and appropriate protection and governance policies to be applied. This reduces the likelihood of sensitive data being shared or stored incorrectly, even in large and complex environments.

Detecting sensitive information

Sensitive information can appear in many forms across organizational content, including personal identifiers, financial data, and confidential business information that organizations need to protect.

Microsoft Purview detects this information by analyzing content stored across Microsoft services without relying on manual review. As a result, sensitive data can be identified at scale without requiring users to manually classify every document.

Detection across Microsoft 365 workloads such as Exchange, SharePoint, OneDrive, and Teams provides a clearer view of how data is distributed. To support this, Microsoft Purview uses several different detection methods to recognize this type of data in organizational content. These are looked at in the following sections.

Sensitive information types

One of the most common ways to identify sensitive information is by detecting specific types of data within documents or messages.

Microsoft Purview includes *built-in definitions* known as **sensitive information types** (**SITs**) that can recognize common forms of sensitive data.

These *definitions* detect **patterns** such as credit card numbers, bank account numbers, national identification numbers, or other personal identifiers. The detection process looks for recognizable formats and supporting context within the content to determine whether the information is likely to be sensitive.

Automatically identifying these types of data supports governance and protection controls by highlighting sensitive information.

Trainable classifiers

Not all sensitive information follows a clear pattern, such as a credit card number or national identifier. In many cases, organizations need to recognize documents based on their *overall content* rather than a specific number or format.

Microsoft Purview **trainable classifiers** help identify these types of documents by using *machine learning* to recognize common document categories. Rather than searching for a specific pattern, classifiers analyze the *structure* and *language* used in documents to determine the type of content they contain.

A common example is classifiers recognizing documents such as contracts, resumes, financial reports, or other business records that may require special handling.

Recognizing these types of documents supports broader data governance efforts by identifying important information.

Exact data match

Some organizations need to identify very specific records within their environment, such as customer account numbers, employee identifiers, or other internal reference values. These types of identifiers may not follow widely recognized patterns, which makes them harder to detect using standard data recognition methods.

Microsoft Purview **Exact Data Match** (**EDM**) allows organizations to detect this type of information by securely comparing content in Microsoft 365 with *reference data* provided by the organization. Instead of searching for a general pattern, the system checks whether the content matches *known values* from the organization's data.

This approach identifies sensitive records unique to the business that may not be found using standard methods.

Detecting these records across documents and messages helps identify sensitive data unique to the organization.

Once this data is identified, organizations can begin applying labels that indicate how it should be protected and shared.

Identifying the use cases for sensitivity labels in Microsoft Purview

Modern organizations rely heavily on digital collaboration. Data moves constantly between people, teams, and departments as part of everyday work.

Employees create documents, share files, send messages, and collaborate across Microsoft 365 services such as SharePoint, OneDrive, Exchange, and Teams. While this improves productivity, it also introduces new risks. *Sensitive information* such as customer data, financial records, or confidential business documents can be shared with the wrong audience if appropriate governance controls are not in place.

Sensitivity labels are one of the key ways organizations manage these risks within Microsoft Purview.

Understanding sensitivity labels

Classification identifies sensitive data, while **sensitivity labels** apply protection and handling rules to that data.

Labels are typically defined as *Public*, *Internal*, *Confidential*, or *Highly Confidential*. These labels give users immediate **context** about the importance of the information and guide how it should be handled and shared.

Sensitivity labels must be **published** through a **label policy** before they are available for users to apply. Without a **policy**, labels exist but cannot be used by users in applications such as Outlook, Word, or SharePoint.

A document labeled as **Confidential** remains protected wherever it is shared because protection is applied directly to the data.

Figure 4.3 shows how sensitivity labels persist with data as it moves across Microsoft 365 services.

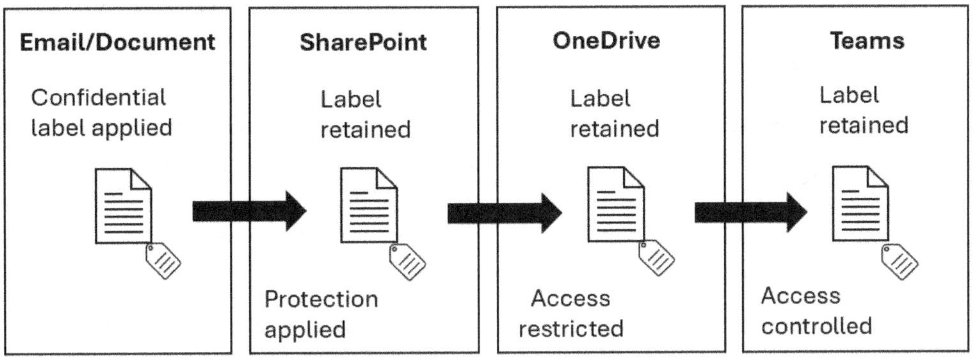

Figure 4.3: Sensitivity label persistence across Microsoft 365 services

As data moves between services such as SharePoint, OneDrive, and Teams, the **sensitivity label** remains attached, enforcing consistent access control and protection regardless of where the data is stored or accessed. In addition, if the data moves locally on the device outside of the M365 services and apps, the **Microsoft Defender for Endpoint** (**MDE**) client can also trigger alerts and prevent unauthorized access based on where the data is being moved (local folder in `c:\` drive or external USB).

In operation, **sensitivity labels** help employees recognize when data requires additional protection. The goal is not only to enforce technical controls but also to guide users in making better decisions when sharing or storing information.

One common use case involves protecting confidential business documents, including regulated data such as customer or employee records, where stricter controls are required. In collaborative environments, sensitivity labels also guide how widely information can be shared and who should have access, helping reduce the risk of accidental exposure.

How sensitivity labels support data protection

Instead of relying only on users to remember how information should be handled, **labels** provide clear guidance that travels with the document or email. When information is labeled, it can influence how that content is shared and accessed.

For example, certain labels may restrict who can open a document or prevent it from being shared outside the organization. Sensitive data remains available only to the intended audience while still allowing employees to collaborate.

By combining clear labeling with *protection policies*, organizations can keep important data secure while still supporting productive collaboration. This reduces the risk of sensitive information being distributed beyond its intended audience.

Sensitivity labels define how data should be protected, while **Data Loss Prevention** (**DLP**) builds on this by preventing sensitive information from being shared in ways that could expose it. It does this by adding controls that monitor how content is handled.

For example, if a user attempts to send an email containing sensitive information or upload a document with confidential data to an external location, DLP policies can detect that activity and take action. Actions include warning the user, blocking the action, or allowing it with justification. Organizations can then move beyond simply identifying sensitive data and instead control how it is shared across Microsoft 365 services.

DLP protects the data itself, while **Communication Compliance** shifts attention to how people communicate using that data. **Insider Risk Management** evaluates user behavior patterns over time, while **Communication Compliance** focuses on the content of individual messages.

It monitors communication across services such as Microsoft Teams and Exchange to identify policy violations or inappropriate behavior. It detects messages that violate regulatory requirements or internal policies, such as inappropriate sharing of sensitive information or language that does not meet organizational standards.

Understanding data lifecycle governance

Documents and messages are created, shared, updated, and eventually become outdated or no longer needed. Managing the lifecycle controls how data is stored and when it is removed.

Without clear **lifecycle governance**, organizations may retain large amounts of unnecessary data, which increases storage costs and makes it harder to locate important information. At the same time, deleting information too early may create legal or regulatory risks if records must be preserved for a certain period.

Data lifecycle governance helps organizations balance these needs by defining rules that determine how long information should be kept and what happens when that period ends.

Microsoft Purview supports this process by allowing organizations to apply retention controls that manage how long information remains available across Microsoft 365 services.

Understanding retention

As organizations create documents, send emails, and collaborate across Microsoft 365, data volume increases rapidly. Without defined rules, information may be retained longer than necessary or deleted too early, increasing both storage costs and compliance risk.

Retention policies define how long information must be kept, ensuring important records remain available while outdated data is removed automatically, eliminating the need for users to manually manage data over time.

Microsoft Purview applies **retention rules** consistently across services such as Exchange, SharePoint, OneDrive, and Teams. **Policies** can retain content for a *defined* period, *delete* it after that period, or *retain* it when required by regulation or business need.

Figure 4.4 shows how Microsoft Purview applies retention policies to enforce data lifecycle control from policy definition through to final disposition.

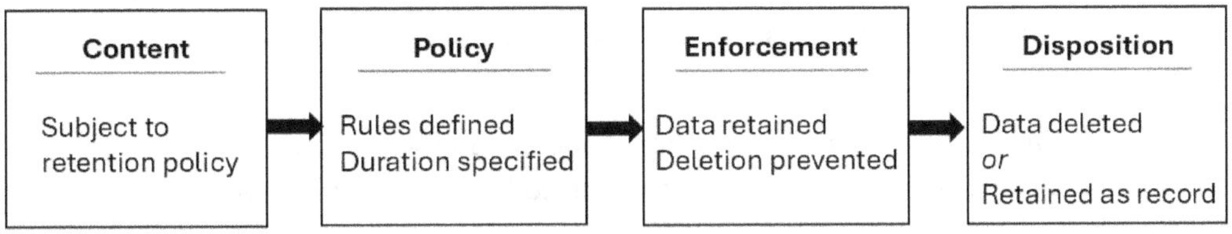

Figure 4.4: Microsoft Purview retention

Data is first brought under a **retention policy**, where *rules* and *duration* are defined. During **enforcement**, the data is retained for the specified period, and deletion can be prevented if required. At the end of this lifecycle, **disposition** determines whether the data is deleted or retained as a record based on regulatory or business needs.

This process is applied automatically across Microsoft 365 services, ensuring consistent retention and compliance without manual intervention.

Defining retention periods reduces unnecessary data storage, maintains compliance, and ensures that information remains available when needed and is removed when no longer required.

Retention labels

Retention labels help organizations apply specific **retention rules** directly to individual documents or emails. This allows different types of content to follow different lifecycle requirements. Each label defines *how long* the content should be kept and *what should happen* when the retention period ends.

For example, certain business records may need to be retained for several years to meet regulatory requirements, while other documents may only need to be kept for a shorter period. This allows organizations to assign the appropriate lifecycle rule to that information.

Retention labels can be applied by users when they create or manage content, helping ensure that documents and messages are categorized according to organizational policies.

By applying retention labels, organizations can manage the *lifecycle* of important information while ensuring that records are preserved or removed according to defined governance requirements.

Retention policies

While retention labels apply lifecycle rules to individual documents or emails, organizations often need broader rules that apply automatically across large volumes of information.

Retention policies allow organizations to define how long content should be kept across Microsoft 365 services such as Exchange, SharePoint, OneDrive, and Microsoft Teams. This means lifecycle rules can be applied automatically at scale without relying on users to manage retention manually.

For example, an organization may define a rule that email messages must be retained for a certain number of years or that documents stored in collaboration sites should be removed after a specific period.

Retention policies applied across services allow organizations to manage information lifecycle requirements consistently while supporting governance and compliance objectives.

In some situations, organizations need to locate and review specific content across Microsoft 365, such as during an investigation or legal request. **eDiscovery** provides this capability by allowing administrators to search for emails, documents, and other data across services.

Data Explorer provides aggregated visibility into where *sensitive data exists*, while **eDiscovery** *retrieves specific items* for investigation.

This helps organizations respond to legal requirements, investigate incidents, or review how information has been used within the environment.

Although **sensitivity labels** and **retention labels** can both be applied to content, they serve different purposes within Microsoft Purview. Understanding how they differ helps clarify how protection and lifecycle governance work together.

Figure 4.5 compares **retention labels** and **sensitivity labels** in Microsoft Purview.

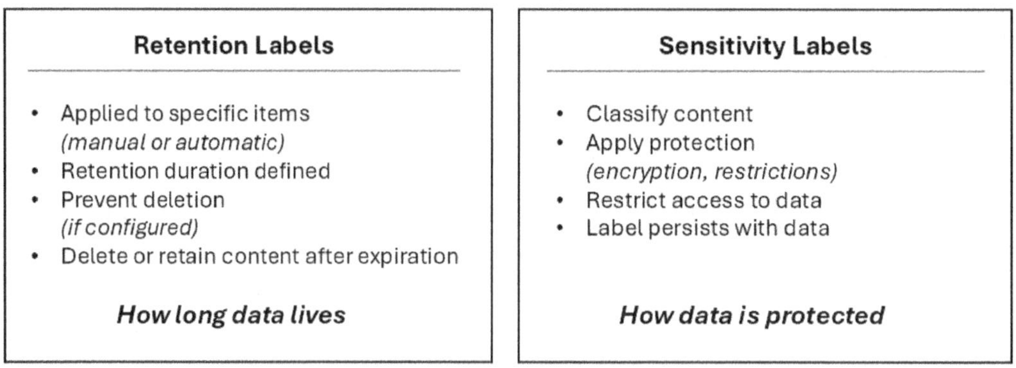

Figure 4.5: Comparison of retention labels and sensitivity labels in Microsoft Purview

Retention labels define how long content is kept and what happens when the retention period ends, governing the lifecycle of data. **Sensitivity labels**, in contrast, classify, and protect data by applying controls such as encryption and access restrictions. While these capabilities serve different purposes, they work together to ensure that data is both protected and managed appropriately throughout its lifecycle.

Summary

As data moves across Microsoft 365, controlling how it is classified, protected, and retained becomes essential. This constant movement across services, users, and systems creates both opportunity and risk.

This chapter showed how Microsoft Purview enables organizations to take control of their data. By combining classification, protection, monitoring, and retention capabilities, Purview provides a consistent approach to managing information across Microsoft 365.

Sensitive data can be identified, protected from exposure, monitored for risk, and retained or removed in line with organizational and regulatory requirements. Capabilities such as **Information Protection** and **Data Loss Prevention** (**DLP**) focus on protecting data, while Insider Risk Management and Communication Compliance provide visibility into how that data is used and where risks may exist.

As organizations adopt AI-powered services, DSPM for AI extends this by identifying how data is accessed by AI systems and where exposure risks may occur, reducing the risk of unintended data exposure.

Retention and lifecycle capabilities ensure that information is kept only for as long as necessary, supporting both compliance requirements and effective data management.

Together, these capabilities enable organizations to maintain control of their data across its entire lifecycle in Microsoft 365.

The next chapter builds on this data protection foundation by looking at how Microsoft 365 Copilot accesses organizational data, how permissions shape responses, and why governance controls are essential when AI can surface information through prompts.

Microsoft Learn reference links

The following table provides official Microsoft Learn references for the main Microsoft Purview topics introduced in this chapter. These links give readers a useful place to return to when reviewing the concepts covered in the AB-900 skills measured for this chapter.

Topic	What it covers	Microsoft Learn reference
Microsoft Purview capabilities	Introduces Microsoft Purview as a unified platform for data governance, data security, risk, and compliance.	`https://learn.microsoft.com/en-us/purview/purview`
Sensitive information types	Explains how Microsoft Purview identifies common sensitive data patterns such as personal, financial, and regulated information.	`https://learn.microsoft.com/en-us/purview/sensitive-information-type-learn-about`
Trainable classifiers	Explains how Microsoft Purview uses machine learning to identify document types that do not rely only on fixed patterns.	`https://learn.microsoft.com/en-us/purview/trainable-classifiers-learn-about`
Exact Data Match	Explains how Microsoft Purview detects sensitive records by matching content against organization-provided reference data.	`https://learn.microsoft.com/en-us/purview/sit-learn-about-exact-data-match-based-sits`
Sensitivity labels	Explains how labels classify and protect content by applying handling rules, encryption, access restrictions, and visual markings.	`https://learn.microsoft.com/en-us/purview/sensitivity-labels`
Sensitivity label use cases	Provides common scenarios for using sensitivity labels in Office apps and Microsoft 365 services.	`https://learn.microsoft.com/en-us/purview/sensitivity-labels-office-apps#common-scenarios-for-sensitivity-labels`

Topic	What it covers	Microsoft Learn reference
Data Loss Prevention	Explains how DLP policies detect sensitive information and reduce inappropriate sharing across Microsoft 365 workloads.	`https://learn.microsoft.com/en-us/purview/dlp-learn-about-dlp`
DLP overview	Provides a broader overview of how DLP works across endpoints, apps, services, and Microsoft 365 content.	`https://learn.microsoft.com/en-us/purview/dlp-overview-plan-for-dlp`
Insider Risk Management	Explains how Insider Risk Management detects and investigates user activity patterns that may indicate data misuse or insider risk.	`https://learn.microsoft.com/en-us/purview/insider-risk-management`
Insider Risk Management policies	Explains how insider risk policies define the activities, indicators, and conditions used to identify potential risks.	`https://learn.microsoft.com/en-us/purview/insider-risk-management-policies`
Communication Compliance	Explains how Communication Compliance identifies communication risks and policy violations in Microsoft 365 messages.	`https://learn.microsoft.com/en-us/purview/communication-compliance`
Communication Compliance overview	Provides a broader overview of Communication Compliance capabilities and supported scenarios.	`https://learn.microsoft.com/en-us/purview/communication-compliance`
DSPM for AI	Explains how Data Security Posture Management for AI identifies data exposure risks related to AI use.	`https://learn.microsoft.com/en-us/purview/dspm-for-ai?tabs=m365`

Topic	What it covers	Microsoft Learn reference
Microsoft Purview and AI	Explains how Microsoft Purview supports data protection and governance for AI scenarios.	`https://learn.microsoft.com/en-us/purview/ai-microsoft-purview`
Data Lifecycle Management	Explains how Microsoft Purview manages data retention, deletion, and lifecycle governance.	`https://learn.microsoft.com/en-us/purview/data-lifecycle-management`
Retention	Explains how retention capabilities keep or delete content based on policy requirements.	`https://learn.microsoft.com/en-us/purview/retention`
Retention policies	Explains how retention policies apply lifecycle rules across Microsoft 365 locations and workloads.	`https://learn.microsoft.com/en-us/purview/retention?tabs=table-overriden`
Microsoft Purview documentation hub	Provides the main Microsoft Purview documentation entry point.	`https://learn.microsoft.com/en-us/purview/`

Table 4.1: Microsoft Learn references for Microsoft Purview topics covered in this chapter

These references provide a structured point of return for the Microsoft Purview topics covered in this chapter. They can be used during revision to connect each capability back to the official Microsoft guidance behind the AB-900 skills measured for this chapter.

Key terms and acronyms

The following table introduces the main Microsoft Purview terms used throughout this chapter. It gives readers a quick reference before they move into the detailed discussion of classification, protection, DLP, risk management, AI governance, and retention.

Term	Meaning
Microsoft Purview	Microsoft's platform for data governance, data security, risk, compliance, and lifecycle management across Microsoft 365 and connected environments.
Data governance	The practice of managing data so it can be discovered, classified, protected, retained, and used appropriately.
Data classification	The process of identifying what type of data exists, where it is located, and whether it contains sensitive information.
Sensitive information type (SIT)	A Microsoft Purview definition that detects common sensitive data patterns, such as credit card numbers, national identifiers, or financial information.
Trainable classifier	A classification method that uses machine learning to recognize document types based on structure, wording, and content patterns.
Exact Data Match (EDM)	A method for detecting sensitive data by matching content against specific reference data supplied by the organization.
Sensitivity label	A label that classifies and protects content by applying handling rules such as encryption, access restrictions, or visual markings.
Data Loss Prevention (DLP)	A Microsoft Purview capability that detects sensitive information and can warn, block, or restrict risky sharing activity.
Insider Risk Management	A Microsoft Purview capability that identifies user activity patterns that may indicate data misuse, policy violations, or insider risk.
Communication Compliance	A Microsoft Purview capability that detects communication risks, policy violations, or inappropriate messages across supported Microsoft 365 communication channels.
DSPM for AI	Data Security Posture Management for AI, which identifies data exposure risks related to AI use and helps organizations understand how sensitive data may be accessed by AI systems.

Term	Meaning
Retention	The process of keeping content for a defined period, deleting it when no longer needed, or preserving it for legal, regulatory, or business reasons.
Retention label	A label that applies lifecycle rules to specific content, defining how long it should be kept and what happens at the end of that period.
Retention policy	A policy that applies retention rules across Microsoft 365 locations such as Exchange, SharePoint, OneDrive, and Teams.
eDiscovery	A Microsoft Purview capability used to search, collect, and review content for investigations, legal requests, or compliance purposes.
Data Explorer	A Microsoft Purview view that helps organizations understand where sensitive data exists across Microsoft 365 workloads.

Table 4.2: Key Microsoft Purview terms and acronyms

These terms summarize the core terminology used throughout the chapter and provide a quick reference for revision. Keeping these definitions clear will help connect Microsoft Purview capabilities to the data protection, governance, risk, AI, and lifecycle scenarios tested in AB-900.

Exam readiness drill – chapter review questions

Apart from mastering key concepts, strong test-taking skills under time pressure are essential for acing your certification exam. That's why developing these abilities early in your learning journey is critical.

Exam readiness drills, using the free online practice resources provided with this book, help you progressively improve your time management and test-taking skills while reinforcing the key concepts you've learned.

HOW TO GET STARTED

1. Open the link or scan the QR code at the bottom of this page
2. If you have unlocked the practice resources already, log in to your registered account. If you haven't, follow the instructions in the *Free Benefits with Your Book* section in this book's *Preface* and come back to this page.
3. Once you log in, click the START button to start this chapter's quiz

4. We recommend attempting a quiz multiple times until you're able to answer most of the questions correctly and well within the time limit
5. You can use the following practice template to help you plan your attempts:

Working On Accuracy		
Attempt	**Target**	**Time Limit**
Attempt 1	40% or more	Till the timer runs out
Attempt 2	60% or more	Till the timer runs out
Attempt 3	75% or more	Till the timer runs out
Working On Timing		
Attempt 4	75% or more	1 minute before time limit
Attempt 5	75% or more	2 minutes before time limit
Attempt 6	75% or more	3 minutes before time limit

The above drill is just an example. Design your drills based on your own goals and make the most out of the online quizzes accompanying this book.

Link to this chapter's quiz

You need to unlock the online practice resources to access the link below. Check the *Free Benefits with Your Book* section in the *Preface* for detailed instructions on how to do this. You only need to unlock the resources once.

Open Quiz `https://packt.link/pyqKhor` scan the QR code

5

Understanding Data Security Implications of Copilot

In the previous chapter, we focused on **Microsoft Purview** and how organizations classify, protect, and govern data across Microsoft 365. Those controls provide the foundation for understanding what happens when data is surfaced through Copilot.

Copilot changes how users access organizational data, shifting from navigating files and messages to retrieving information through prompts. This affects how data is surfaced, how permissions are applied, and how protection controls influence what can be returned.

The chapter focuses on the **Understand data protection and governance tasks for Microsoft 365 and Copilot** module from the *Skills Measured* section of the **AB-900** exam.

This chapter covers the following topics:

- Understanding how Copilot accesses data
- Understanding how Microsoft Graph influences Copilot responses
- Understanding how Copilot uses permissions controls
- Understanding responsible AI principles

Copilot's impact on data security begins with how it accesses organizational data within Microsoft 365.

Understanding how Copilot Accesses Data

Copilot interacts with organizational data through the existing Microsoft 365 service model, retrieving information from established services rather than introducing a new access path. Users express **intent** through **prompts** instead of navigating files, messages, and sites directly.

The process still follows the same service boundaries used by Exchange, SharePoint, OneDrive, and Teams, meaning visibility is defined by how data is structured, secured, and shared.

Prompts simplify how data is *accessed*, while **permissions** determine *what can be returned.* **Responses** reflect both user **intent** and existing **permissions**, forming a single flow from user input through service queries to response generation.

While Copilot retrieves data within existing boundaries, Microsoft Purview and Microsoft Defender apply classification, protection, and monitoring controls that govern how sensitive information is handled during and after retrieval.

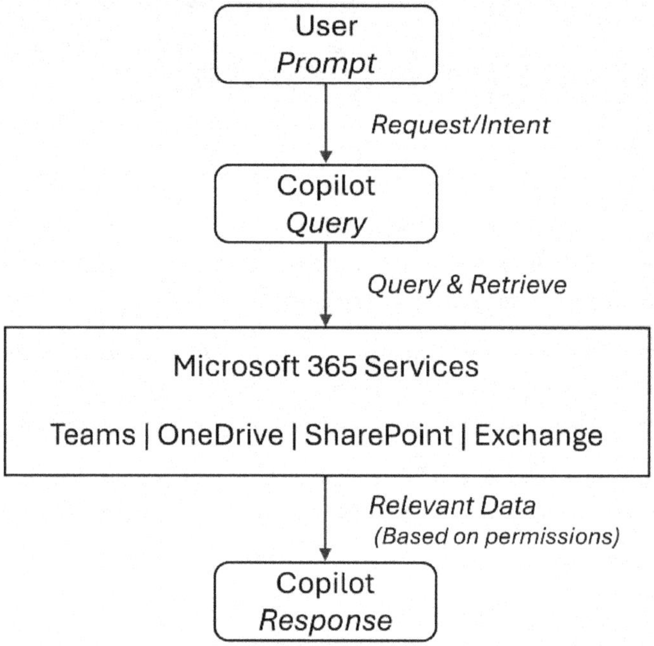

Figure 5.1: Copilot retrieval flow across Microsoft 365 services

Figure 5.1 shows how **Copilot** translates a *prompt* into *queries* across Microsoft 365 services and assembles results into a single response.

The model highlights that Copilot does not query a single service in isolation, but instead assembles responses by correlating data across multiple Microsoft 365 workloads, all within the same permission boundaries that already govern user access.

Because retrieval depends on those relationships and boundaries, well-structured content, clear ownership, and controlled sharing produce more accurate results, while fragmented storage or broad access increase the likelihood of unintended data exposure and reduce response precision.

Microsoft 365 data sources accessed by Copilot

Copilot retrieves information from the Microsoft 365 services where users already create, store, and share data.

Email and calendar content from Exchange, documents in SharePoint and OneDrive, and conversations in Teams all contribute to what can be surfaced in a response. The data remains in those services, and retrieval occurs against it rather than through a separate data copy or repository.

What gives Copilot reach across services is the ability to **query relationships** between people, files, meetings, chats, and sites, where files are linked to locations and owners, messages are tied to conversations and participants, and meetings connect users, documents, and discussions over time.

When a *prompt* references a meeting, project, or person, retrieval can draw from related emails, shared documents, calendar context, and Teams conversations, bringing together information from multiple workloads when those connections exist and access is allowed.

Where content is stored still affects how it contributes to results. A document stored in a private OneDrive location behaves differently from one in a shared SharePoint site, and a Teams conversation only appears when it falls within the user's accessible chats or channels. Results are shaped by both where data is stored and how it is connected, not just the content itself.

Well-organized files, clear naming, consistent storage, and conversations tied to the work they support produce more relevant results.

Fragmented storage, inconsistent naming, over-sharing, or disconnected discussions reduce the clarity of what Copilot can assemble, even when access exists. Copilot exposes these conditions in its responses rather than compensating for them.

Structured data analysis across multiple files is handled by specialist agent capabilities covered later in the book. For this chapter, the important point is that Copilot responses depend on the data, relationships, permissions, and service boundaries available in Microsoft 365.

User identity as the data access context

Every **response** is built from the perspective of the *signed-in user* and uses the same permissions that control access to emails, files, sites, and conversations, returning only what that user is allowed to see. Access granted through group membership, sharing links, site permissions, mailbox delegation, or inherited access all shape what Copilot can return. Changes to those controls are reflected as those changes are applied across Microsoft 365 services and appear in responses.

Prompt-driven data retrieval in Copilot

Copilot interprets each prompt as **intent**, using its specificity to determine how narrowly or broadly content is retrieved, which means the same data can produce different responses depending on how a request is framed.

Copilot does not follow a fixed query pattern; it adapts the search based on the structure and detail of the prompt.

Copilot limitations

Copilot operates within boundaries defined by *data availability* and *service scope*. It can only return what exists, what is connected, and what the user can access at that moment.

Gaps in data coverage affect retrieval. Content that is stored outside Microsoft 365, not indexed, or delayed in becoming searchable, does not contribute to responses. Timing also plays a role, as recently created or updated content may not immediately appear if it has not yet been processed into the searchable data layer.

Disconnected files, unclear naming, or fragmented collaboration patterns reduce how effectively Copilot can assemble relevant results. Even when access is available, weak context limits how well related content can be identified and combined.

Copilot should not be relied on as a source of verified or authoritative results, as it assembles responses from available data without independent validation.

Data retrieval changes with Copilot, while access continues to be defined by existing permissions. **Retrieval** is driven primarily by *data relationships*, with storage location influencing how effectively related content can be combined. Prompts drive the interaction, but the outcome reflects the structure, availability, and accessibility of the underlying data.

Understanding how Microsoft Graph Influences Copilot Responses

Microsoft Graph is the **unified API layer** that exposes **data** and **relationships** across Microsoft 365 services, enabling Copilot to retrieve information across those services as a *single result*.

This relationship model can be visualized as a central layer linking services and the data they expose.

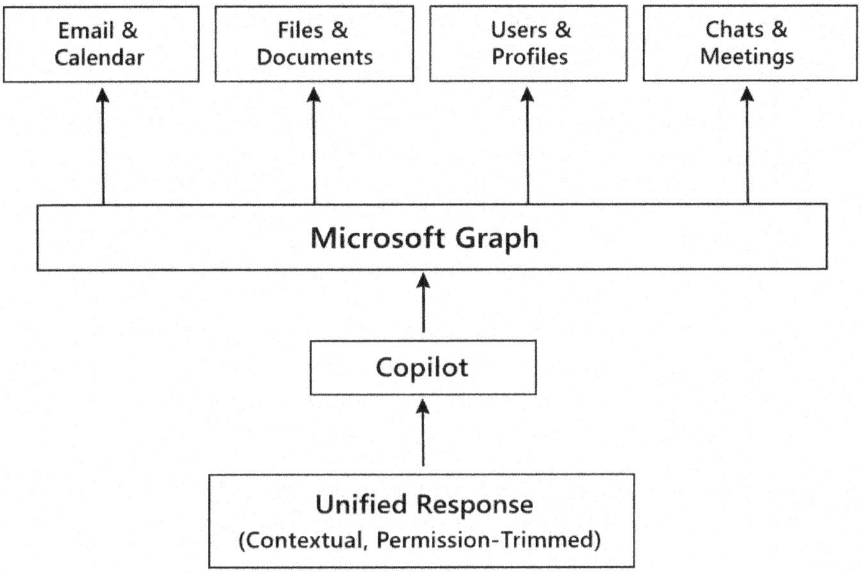

Figure 5.2: Microsoft Graph exposing data and relationships across Microsoft 365

Figure 5.2 shows **Microsoft Graph** acting as the central layer that links services across Microsoft 365.

The quality and scope of responses depend on the signals available through Microsoft Graph. Strong relationships, consistent metadata, and well-connected content produce more relevant results. Where connections are weak, incomplete, or inconsistent, Copilot has less context to work with and the response reflects those limitations.

Microsoft Graph as the data aggregation layer

Microsoft Graph provides a *common data model* that allows Copilot to query across Microsoft 365 services in a consistent way, so retrieval can span multiple services without separate lookups or manual correlation.

Copilot does not retrieve information as isolated items. It follows the relationships defined within Graph, where users are connected to their files, meetings link participants and shared content, and conversations tie back to documents and actions. These relationships determine how data is combined at query time, so responses reflect connected activity rather than separate pieces of content.

Content is not *moved* or *duplicated*. It remains in its original service, while Graph maps where that data lives and how it connects. Copilot uses that mapping during retrieval to resolve relationships across the tenant before assembling a response.

Prompt grounding using Microsoft Graph

Prompts are **grounded** through **Microsoft Graph** before any response is assembled.

Grounding refers to linking a prompt to real *data* and *relationships* within Microsoft 365 so responses are based on actual content rather than generated in isolation.

Copilot interprets the request and uses Microsoft Graph to identify relevant entities such as users, files, meetings, and conversations. These entities anchor the retrieval process and ensure results are tied to actual content and relationships within Microsoft 365.

Microsoft Graph resolves the *context* within the prompt. References to a project, meeting, or person are matched against known objects and activity across the tenant. That matching narrows the search space and directs retrieval toward content that is connected to those entities, shaping how results are selected and combined.

Grounding also influences how responses stay aligned with available data. When grounding *is strong*, responses align closely with user intent. When references *are unclear* or *loosely defined*, retrieval widens and results become less precise.

Permissions trimming in Microsoft Graph data retrieval

Permission trimming is applied during **data retrieval** to ensure that only content the user can access is returned. Permission checks are applied during retrieval, so **Microsoft Graph** and the underlying Microsoft 365 services return only content the signed-in user is allowed to access before Copilot assembles a response.

Retrieval operates within the same access boundaries that govern files, messages, sites, and conversations across Microsoft 365.

The permission trimming process evaluates access tied to each item. Access defined through sharing, group membership, site permissions, and inherited rights determines whether content is included or excluded. Items outside that boundary are not returned, even if they are closely related to the request or connected through other entities.

This filtering shapes what Copilot can use to build a response. Retrieval may span multiple services and relationships, but every element is constrained by the user's effective permissions. The response reflects a permission-scoped view of the data rather than a complete view of all related content.

Microsoft Graph limitations

Microsoft Graph does not provide complete or immediate visibility into all Microsoft 365 data. Retrieval depends on what has been indexed, how services expose their data, and how consistently relationships are maintained across workloads. Content that is not indexed or not represented through Graph does not contribute to Copilot responses.

Timing affects what can be retrieved. Changes in files, messages, or conversations may take time to appear through Graph, so recent activity is not always immediately available. Retrieval reflects the current state of the indexed data rather than real-time system activity.

Coverage also varies across services and data types. Some workloads expose richer relationships and metadata than others, which affects how well content can be connected and retrieved. Where relationships are limited or inconsistent, Copilot has less context to work with when assembling a response.

The graph also does not interpret or validate the meaning of the content. It provides structured access to data and relationships, but it does not determine accuracy or resolve conflicting information. Copilot responses reflect what Graph can retrieve, shaped by data availability, structure, and permissions.

Copilot builds responses from what can be located and related through Graph, so gaps in indexing, weak relationships, or inconsistent data structures appear directly in the output. Governance and control layers determine how data is exposed through Graph, influencing what can be accessed before retrieval begins.

Understanding how Copilot uses permissions and controls

Permissions determine what data can be accessed. Microsoft Purview applies classification and protection policies, while Microsoft Defender analyzes activity for risk and monitors how data is used after access. Copilot operates across these layers, so output reflects access rights as well as protection and monitoring controls.

Microsoft 365 permissions model

Access to data in Microsoft 365 is controlled through a *layered permissions model.* Copilot operates within the same access boundaries already defined for the user.

Users gain access through direct assignment, group membership, sharing links, and inherited permissions across sites, files, mailboxes, and teams. That model defines what content is visible and forms the boundary within which Copilot operates.

This layered control model can be visualized as an access boundary that shapes how data is retrieved and used.

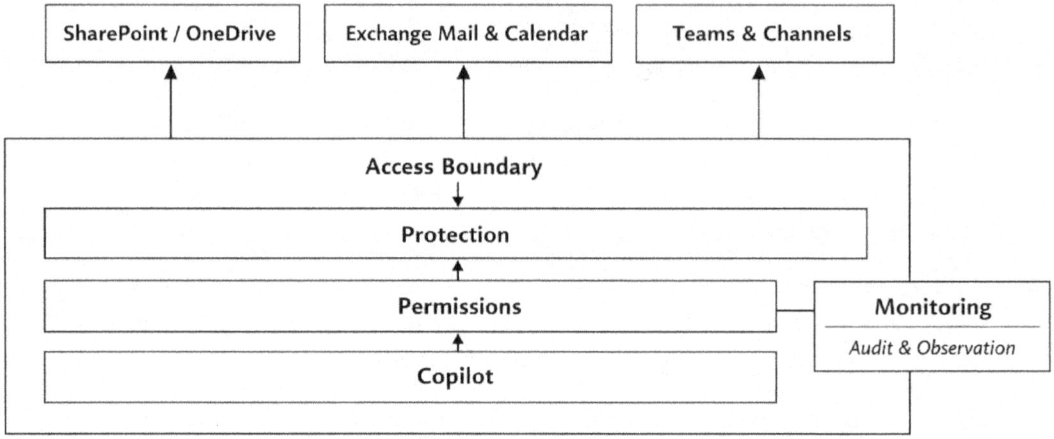

Figure 5.3: Permission, protection, and monitoring layers shaping Copilot responses

Figure 5.3 shows how permissions and protection form the control layers that govern how Copilot interacts with data, while monitoring provides visibility into how those controls are exercised. Permissions define what content can be accessed, establishing the boundary within which retrieval occurs. Protection policies apply constraints to that data, shaping how it can be used once accessed. Monitoring observes activity across these layers, providing visibility into how access is exercised.

Permissions are applied at multiple levels, where SharePoint and OneDrive control access to files and sites, Exchange governs mailboxes and calendars, and Teams enforces access through team and channel membership.

These controls are interconnected, so access granted in one context often extends to related content, shaping how broadly data can be retrieved.

The model is dynamic. Changes to group membership, sharing settings, or resource permissions are reflected as those changes are applied across Microsoft 365 services, altering what data is available at the time of a request. Copilot does not maintain its own access model. It relies on these existing controls, so the scope of responses directly reflects the current state of permissions across Microsoft 365.

Copilot enforcement of existing permissions

Access checks are applied at *retrieval time* across all contributing services, with queries running in the context of the signed-in user and each source returning only the items that the user is permitted to access.

When a prompt spans emails, files, meetings, and conversations, those permission checks are enforced independently by each service, and Copilot combines only the permitted results into a single response. The output reflects the user's effective permissions at that moment.

Permission changes take effect as those changes are applied across Microsoft 365 services. Updates to group membership, sharing settings, or resource permissions alter what Copilot can access without any additional configuration. As access expands or contracts, the scope of results adjusts in the same way.

Results reflect a *permission-scoped* view of the tenant. Even when content is related or highly relevant, it is excluded if the user does not have access. Copilot does not infer or expose restricted information; it assembles output strictly from what is allowed.

Data protection using Microsoft Purview

Microsoft Purview applies **classification** and **protection policies** that control how data is labeled, protected, and used during retrieval and after access is **granted**. Where labels apply encryption or access restrictions, those controls also affect whether Copilot can use the protected content in a response.

Sensitivity labels, **encryption**, and **access restrictions** define how content can be used, shared, and exposed across Microsoft 365. Copilot operates within those controls, so protected content remains governed by the policies applied to it.

For exam scenarios that ask where to identify sensitive content used during Copilot interactions, analyze usage patterns, and receive recommendations for protection, use Microsoft Purview Data Security Posture Management for AI.

Labels attach meaning and handling requirements to data. A document marked as confidential may carry restrictions that limit access, prevent external sharing, or enforce encryption. When Copilot retrieves labeled content, those protections remain in effect and shape what can be included in output. Where a sensitivity label applies encryption, Copilot can only interact with that content when the signed-in user has both `VIEW` and `EXTRACT` usage rights. View access alone is not enough for Copilot to use the encrypted content in a response.

Protection travels with the data. Files and emails retain their classification and enforcement settings regardless of where they are accessed from, including through Copilot. Retrieval does not strip or bypass those controls, so responses reflect both the content and the restrictions applied to it.

Policy enforcement influences what can be returned. Content that is restricted, encrypted, or scoped to specific users or groups is only included when the requesting user meets those conditions. Copilot builds output from data that satisfies both permission checks and protection policies, aligning output with the organization's data governance model.

Data loss prevention using Microsoft Purview DLP

Microsoft Purview Data Loss Prevention (**DLP**) can affect Copilot interactions at several points. A policy can stop a prompt from being processed when it contains defined sensitive information types, prevent external web search from being used to ground a sensitive prompt, or stop supported labeled files and emails from being processed into a response.

Those decisions sit around the Copilot interaction rather than replacing Microsoft 365 permissions. The user may still have access to the underlying content, but DLP can control whether sensitive prompt text, web grounding, or labeled source content is used during the response flow. If prompt processing is blocked, Copilot does not return a response based on that prompt. If web grounding is blocked, Copilot can still use permitted internal Microsoft 365 data where applicable.

For labeled source content, the item may still appear as a citation, but its content is not used to generate the summary or answer. DLP therefore shapes what Copilot can process and include in output without changing what data exists or replacing the permissions that determine what the user can access.

Risk detection using Microsoft Defender

Microsoft Defender monitors *user activity*, *identities*, and *data interactions* for signals that indicate risk. It analyzes *patterns* such as unusual access behavior, anomalous data movement, and indicators of compromise across Microsoft 365 services. Those signals are evaluated continuously and contribute to identifying potentially risky activity linked to users or content.

Copilot activity becomes part of the same monitoring and risk detection processes as any other data access.

These interactions are analyzed alongside other activities within Microsoft 365. When a user interacts with data through prompts, those interactions are part of the same activity stream that Defender evaluates. Patterns such as rapid access to large volumes of data, access outside normal behavior, or interaction with sensitive content can contribute to risk signals associated with that user.

Risk signals influence how activity is viewed and managed. Elevated risk can lead to further investigation, alerting, or automated response actions depending on how Defender is configured. While Copilot continues to operate within permissions and policies, the activity it generates contributes to the broader detection and response pipeline, without altering the response itself.

The response itself is not altered by Defender, but the interaction is visible within the monitoring layer. Copilot does not suppress or bypass detection mechanisms, so usage patterns are assessed in the same way as any other data access activity within Microsoft 365.

Defender identifies and responds to risk after data access occurs, rather than restricting what data can be retrieved.

This means Defender monitors how data is used after access decisions have been made, rather than determining whether it can be accessed. Access remains controlled by permissions and policies, while Defender provides visibility into how that access is exercised.

Security control limitations in Copilot

Copilot follows the *controls applied* across **Microsoft 365**, **Microsoft Purview**, and **Microsoft Defender** without extending or strengthening them. The system enforces what is already defined through permissions, classification, DLP policies, and monitoring, so any gaps in those areas are reflected in how data can be retrieved and used.

Permissions define the *access boundary*, but broad or inherited access increases the range of data available for retrieval. Copilot follows that boundary without narrowing it, so overexposed content remains visible in responses when access is allowed. The system does not evaluate whether access should be restricted; it applies the permissions as configured.

Protection policies also depend on how consistently they are applied. Unlabeled content, incomplete classification, or gaps in DLP coverage reduce how effectively sensitive data is governed. Copilot retrieves based on what is available and permitted, so inconsistent policy application leads to uneven protection in responses.

Monitoring identifies risk after activity occurs rather than preventing retrieval. Defender detects patterns and raises signals based on behavior, but it does not block Copilot from accessing data within permitted boundaries. The interaction contributes to detection and response workflows, while retrieval continues under existing controls.

Copilot reflects the combined state of permissions, protection, and monitoring across the environment, operating within the security model already defined across Microsoft 365.

Output is built from data that satisfies both access rights and policy enforcement, so gaps in permissions, classification, or coverage appear directly in the output. Strength in those controls produces predictable and governed behavior, while weaknesses increase exposure and reduce control over how data is surfaced.

The way these controls are configured determines how Copilot behaves before data is accessed.

Understanding responsible AI principles

Copilot *responses* are shaped by **guardrails** that control how prompts are processed and what can be returned without changing the underlying data access permissions.

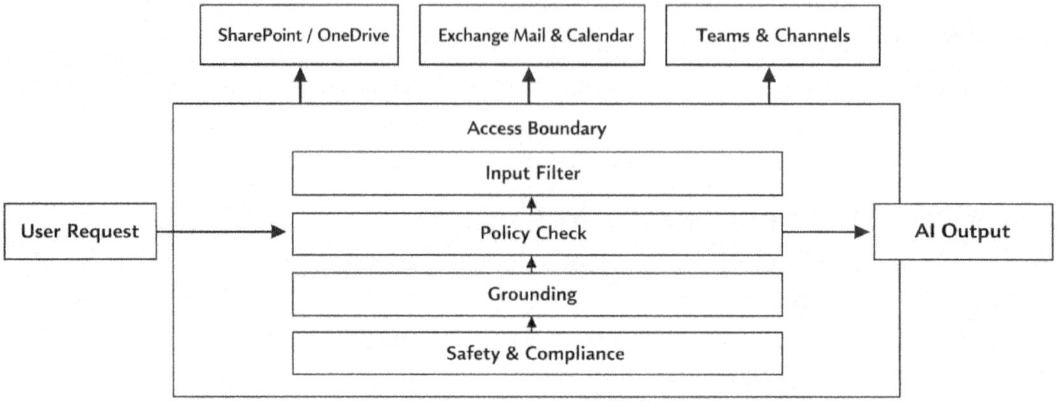

Figure 5.4: Responsible AI guardrails applied to prompts and responses

Figure 5.4 shows how *responsible AI guardrails* are applied across the request and output flow. **Input filtering** evaluates prompts as they enter the system, preventing unsafe or non-compliant requests from progressing further. **Policy checks** then ensures that requests and retrieved content align with organizational rules and constraints.

Grounding anchors output in available data, so responses are based on retrieved content rather than unsupported or fabricated information. During this process, the data used to generate Copilot responses is encrypted in transit. Safety and compliance controls are then applied during generation, shaping the final result so it remains appropriate, policy-aligned, and within defined boundaries.

These controls function as a single processing path, shaping both what enters the system and how output is generated. Each interaction passes through this sequence, so both inputs and outputs are constrained in real time, reducing the likelihood of unsafe, non-compliant, or ungrounded responses.

Enterprise guardrails controlling Copilot behavior

Enterprise guardrails define the boundaries within which Copilot operates.

These guardrails apply organizational policies to both prompts and output, shaping how the system behaves across different scenarios. They sit in the execution path of every interaction, ensuring that content generation aligns with internal standards, compliance requirements, and acceptable use expectations.

Requests are evaluated against defined conditions. Prompts that conflict with policy can be restricted, modified, or rejected before processing continues. This prevents the system from acting on instructions that fall outside approved use, reducing the risk of unsafe or non-compliant output entering the response pipeline.

Response generation is also constrained by these controls. Even when a prompt is accepted, the output is shaped to remain within policy boundaries. Content that could introduce risk, violate compliance requirements, or produce inappropriate results is adjusted or excluded as part of the generation process.

They operate continuously and consistently across interactions. They do not rely on user awareness or manual enforcement, and they apply regardless of how broadly a user can access data. Copilot behavior is therefore governed by both what the user can retrieve and what the system is permitted to generate.

Prompt filtering in Copilot

Prompt filtering evaluates user input against safety rules and policy conditions before it is processed into output.

In practice, this means unsafe or non-compliant requests are stopped before they can influence retrieval or response generation.

Both *intent* and *content* are evaluated during filtering. Prompts that attempt to generate harmful, unsafe, or non-compliant output are intercepted early, reducing the likelihood of inappropriate responses. In some cases, the request is adjusted to align with policy, while in others it is rejected outright depending on severity and context.

This step directly affects what Copilot can act on. Retrieval and response generation only occur after the prompt passes filtering, so disallowed instructions never influence downstream behavior. The system, therefore, limits risk at the point of entry, preventing unsafe requests from progressing through the pipeline.

Filtering operates consistently across interactions without requiring user awareness. Copilot evaluates each prompt independently, applying the same rules regardless of user role or access level. Behavior is constrained at the input stage before any data is retrieved or combined.

Prompts that fall outside defined policy boundaries can be blocked before retrieval begins.

Policy-aligned response generation in Copilot

Response generation is constrained by **policy rules** that apply after retrieval and during content assembly, so Copilot does not return raw results from data sources. Retrieved content is evaluated before being returned, and policy alignment ensures it remains within safety, compliance, and organizational boundaries.

This control affects how information is presented rather than what exists in the underlying data. Copilot may have access to relevant content, but the output only includes what satisfies policy constraints. The output is therefore a filtered representation of retrieved data, aligned with defined rules.

Response shaping occurs continuously during generation. As content is assembled, policy checks influence structure, wording, and inclusion decisions, ensuring that the final result remains within acceptable boundaries without requiring manual intervention.

System messages and grounding controls in Copilot

System messages define the internal instructions that guide how Copilot interprets prompts and generates output.

These instructions are not visible to the user but influence how the model behaves, setting constraints on tone, scope, and acceptable output. They operate alongside user input, shaping how requests are understood before retrieval and generation occur.

Grounding controls connect output to verifiable data. Copilot uses signals from Microsoft 365 content, Microsoft Graph relationships, and contextual inputs to anchor responses in actual information rather than generating unsupported output. This reduces the likelihood of irrelevant or fabricated responses by tying generation to known data sources and relationships.

System messages and **grounding controls** work together during execution. Internal instructions define how the model should behave, while grounding ensures that output remains connected to available data. The result reflects both behavioral constraints and data-backed context.

These controls influence both interpretation and output. Prompts are processed within defined behavioral limits, and output is constructed using grounded data, keeping the interaction aligned with policy and reducing the risk of unsupported or inappropriate results.

Responsible AI controls shape how Copilot interprets requests and generates output, with guardrails, prompt filtering, policy alignment, and grounding working together during each interaction to ensure results remain aligned with both policy and available data.

Prompts, responses, and data accessed through Microsoft Graph are not used to train the foundation large language models that power Microsoft 365 Copilot.

When these controls are weak or inconsistently applied, Copilot can still generate output that reflects biased, incomplete, or misinterpreted data.

Summary

Copilot changes how data is accessed across Microsoft 365 by shifting from manual navigation to prompt-based retrieval, while keeping access boundaries unchanged.

Microsoft Graph exposes data and relationships across services, allowing retrieval to follow relationships between users, content, and activity so responses reflect how information is connected rather than where it is stored.

Output is shaped across multiple control layers. The Microsoft 365 permissions model defines access, while enforcement occurs during retrieval, and Microsoft Purview applies classification and protection to sensitive data. Data loss prevention policies restrict how information can be used, while Microsoft Defender monitors activity for risk as users interact with data.

Responsible AI controls shape behavior during each interaction. Prompt filtering governs what enters the system, policy-aligned generation shapes how output is formed, and grounding ties output to available data. System instructions guide how output is constructed so it remains within defined boundaries.

Effectiveness depends on how these controls are configured and maintained. Access design, data classification, policy coverage, and monitoring influence what can be retrieved and how it is presented. Well-governed environments produce predictable results, while gaps in control appear directly in output.

Retrieval, protection, and control operate together. Copilot depends on these layers rather than replacing them, making their design and consistency visible in every output.

The next chapter builds on this foundation by looking at how data protection and governance risks are identified across Microsoft 365 and Copilot. It moves from how data is accessed, protected, and surfaced to how organizations assess compliance posture, discover sensitive information, analyze user activity, and investigate potential exposure.

Microsoft Learn reference links

The following table provides official Microsoft references for the main Copilot data access, Microsoft Graph, permission control, data protection, and responsible AI topics introduced in this chapter:

Topic	What it covers	Microsoft Learn reference
Microsoft 365 Copilot architecture	Explains how Microsoft 365 Copilot works across Microsoft 365 services, Microsoft Graph, grounding, prompts, responses, and security boundaries.	`https://learn.microsoft.com/en-us/microsoft-365/copilot/microsoft-365-copilot-architecture`

Topic	What it covers	Microsoft Learn reference
Microsoft 365 Copilot data and compliance readiness	Explains the data protection, permissions, compliance, and governance requirements organizations should understand before using Microsoft 365 Copilot.	`https://learn.microsoft.com/en-us/microsoft-365/copilot/microsoft-365-copilot-minimum-requirements-data-compliance`
Information used by Copilot to answer prompts	Explains what information Copilot can use when answering a prompt, including Microsoft 365 content and the user's accessible work data.	`https://support.microsoft.com/en-us/topic/what-information-does-copilot-use-to-answer-my-prompt-934f537d-ff7d-4059-9fec-a751e4651307`
Microsoft Graph and Copilot grounding	Explains how Microsoft Graph connects Microsoft 365 data, relationships, and user context so Copilot can ground responses in available organizational information.	`https://learn.microsoft.com/en-us/microsoft-365/copilot/microsoft-365-copilot-architecture`
Copilot permission and protection controls	Explains how Copilot works within existing Microsoft 365 permissions, identity access, Conditional Access, sensitivity labels, encryption, and data protection boundaries.	`https://learn.microsoft.com/en-us/microsoft-365/copilot/microsoft-365-copilot-minimum-requirements-data-compliance`
Copilot APIs and permission trimming	Explains how Copilot APIs respect identity access, Conditional Access, sensitivity labels, and permission trimming by default.	`https://learn.microsoft.com/en-us/microsoft-365/copilot/extensibility/copilot-apis-overview`

Topic	What it covers	Microsoft Learn reference
Copilot data protection and auditing	Explains how Copilot interacts with protected content, including sensitivity labels, encryption, usage rights, and auditing.	`https://learn.microsoft.com/en-us/microsoft-365/copilot/microsoft-365-copilot-architecture-data-protection-auditing`
DLP for Microsoft 365 Copilot and Copilot Chat	Explains how Microsoft Purview DLP can apply to Copilot prompts, web grounding, and supported labeled files or emails.	`https://learn.microsoft.com/en-us/purview/dlp-microsoft365-copilot-location-learn-about`
Microsoft 365 Copilot privacy	Explains Microsoft's privacy commitments for Copilot, including how prompts, responses, and Microsoft Graph data are handled.	`https://learn.microsoft.com/en-us/microsoft-365/copilot/microsoft-365-copilot-privacy`
Microsoft Responsible AI	Introduces Microsoft's responsible AI approach and the principles used to guide AI system design and use.	`https://www.microsoft.com/en-us/ai/responsible-ai`
Responsible use of AI overview	Explains responsible AI concepts used when designing and operating AI systems safely and appropriately.	`https://learn.microsoft.com/en-us/azure/ai-services/responsible-use-of-ai-overview`

Topic	What it covers	Microsoft Learn reference
Microsoft AI principles and approach	Provides Microsoft's responsible AI principles, including fairness, reliability and safety, privacy and security, inclusiveness, transparency, and accountability.	`https://www.microsoft.com/en-us/ai/principles-and-approach`

Table 5.1: Microsoft references for Copilot data access, governance, and responsible AI topics covered in this chapter

Together, these references support the chapter's focus on how Copilot works with Microsoft 365 data, how existing controls shape retrieval and output, and how responsible AI principles guide the way prompts and responses are handled.

Key terms and acronyms

The following table introduces the main Copilot, Microsoft Graph, permission, data protection, and responsible AI terms used throughout this chapter. It gives readers a quick reference as they review how Copilot accesses Microsoft 365 data, how responses are grounded, and how existing controls shape what can be returned:

Term	Meaning
Microsoft 365 Copilot	An AI-powered Microsoft 365 experience that uses prompts, Microsoft Graph, and Microsoft 365 data to generate responses within the user's existing access boundaries.
Prompt	A natural language request entered by a user to ask Copilot for information, analysis, summarization, or assistance.
Response	The output generated by Copilot after the prompt is processed, grounded, filtered, and shaped by available data and policy controls.
Grounding	The process of connecting a prompt to available Microsoft 365 data and context so the response is based on retrieved information rather than generated in isolation.

Term	Meaning
Microsoft Graph	The Microsoft API and relationship layer that connects users, files, messages, meetings, chats, sites, and other Microsoft 365 objects.
Permission trimming	The process of filtering retrieval results so only content the signed-in user is permitted to access can be used by Copilot.
Signed-in user	The user account currently interacting with Copilot. This identity determines the permissions and access scope used during retrieval.
Effective permissions	The actual access a user has after direct permissions, group membership, sharing links, inherited permissions, and other access controls are evaluated.
Sensitivity label	A Microsoft Purview label that classifies content and can apply protection settings such as encryption, access restrictions, and visual markings.
Encryption	A protection method that restricts access to content so only authorized users with the required usage rights can open or use it.
VIEW usage right	A usage right that allows a user to view protected content when encryption is applied.
EXTRACT usage right	A usage right is required for Copilot to use encrypted labeled content in a response. View access alone is not enough.
Microsoft Purview	Microsoft's platform for data governance, data security, risk, compliance, and lifecycle management across Microsoft 365 and connected environments.
Data Loss Prevention (DLP)	A Microsoft Purview capability that detects sensitive information and can restrict how prompts, web grounding, or supported labeled content are processed in Copilot interactions.
Web grounding	The use of web search as an additional grounding source for a response, subject to policy and configuration.

Term	Meaning
Microsoft Defender	Microsoft's security platform that can monitor activity, detect risk signals, and support investigation and response across Microsoft 365 activity.
Risk signal	An indicator generated from activity or behavior that may suggest suspicious, risky, or policy-relevant activity.
Responsible AI	Microsoft's approach to designing and operating AI systems according to principles such as fairness, reliability and safety, privacy and security, inclusiveness, transparency, and accountability.
Guardrails	Controls that shape how prompts are processed and how responses are generated so Copilot behavior remains within defined safety, policy, and compliance boundaries.
Prompt filtering	The process of evaluating prompt content before it is processed, so unsafe or non-compliant requests can be blocked or restricted.
Policy-aligned response generation	The process of shaping Copilot output so the final response remains within safety, compliance, and organizational policy boundaries.
Foundation large language model (foundation LLM)	The underlying AI model used by Copilot to understand prompts and generate responses. Microsoft 365 Copilot does not use prompts, responses, or Microsoft Graph data to train these foundation models.

Table 5.2: Key Copilot data security terms and acronyms

These terms help connect the chapter's terminology to the AB-900 skills measured. They also give readers a simple reference point for understanding Copilot data access, permission trimming, Purview protection, DLP behavior, Defender monitoring, and responsible AI controls.

Exam readiness drill – chapter review questions

Apart from mastering key concepts, strong test-taking skills under time pressure are essential for acing your certification exam. That's why developing these abilities early in your learning journey is critical.

Exam readiness drills, using the free online practice resources provided with this book, help you progressively improve your time management and test-taking skills while reinforcing the key concepts you've learned.

HOW TO GET STARTED

1. Open the link or scan the QR code at the bottom of this page
2. If you have unlocked the practice resources already, log in to your registered account. If you haven't, follow the instructions in the *Free Benefits with Your Book* section in this book's *Preface* and come back to this page.
3. Once you log in, click the START button to start this chapter's quiz
4. We recommend attempting a quiz multiple times till you're able to answer most of the questions correctly and well within the time limit
5. You can use the following practice template to help you plan your attempts:

Working On Accuracy		
Attempt	**Target**	**Time Limit**
Attempt 1	40% or more	Till the timer runs out
Attempt 2	60% or more	Till the timer runs out
Attempt 3	75% or more	Till the timer runs out
Working On Timing		
Attempt 4	75% or more	1 minute before time limit
Attempt 5	75% or more	2 minutes before time limit
Attempt 6	75% or more	3 minutes before time limit

The above drill is just an example. Design your drills based on your own goals and make the most out of the online quizzes accompanying this book.

Link to this chapter's quiz

You need to unlock the online practice resources to access the link below. Check the *Free Benefits with Your Book* section in the *Preface* for detailed instructions on how to do this. You only need to unlock the resources once.

Open Quiz `https://packt.link/tc1Ys` or scan the QR code

6

Identifying Data Protection and Governance Risks for Microsoft 365 and Copilot

Microsoft Copilot changes how data is accessed, surfaced, and shared across **Microsoft 365 services**. Instead of users manually searching for information, **AI** can pull together content from multiple sources and present it instantly. That shift increases the importance of understanding where sensitive data exists, how it is used, and how it is protected across the environment. This chapter focuses on how **Microsoft Purview** helps identify and manage those risks.

You will explore how compliance posture is assessed, how sensitive information is discovered, and how user activity and behavior are analyzed to detect potential exposure. You will also look at how policies enforce protection, how communication risks are identified, and how activity can be investigated across the environment.

The content primarily supports the **Understand data protection and governance tasks for Microsoft 365 and Copilot** module from the *Skills Measured* section of the AB-900 exam.

By the end of this chapter, you will be able to confidently answer questions on the following topics:

- Identifying Compliance Risks with Compliance Manager
- Identifying Sensitive Information with Data Explorer
- Identifying Risks with Insider Risk Management
- Identifying and Responding to DLP Alerts
- Identifying Violations in Communication Compliance

- Identifying User Activities in Activity Explorer
- Discovering and Managing AI Activity with DSPM for AI
- Searching Data Using Purview eDiscovery Content Search

These capabilities equip readers to detect, investigate, and manage risks that impact Copilot readiness.

Before examining data, activity, or AI-driven exposure, organizations must first determine whether the controls that govern it are correctly implemented. This baseline shapes how every signal that follows should be interpreted.

> Note
>
> **Important information regarding Microsoft Portal experiences and UI elements**
>
> Microsoft frequently updates portal experiences and UI elements. As a result, some screenshots, navigation paths, or interface details shown in this book may differ slightly from your individual tenant's environment at the time of reading.

Identifying compliance risks and recommendations using Microsoft Purview Compliance Manager

Microsoft Purview Compliance Manager evaluates compliance posture by assessing controls in selected assessments, showing which Microsoft-managed and organization-managed actions are complete, incomplete, or require attention.

Figure 6.1 introduces the **Microsoft Purview risk lifecycle** and positions each capability according to its role in managing risk.

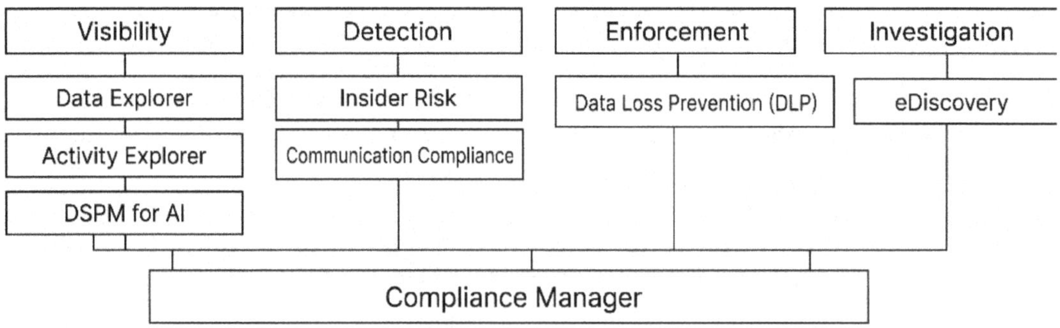

Figure 6.1: Microsoft Purview risk lifecycle across visibility, detection, enforcement, and investigation

Figure 6.1 shows how risk is addressed across distinct functional layers. Each layer plays a specific role.

Visibility provides insight into data location and usage, **Detection** identifies risky behavior patterns, **Enforcement** applies controls to prevent data exposure, and **Investigation** enables detailed examination of specific content. These capabilities operate independently but depend on the same underlying environment. **Compliance Manager** sits beneath them, evaluating whether the required controls are configured correctly before any of these stages act on user activity.

Where to find this: In the **Microsoft Purview** portal, **Compliance Manager** is available from the **Solutions** area in the left navigation bar. This is where assessments, improvement actions, and compliance scores are reviewed.

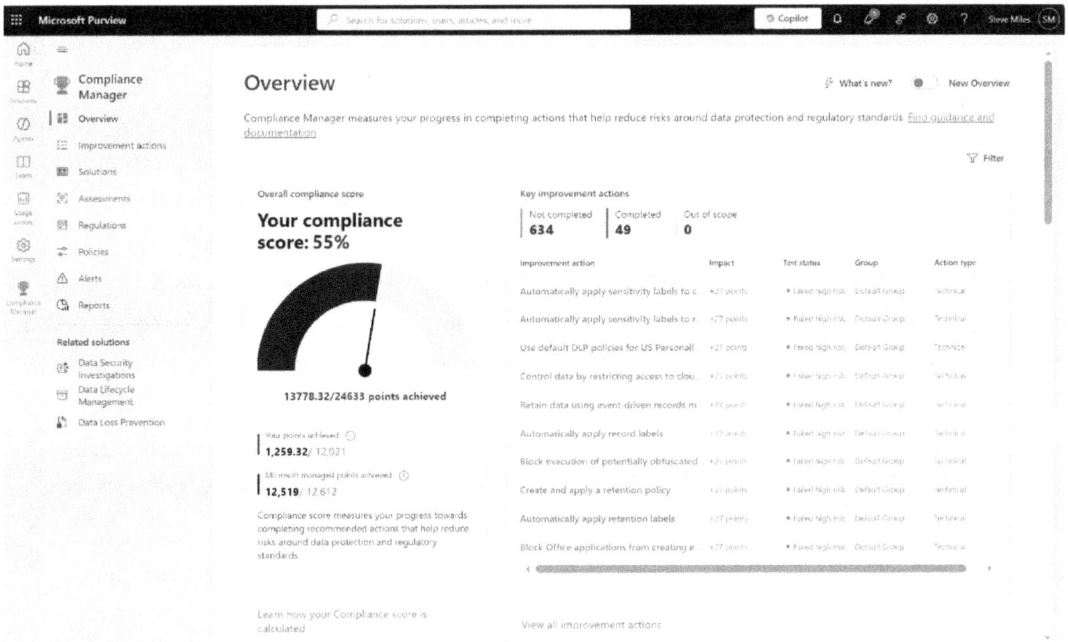

Figure 6.2: Microsoft Purview Compliance Manager

This view gives readers a practical anchor for understanding how Compliance Manager turns control status into measurable compliance posture.

With this lifecycle in place, focus shifts to how **Compliance Manager** *identifies gaps* and translates them into actionable recommendations.

Compliance posture through control-based assessments

Compliance Manager translates regulatory requirements into measurable controls, where each control represents a condition that must exist within the environment, such as ensuring data is protected, access is restricted, and activity is auditable.

Controls are grouped into assessments aligned to specific regulatory frameworks, allowing organizations to track which controls are implemented and which remain incomplete, and to evaluate compliance based on actual conditions rather than assumptions.

Posture is built directly from those control states. When controls are fully implemented and validated, they contribute to a stable baseline. When they are incomplete or missing, they expose gaps that represent structural risk. A clear picture of exposure emerges based on what is actually configured, not what is assumed to be in place.

Responsibility is defined at the control level. Some controls require action from the organization, while others are already enforced by Microsoft. This separation ensures that effort is focused only on areas where change is possible, avoiding confusion between controllable and fixed conditions.

Compliance scores and control responsibility

The **compliance score** provides a way to understand control coverage as a measurable outcome. Each **control** contributes to the *score* based on its *importance* and its level of *completion*, turning the state of the environment into a numerical representation.

What matters is how that score moves. As controls are implemented and validated, the score *increases*, reflecting *improved coverage*. When controls remain incomplete, the score reflects that gap. This makes the score a direct indicator of how the environment is evolving, not in terms of threat activity, but in terms of structural readiness.

Responsibility plays a key role in how the score can change. Organizational controls can be improved through action, while Microsoft-managed controls remain constant. This ensures that movement in the score reflects only what can actually be influenced.

The result is a metric that tracks progress in strengthening the environment, rather than reacting to events that have already occurred.

Improvement actions for control gaps

Where *gaps* exist, Compliance Manager generates *improvement actions*. These actions are not generic recommendations. Each one is tied directly to a *control requirement*, defining a specific condition that must be met for the control to be considered complete.

This creates a direct link between exposure and remediation. Instead of identifying a problem and leaving interpretation to the reader, the system defines what needs to change to close that gap. Ownership is assigned so that responsibility is clear, and progress is tracked as actions move toward completion. As actions are resolved and validated, the associated controls transition to a fully implemented state, and the overall posture improves.

These actions guide remediation but do not enforce it. They define what needs to be done without applying the change automatically, keeping control in the hands of the organization.

Compliance posture compared to detection and enforcement

Compliance Manager sits at the very start of the risk lifecycle. It establishes whether the environment is configured correctly before any activity is evaluated.

Detection systems operate after this point, analyzing activity to identify patterns, anomalies, or known indicators. Enforcement mechanisms follow, applying restrictions or protections based on those findings. Both depend on the consistency and completeness of the control framework already in place.

If controls are incomplete, detection becomes less reliable and enforcement less effective. If controls are well implemented, activity is more predictable, signals are clearer, and responses operate within defined boundaries.

Data Lifecycle Management operates differently. Instead of reacting to activity or enforcing controls at the point of interaction, it applies time-based rules that retain data for a defined period and then delete it automatically, independent of how that data is used.

Identifying sensitive information by using Microsoft Purview Data Explorer

Before data can be protected, monitored, or controlled, it must first be identified and understood in terms of what it is and where it resides.

Microsoft Purview Data Explorer provides that perspective. It does not look at how data is used or whether it has been exposed. Instead, it focuses on what data exists across the environment and how it is distributed, using classification signals to make sensitive information visible at scale.

Where to find this: In the **Microsoft Purview** portal, **Data explorer** is available under **Information Protection** | **Explorers** | **Data explorer**. This is where classified and sensitive data can be reviewed at an aggregated level.

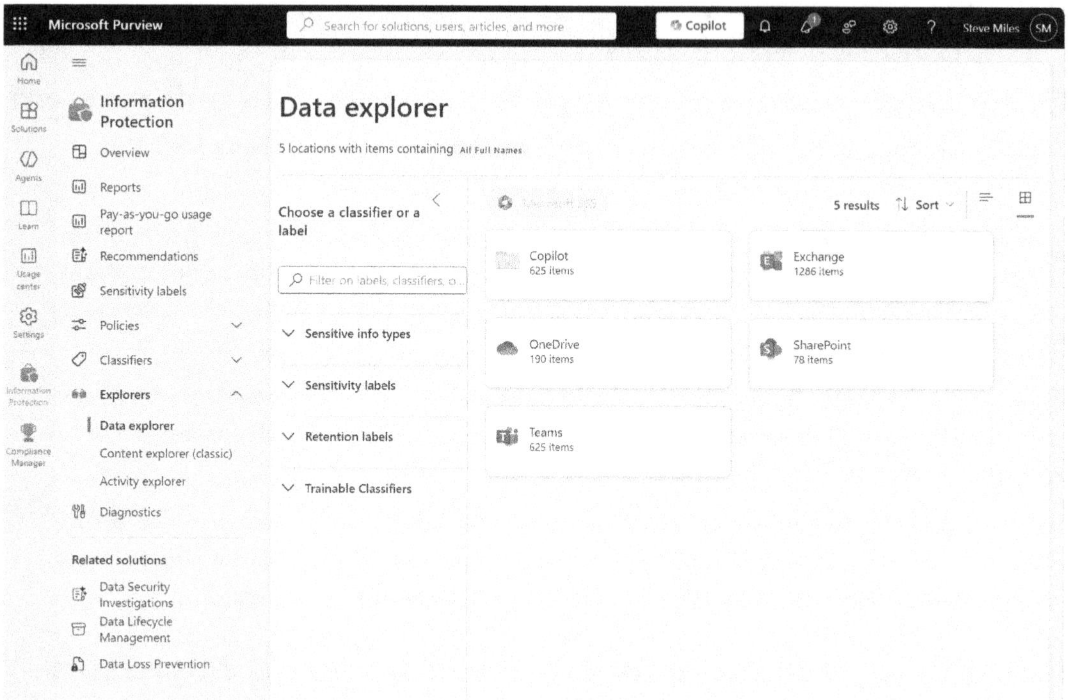

Figure 6.3: Microsoft Purview Data Explorer

This reinforces that Data Explorer is used to understand where sensitive data exists at scale, rather than to investigate individual files.

In practice, this means organizations can see where sensitive data exists without needing to examine individual files.

Classification signals from labels and sensitive information types

Data Explorer builds its view from classification signals that are applied across Microsoft 365. These signals originate from *sensitivity labels* and *sensitive information types*, both of which identify content based on predefined or custom patterns.

As content is created or processed, these signals become part of its classification state. A document labeled as confidential or containing financial data is no longer just a file; it becomes a known instance of sensitive information within the environment.

This allows visibility to scale by relying on classification already applied to content, turning it into a structured view of where sensitive data exists.

Aggregated insights from classified data

Rather than presenting individual files or messages, Data Explorer aggregates classification signals into a broader view. Counts and volumes replace item-level detail, allowing patterns to emerge across large datasets.

Exposure is assessed at an aggregate level. Attention moves from individual items to how much sensitive data exists and where it is concentrated across the environment.

As data changes, the pattern shifts, allowing exposure trends to be tracked over time.

Distribution of classified data across services

Sensitive data does not exist in a single location. It is spread across services such as Exchange Online, SharePoint, and OneDrive, each of which handles data differently.

Data Explorer reflects this distribution by showing where classified data resides across those services. This allows exposure to be understood in terms of location, not just volume.

Patterns begin to emerge from this distribution. Large volumes in collaboration platforms may indicate broad sharing and access, while concentration in mailboxes may reflect communication-driven exposure. These differences shape how risk should be interpreted.

The important point is that this view shows where sensitive data exists, not how it is being used. It provides location-based visibility, not behavioral insight.

Data Explorer limitations

The visibility provided by Data Explorer depends entirely on *classification*. If data has not been labeled or does not match a defined sensitive information type, it does not appear in the view.

Blind spots emerge where sensitive data exists but is not recognized because only classified data contributes to this view.

It also operates at an *aggregated level*. Individual items are not exposed, which means deeper investigation requires other tools. **Data Explorer** highlights where to look, but it does not provide the content itself.

Its focus remains on where data exists, not how it is used. Alerting and enforcement are handled by other capabilities. Its role is to make sensitive data visible so that other systems can act on that understanding.

Figure 6.4 shows how *classification* drives visibility, detection, enforcement, and investigation across Microsoft Purview.

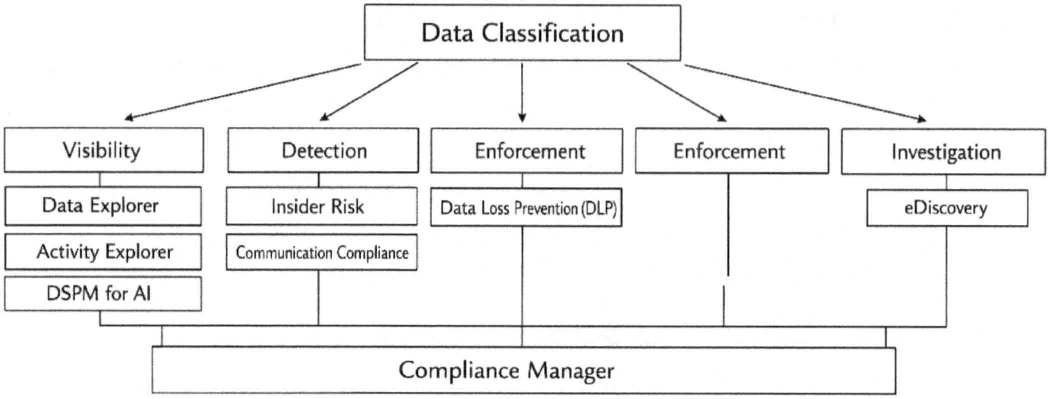

Figure 6.4: Flow from classification to visibility, enforcement, and investigation

Figure 6.4 shows how classification acts as the starting point for all downstream capabilities. Labels and sensitive information types determine what content is recognized as sensitive, which in turn controls what appears in visibility tools such as Data Explorer and Activity Explorer. The same classification context is used by detection capabilities, including Insider Risk Management and Communication Compliance, to identify patterns of risky behavior.

Enforcement is applied through **Data Loss Prevention** (**DLP**), where classification determines when policies are triggered and what actions are taken. Investigation relies on that same context, allowing **eDiscovery** to retrieve and analyze content that has already been identified as sensitive. These capabilities operate independently but rely on consistent classification to function correctly. **Compliance Manager** underpins the model by evaluating whether the controls that support classification and protection are properly configured.

Identifying risks using Insider Risk Management

Risk only becomes meaningful when activity is understood in context. A single action rarely tells you anything on its own. Opening a file, downloading content, or sharing information can all be completely normal depending on who is doing it and why. The challenge is not identifying activity, but understanding when that activity begins to form a pattern that no longer fits expected behavior.

Microsoft Purview Insider Risk Management is designed around that problem. Instead of looking at events in isolation, it builds a view of behavior that develops over time, linking actions to identity and evaluating how those actions relate to one another.

Where to find this: In the **Microsoft Purview** portal, **Insider Risk Management** is available from the **Solutions** area in the left navigation bar. This is where policies, alerts, and cases are managed.

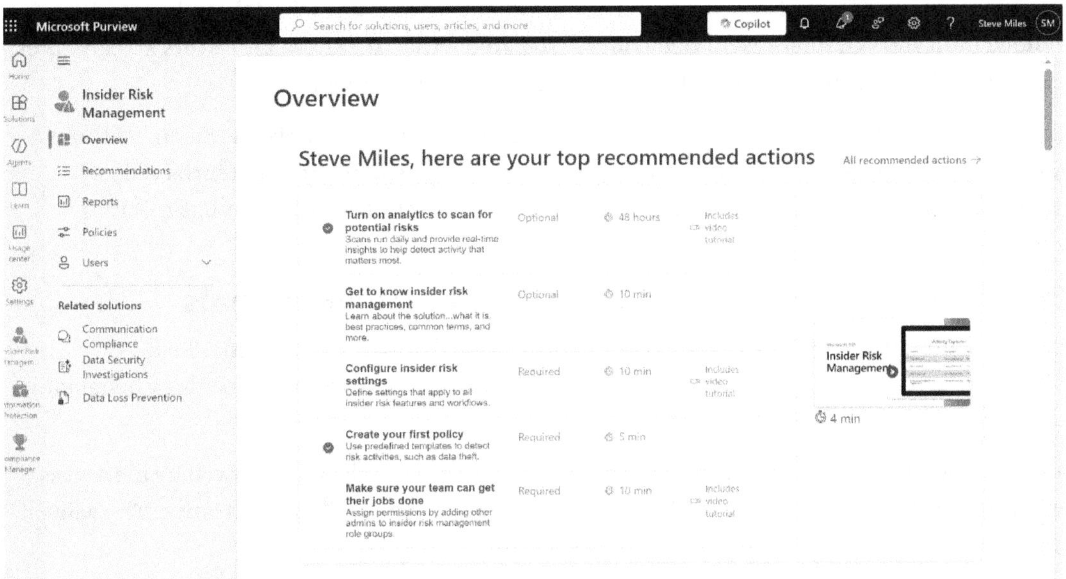

Figure 6.5: Microsoft Purview Insider Risk Management

This helps connect the section's behavioral risk model to the policy and case-based workflow used in the portal.

User-centric risk model

At the center of **Insider Risk Management** is the user. Every action is tied back to an identity, allowing activity across services to be connected into a single behavioral timeline. This changes the way risk is interpreted.

Two users can perform the same action, yet only one may represent a risk. A large file download by an administrator working on a migration is expected. The same action performed by a user who rarely accesses that data, or who is about to leave the organization, carries a very different meaning. The system does not treat actions equally. It evaluates them in the context of who is performing them and how that behavior compares to what is expected.

This is what separates Insider Risk from **activity logs**. It is not concerned with recording what happened, but with understanding whether what happened fits the user's normal pattern of behavior.

Signals and indicators from user activity

As users interact with data, each action generates signals. Accessing a document, copying files, downloading content, or sharing information all produces traceable activity across Microsoft 365 services.

On their own, these signals are neutral. They only become relevant when they align with defined indicators that represent behaviors associated with risk. These indicators act as a filter, narrowing the focus to actions that matter in the context of insider risk.

This distinction is important. Not every action should contribute to a risk decision. Without filtering, normal business activity would appear indistinguishable from potential risk. By mapping signals to indicators, the system isolates the subset of activity that has meaning within a risk model.

Behavioral patterns from correlated activity signals

The real shift happens when signals are no longer viewed individually. Insider Risk Management connects related actions over time, forming patterns that reflect how behavior is evolving.

A single download might not raise concern. A sequence of downloads, followed by file access across multiple locations, followed by external sharing, begins to form a narrative. The value is not in any one action, but in how those actions connect.

This correlation introduces continuity. Behavior is no longer a series of disconnected events, but a progression that can be observed and evaluated. Patterns become stronger when actions are closely related in time and context, and weaker when they are isolated or unrelated. Risk emerges from that pattern, not from the individual signals that make it up.

Risk scenarios and policies

Patterns only become meaningful when they are evaluated against defined conditions. This is where policies and risk scenarios come into play.

Each scenario represents a type of risk the organization is concerned about, such as data exfiltration or misuse of access. Policies determine which signals contribute to that scenario and how those signals are interpreted.

The same behavior can carry different weight depending on the scenario applied. Downloading files may be insignificant in one context, but critical in another. By shaping evaluation through scenarios, the system avoids applying a single, generic interpretation to all activities.

This keeps detection focused and relevant, aligning behavior with the specific risks the organization needs to manage.

Cases for investigation and management

When patterns reach thresholds defined by risk policies, they are grouped into cases. A case brings together the related signals, the pattern they form, and the context surrounding the user into a single investigative unit.

This removes the need to manually piece together activity from multiple sources. Instead of working backward from scattered events, investigators are presented with a structured view of behavior that already reflects how those actions are connected.

The case does not provide a final answer. It provides a complete picture. The responsibility for interpreting that behavior and determining the appropriate response still sits with the analyst or process reviewing it.

Insider risk limitations

Insider Risk Management is only as complete as the signals it can observe and the indicators it is configured to evaluate. Activity that falls outside those definitions remains invisible to the model.

It also does not determine intent. **Patterns** can indicate that something may be wrong, but they do not explain why the behavior occurred. That distinction matters because the same pattern can represent different outcomes depending on context.

The system highlights potential risk conditions, leaving enforcement, response, and final determination to other processes. Its role is to provide enough context for a decision to be made, not to make that decision itself.

Identifying and responding to alerts generated by Microsoft Purview DLP

Sensitive data protection only becomes meaningful at the point where data is actually used. It is one thing to know that sensitive information exists, and another to control what happens when someone tries to access it, share it, or move it. That transition—from visibility into action—is where **Microsoft Purview Data Loss Prevention** (**DLP**) operates.

DLP evaluates data as users interact with it in supported locations, applying policy-driven decisions that determine whether those interactions are allowed, restricted, or blocked. This moves data protection from simply identifying where sensitive data exists to controlling how it is used at the moment of access.

Where to find this: In the **Microsoft Purview** portal, **Data Loss Prevention** is available from the **Solutions** area in the left navigation bar. This is where DLP policies, alerts, and activity are managed.

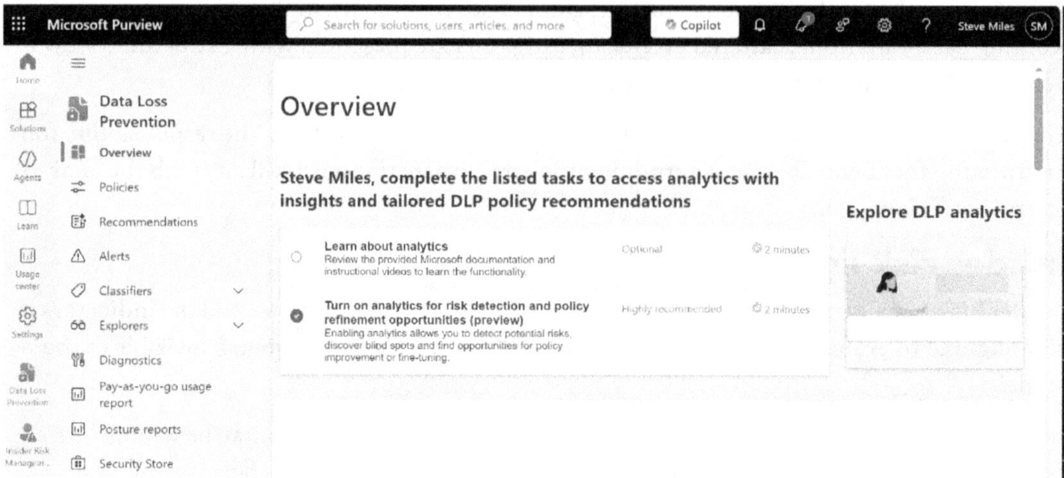

Figure 6.6: Microsoft Purview Data Loss Prevention

This view shows how DLP moves from policy definition to alert review when sensitive data activity matches configured conditions.

Policy conditions based on classification signals

At the core of DLP is the idea that data must be identified before it can be protected. Policies rely on **classification signals**, such as *sensitivity labels* and *sensitive information types*, to define what qualifies as sensitive.

These signals act as the foundation for evaluation. When a user interacts with data, the system checks whether those signals are present and whether they meet the conditions defined in the policy. The outcome does not depend on interpretation or intent. It depends entirely on whether the data meets the defined criteria.

This creates a consistent policy basis, while the final outcome can still vary by user, location, policy scope, exception, and configured action.

Policy matches for classified or sensitive data

When data meets the *conditions* defined in a *policy*, a **match occurs**. This is the moment where the system recognizes that the interaction involves data that requires protection.

A **match** does not immediately apply a response. Instead, it establishes a decision point. From this point forward, the policy determines what should happen next. This separation between identifying a condition and acting on it is what allows DLP to support both monitoring and enforcement scenarios.

It also means that not every match results in disruption. Some matches are simply observed, while others trigger stronger responses depending on how the policy is configured. Policies can operate in monitoring or enforcement modes, depending on how they are configured.

Alerts for sensitive data events

Alerts are generated when a *policy match* meets conditions that require **visibility** or **escalation**. Not every interaction with sensitive data produces an alert. Alerting is selective, designed to surface events that are significant enough to require attention.

When an alert is created, it captures the key elements of the interaction: who performed the action, what action was taken, and what data was involved. This provides enough context to understand what happened without needing to reconstruct the event from multiple sources.

The value of alerting lies in **focus**. Without it, organizations would need to review every instance of sensitive data interaction. With it, attention is directed only to events that meet defined thresholds of concern.

Enforcement actions for data protection

The defining characteristic of DLP is that **enforcement** happens at the *moment of interaction*. When a *policy match occurs*, the system applies the configured action **immediately**, shaping the outcome of that interaction in real time.

These actions take different forms. An action may be blocked entirely, allowed with conditions, or restricted in a way that limits how the data can be used. The important point is that the decision is applied before the action is completed, not after the data has already been exposed.

This is what separates DLP from investigation tools. Rather than describing what has already happened, DLP influences what is allowed to happen at the moment of interaction. Insider Risk Management, by contrast, evaluates behavior over time to identify patterns.

DLP limitations

DLP operates within the boundaries of what it can evaluate. If data is not classified or if it falls outside the scope of a policy, it will not be assessed. This creates gaps where protection does not apply.

It evaluates interactions at a specific point in time, assessing each interaction independently, without building behavioral patterns over time. That type of analysis belongs to other systems.

Decisions are applied based on defined conditions rather than interpretation of intent, ensuring consistent outcomes without subjective evaluation. Whether an action is accidental or deliberate is outside its scope.

Its role is precise: to evaluate data at the moment it is used and to apply policy-based control to that interaction.

Identifying policy violations generated by communication compliance

Not all risk comes from how data is handled. Some risk comes from how people communicate. Messages can carry inappropriate content, disclose sensitive information in ways that fall outside policy, or create regulatory exposure simply through what is said and how it is expressed. Unlike data protection, where the focus is on controlling access and movement, communication risk is centered on understanding the content of interactions themselves.

Microsoft Purview Communication Compliance analyzes message content to identify policy violations across communication channels. It evaluates communication content across supported channels, identifying messages that meet defined policy conditions and surfacing them for review. The goal is not to block communication in real time, but to ensure that potentially non-compliant interactions are consistently identified and assessed.

Where to find this: In the **Microsoft Purview** portal, **Communication Compliance** is available from the **Solutions** area in the left navigation bar. This is where policies and reviewable items are managed.

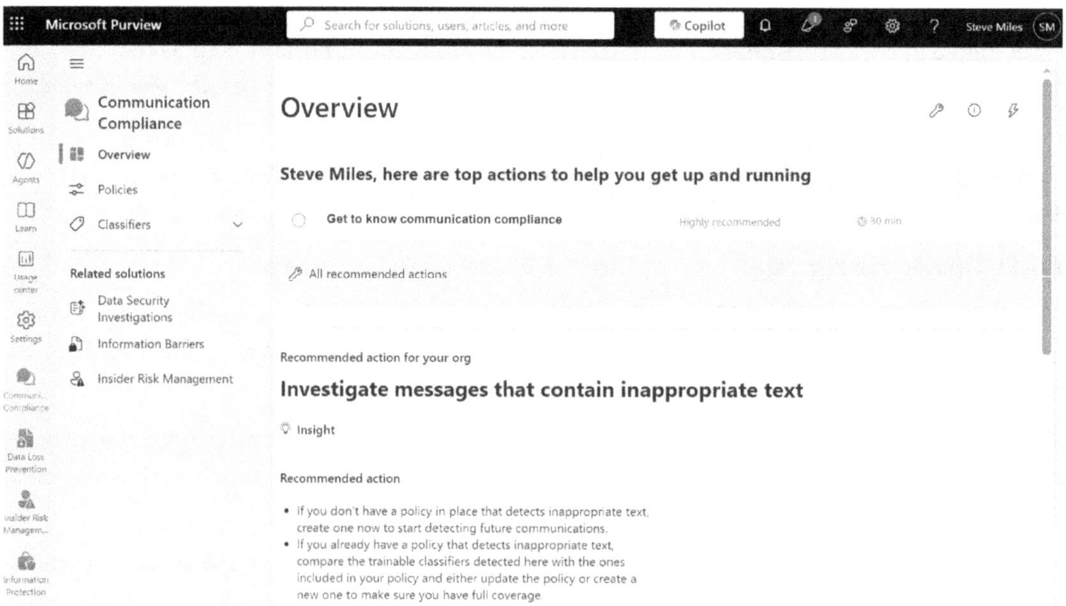

Figure 6.7: Microsoft Purview Communication Compliance

This gives readers a concrete view of how communication risks are surfaced for review rather than blocked automatically.

Message content analysis across communication channels

Communication Compliance operates directly on message content across services such as Exchange Online and Microsoft Teams.

It can also analyze supported prompts and responses from Microsoft 365 Copilot, Microsoft 365 Copilot Chat, and other supported generative AI applications, allowing risky or non-compliant AI interactions to be surfaced through the same review workflow.

Each message becomes part of a broader stream of communication that can be analyzed for patterns, language, and contextual meaning.

The nature of communication varies by channel. Email tends to contain longer, more structured exchanges, while chats and Copilot interactions are usually shorter and more frequent. Despite these differences, the system evaluates content against the same policy conditions, ensuring consistent analysis across formats.

The emphasis remains on what is communicated. It does not evaluate how data is stored or accessed, nor does it build behavioral patterns over time. Instead, it evaluates the content of each interaction against defined conditions.

Conditions for non-compliant communication content

Policies define what constitutes *non-compliant communication*. These conditions are based on **patterns** such as offensive language, regulatory violations, or inappropriate sharing of information.

When messages are processed, their content is evaluated against these conditions. Matches occur when language or context aligns with what the policy defines as a potential violation.

Context plays an important role in this evaluation. Words and phrases can carry different meanings depending on how they are used. The system evaluates surrounding content to determine whether a condition is met, reducing the likelihood of treating isolated terms as violations without context.

This keeps detection aligned with how communication actually occurs, rather than relying on simple keyword matching.

Violations as reviewable items

When a message meets a policy condition, it is surfaced as a **reviewable item**. This is not a final judgment. It is a signal that the content requires further assessment.

Each item preserves the context of the communication, including the message, the participants involved, and the conditions that were matched. This allows reviewers to evaluate the interaction as it occurred, rather than as an isolated fragment of text.

The purpose of the **reviewable item** is to narrow the focus. Instead of analyzing all communication, reviewers are presented with a filtered set of interactions that have already met defined criteria.

Structured review workflows for investigation

Once surfaced, reviewable items move through structured workflows that guide how they are assessed. These workflows define how items are reviewed, classified, escalated, or resolved.

This introduces consistency into the review process. Similar types of communication are evaluated in the same way, reducing variability in how decisions are made. It also ensures that policy conditions are applied in a controlled and repeatable manner.

The workflow does not determine whether a violation has occurred. It provides the structure within which that decision is made.

Communication compliance limitations

Communication compliance operates within the scope of supported channels and defined policy conditions. Messages outside those channels or conditions are not evaluated.

Classifier results also require review. Communication Compliance can surface messages that appear to match policy conditions, but false positives and false negatives can occur, and coverage depends on supported channels, languages, and policy scope. User-reported or matched messages are therefore treated as reviewable items, not automatic proof that a violation has occurred.

It focuses on content at a specific point in time. It does not correlate behavior across multiple interactions or build long-term behavioral profiles. That type of analysis is handled elsewhere.

Enforcement is not applied at the point of communication, as the focus remains on review rather than control. Its role is to identify and present potentially non-compliant content for review, leaving investigation and response to follow-on processes.

Identifying user activities reported by Microsoft Purview Activity Explorer

Understanding risk at the activity level requires more than knowing that an action occurred. It requires seeing exactly what was done, by whom, and in what sequence. Without that level of detail, it becomes difficult to reconstruct events, validate concerns, or move from suspicion to evidence.

Microsoft Purview Activity Explorer provides *event-level visibility* into user interactions with data based on *audit logs*. It does not attempt to interpret behavior or assign risk. Instead, it exposes activity as it actually occurred, capturing user interactions with data and presenting them in a way that allows those actions to be examined, connected, and understood.

Where to find this: In the **Microsoft Purview** portal, **Activity Explorer** is available under **Information Protection** | **Explorers** | **Activity explorer**. This is where audit-based user activity can be filtered and reviewed.

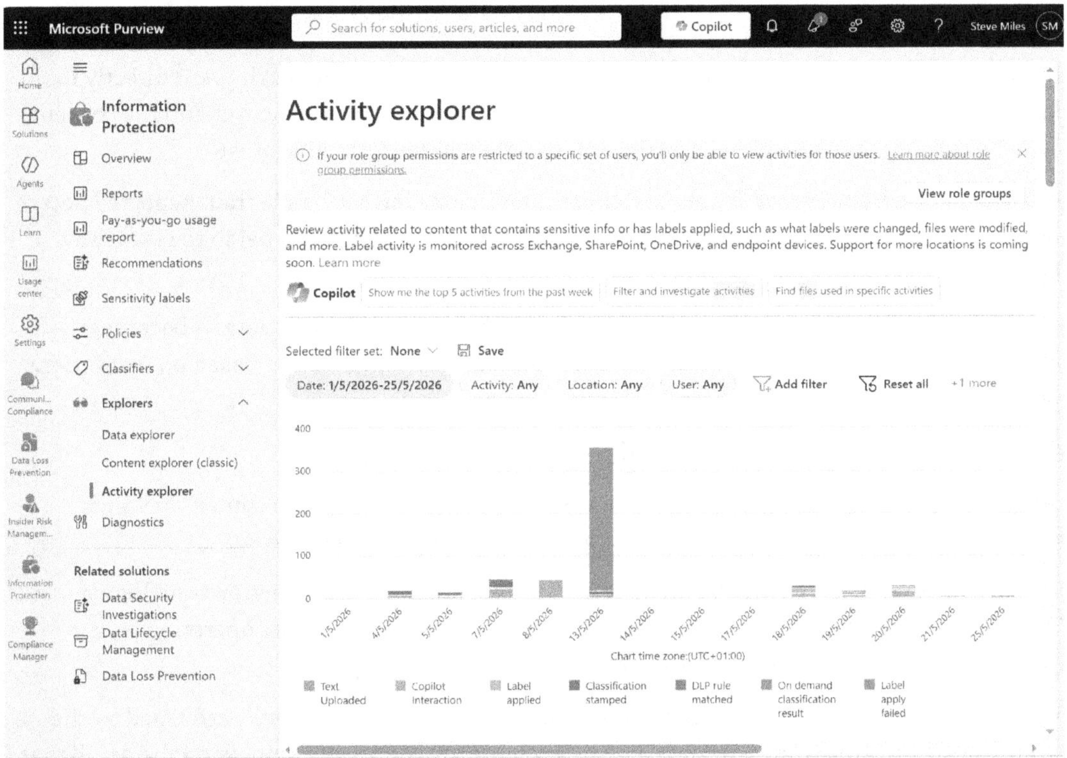

Figure 6.8: Microsoft Purview Activity Explorer

This view supports the distinction between aggregated data visibility and event-level activity review.

Audit-derived activity events

Activity Explorer is built on **audit events** generated across Microsoft 365 services. Every interaction with data—whether it is accessing a file, modifying content, downloading information, or sharing it—can be recorded as a discrete event tied to a specific point in time.

Each event includes more than just the action itself. It carries *metadata* such as the user identity, the type of operation performed, and the object involved. This transforms raw activity into structured records that can be analyzed without needing to reconstruct context from multiple sources.

The completeness of this view depends on audit coverage. If an action is not captured at the audit layer, it does not appear. What Activity Explorer presents is not an approximation of activity, but a direct reflection of what has been recorded.

User interactions with data

Rather than presenting activity as abstract logs, Activity Explorer ties each event directly to the data being interacted with. This creates a clear relationship between the user and the content, showing not just that an action occurred, but what it was performed against.

As users open, edit, move, or share data, those interactions form a visible trail. Repeated access to the same content, movement across locations, or patterns of sharing begin to reveal how data is actually being used in practice.

This shifts visibility from *system-level events* to *user-level interaction* with data. It becomes possible to understand how information flows through the organization based on real actions rather than assumptions.

Activity events: users, actions, and context

Each event includes the action performed, the user responsible, and the context in which it occurred, such as location, device, application, or the specific data involved.

This structure allows events to be interpreted in a meaningful way. An action is no longer just "*a download*" or "*a share*." It becomes a specific user performing a specific operation on a specific piece of data within a defined context.

As events accumulate, connections emerge across related activity. Actions performed by the same user, or targeting the same data, can be examined together without losing the detail that makes them meaningful.

Activity timelines for investigation

A key aspect of **Activity Explorer** is how events are presented over time.

Activity is not shown as isolated records, but as a sequence that reflects how actions unfold. A file may be accessed first, then modified, downloaded, and shared, creating a clear progression rather than a set of disconnected actions.

Timing adds another layer of meaning. Rapid sequences may indicate automated or bulk behavior, while gaps between actions may suggest deliberate steps. The timeline provides the structure needed to interpret that activity.

Event-level activity compared to aggregated data insights

Activity Explorer operates at the **event level**, preserving the detail of individual actions. This is fundamentally different from tools that present aggregated insights, where data is summarized into counts, trends, or distributions.

Aggregated views are useful for understanding **where** data exists or **how much** of it there is. They provide scale, but they remove detail. Activity Explorer does the opposite. It *preserves detail,* allowing individual actions to be examined in context.

This distinction is critical. When the goal is to understand *behavior* or investigate a *specific scenario,* aggregated data is not enough. The **underlying events** are required.

Activity Explorer limitations

Activity Explorer reflects only what has been captured through *audit logging.*

If activity is not *recorded,* it cannot be *analyzed.* This creates gaps where visibility is dependent on logging coverage.

It presents activity without classification or judgment, providing the foundation on which alerting and enforcement decisions are made. By exposing activity exactly as it occurred, it allows behavior to be examined and understood before any conclusions are drawn.

Discovering and managing AI Activity by using DSPM for AI

The introduction of AI changes the nature of data exposure. Traditionally, access has been shaped by how users interact with information—what they search for, what they open, and what they share. AI shifts that model. Instead of navigating data step by step, it can retrieve, combine, and process large volumes of information in a single interaction. This does not introduce new access, but it amplifies the reach of existing access.

Microsoft Purview DSPM for AI identifies where sensitive data is exposed through AI by analyzing *classification*, *permissions*, and *access scope*. It evaluates how data, classification, and permissions combine to define what AI systems can reach, exposing conditions where sensitive information may be more broadly accessible than intended.

DSPM for AI also surfaces AI activity, including prompts and responses from Microsoft 365 Copilot, Microsoft 365 Copilot Chat, and other supported AI applications. This allows administrators to see where AI interactions involve sensitive information, connecting actual AI usage with the classification and permission context that shapes exposure risk.

Where to find this: In the **Microsoft Purview** portal, **DSPM for AI** is available from the **Solutions** area in the left navigation bar. This is where AI activity, sensitive data exposure, and oversharing risks can be reviewed.

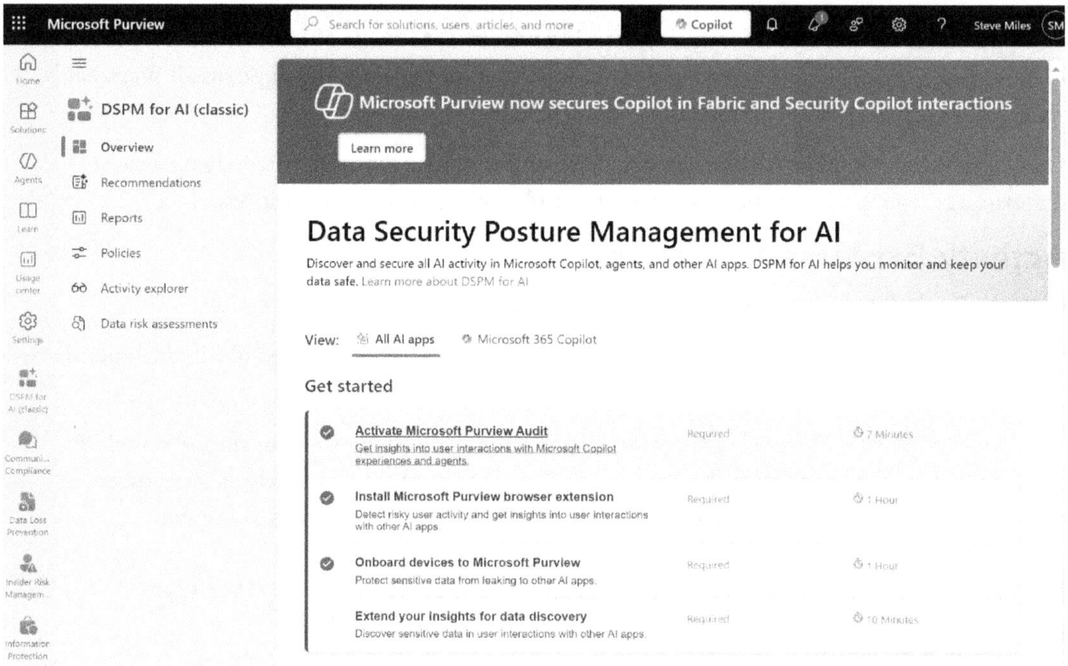

Figure 6.9: Microsoft Purview DSPM for AI

This connects DSPM for AI to both exposure analysis and the AI activity signals that help administrators understand how sensitive data may surface through Copilot experiences.

Data exposure from AI access

In an *AI-driven* environment, exposure is determined by how much data can be accessed in a single interaction. A user might access a limited set of files during normal activity, but an AI system can retrieve and process a much larger set of data in response to a single prompt.

Exposure is understood differently in this context. The question is no longer **how often** data is accessed, but **how much** data can be accessed at once. Large repositories, shared locations, and broadly accessible datasets increase exposure because they allow more information to be retrieved in a single operation.

The scale of access becomes the risk factor. The broader the accessible dataset, the greater the potential exposure.

AI access to data through existing permissions

AI systems do not bypass access controls. They operate within the same permission model that governs user access, inheriting permissions from identities, groups, and sharing configurations.

This is what makes exposure difficult to detect without analysis. Permissions that were originally granted for collaboration or convenience can unintentionally allow AI systems to retrieve data far beyond what users would typically access in practice.

Access accumulates over time. Shared folders, inherited permissions, and broad group membership all expand the scope of what is reachable. AI simply makes that scope visible in a new way.

Exposure risk from classification and access

Understanding exposure requires combining *two dimensions:* **what** data is sensitive and **where** it is accessible.

Classification identifies *sensitivity*, while **permissions** defines *reach*. **Risk** emerges where these two overlap. When sensitive data is broadly accessible, AI can retrieve that information at scale.

Figure 6.10 shows how exposure risk emerges from the intersection of **classification**, **permissions**, and **retrieval scale**.

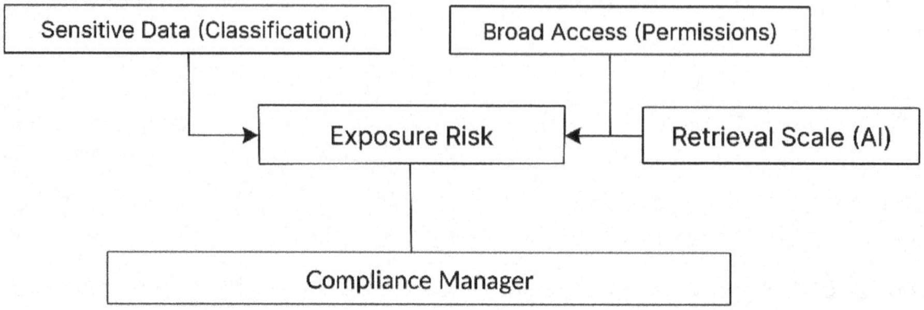

Figure 6.10: AI exposure from classification, permissions, and retrieval scale

Figure 6.10 illustrates how sensitive data becomes exposed when it is both classified as *sensitive* and broadly accessible through *permissions*. AI increases this exposure by retrieving and combining information at scale, extending the impact of any misconfiguration.

Gaps in **classification** complicate this further. Data that has not been *labeled* appears no different from *non-sensitive content*, even if it carries risk. This creates hidden exposure, where sensitive information is present but not recognized as such.

DSPM for AI brings these dimensions together, showing not just where sensitive data exists, but where it is both present and accessible.

AI exposure scenarios for sensitive data

Rather than presenting exposure as isolated instances, **DSPM for AI** groups conditions into scenarios. These scenarios represent *patterns of exposure*, such as sensitive data stored in broadly accessible locations or shared across large groups.

This approach makes exposure easier to understand. Instead of analyzing individual files or permissions, organizations can identify recurring conditions that create risk.

By focusing on *patterns*, it becomes possible to address root causes rather than individual symptoms. Reducing exposure in one scenario often reduces it across many instances.

Governance through classification and access

Managing exposure in an AI context is not about introducing new controls; it is about refining what already exists.

Permissions can be adjusted to reduce unnecessary access, limiting how broadly data can be reached.

Classification can be improved to ensure that sensitive data is clearly identified and can be managed appropriately.

When these two elements are aligned, exposure is reduced. Sensitive data is both visible and controlled, and access reflects actual need rather than accumulated permissions.

This shifts governance from *reactive* to *preventative*. Instead of responding to how AI uses data, the focus is on controlling what AI is able to access in the first place.

DSPM limitations

DSPM for AI identifies *exposure conditions* and also surfaces *supported AI activity*. Exposure findings show where sensitive data could be accessed through AI, while activity findings show observed AI interactions where supported. It does not replace investigation, classification, permission remediation, or policy enforcement.

Searching data using content search in Microsoft Purview eDiscovery

At some point, *visibility* and *detection* are no longer enough. Knowing that data exists, or that activity has occurred, does not answer the most important question—*what exactly is in that data?*

When an investigation reaches that stage, the focus shifts from signals and summaries to the underlying content itself.

In the current Microsoft Purview portal, **Content Search** is part of the unified eDiscovery experience rather than a separate standalone tool. It allows organizations to search for and retrieve specific items—emails, documents, and other data—across Microsoft 365 based on query conditions, making it possible to move from indicators of risk to the actual evidence behind them.

Where to find this: In the **Microsoft Purview** portal, **Content Search** is accessed through the **eDiscovery experience**, either as a search within an eDiscovery case or by using the Content Search case type.

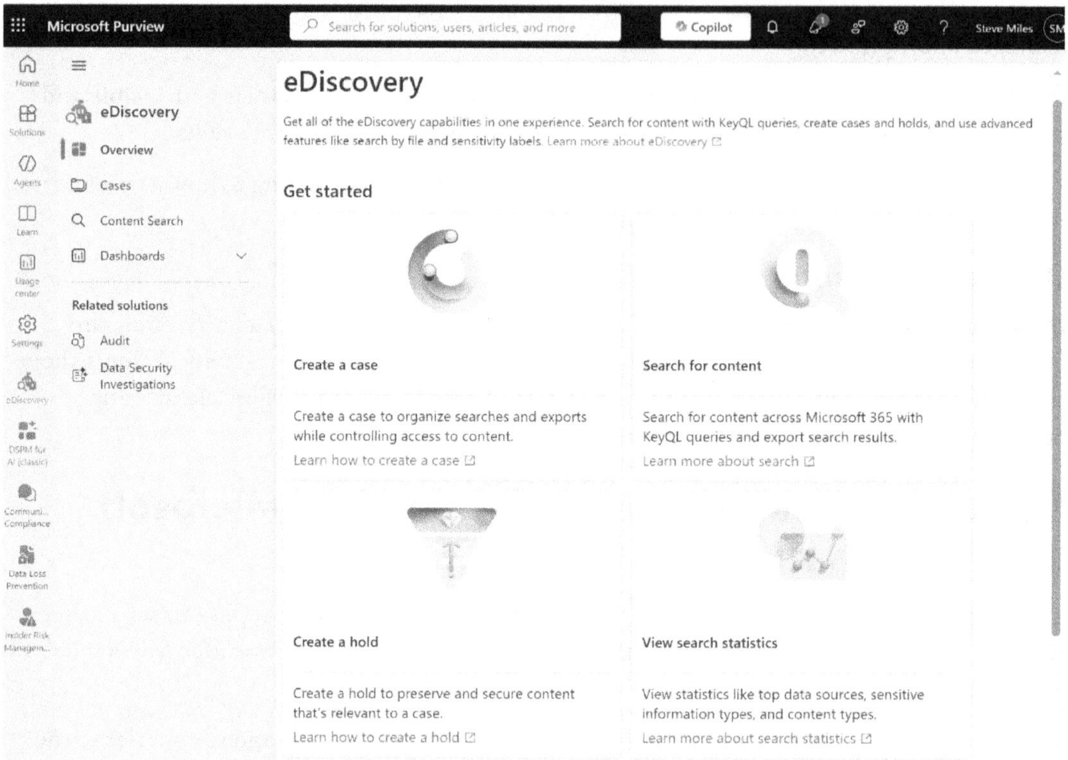

Figure 6.11: Content Search accessed through the unified Microsoft Purview eDiscovery experience

This reinforces that Content Search is accessed through eDiscovery, rather than from a separate top-level Content Search tool.

Query-based data retrieval across Microsoft 365

Content Search begins with a *query*. Instead of browsing data manually, investigators define what they are looking for using criteria that can span multiple services, including Exchange Online, SharePoint, OneDrive, and Teams.

As the query runs, it evaluates indexed content across those services and returns items that match the defined conditions. This allows a single search to retrieve data from multiple locations, bringing together information that would otherwise remain distributed across the environment.

The outcome is shaped entirely by how the query is defined. A broad query returns a large volume of results, while a more targeted query narrows the focus to a smaller, more relevant dataset. Results depend on both the query conditions and the locations included in the search.

Filtering using keywords, locations, and conditions

To make retrieval useful, queries can be refined using filters.

Keywords allow searches to focus on specific terms or phrases within content.

Location filters restrict the search to selected mailboxes, sites, or services, narrowing the scope of where results are drawn from.

Additional conditions, such as **date ranges** or **participant details**, further refine the results. These filters *reduce noise*, allowing investigators to concentrate on the subset of data that is most relevant to the scenario they are examining.

The precision of the results depends on how these filters are combined. Effective filtering reduces the need to manually sift through large datasets, making it easier to move quickly from search to analysis.

Indexed data in Microsoft 365 services

Content Search relies on indexed data rather than scanning content directly at the time of the query. As data is created and stored across Microsoft 365 services, it is processed into an index that allows it to be searched efficiently.

This **index** acts as a structured representation of the data, enabling queries to return results quickly without examining every item individually. It also defines where **what** can be found. If content is not indexed, or has not yet been processed into the index, it will not appear in search results.

This dependency on **indexing** shapes both performance and coverage. Retrieval is fast and scalable, but it is limited to what the index contains.

Content retrieval to support investigation workflows

When results are returned, each item includes both the content and its associated metadata. This allows investigators to examine not just the content returned, but where it came from and how it relates to other activity.

These results form a working dataset that can be reviewed, analyzed, or exported for further investigation. Instead of working from signals such as alerts or activity logs, investigators now have direct access to the underlying data that those signals represent.

This is the point where the investigation moves from *inference* to *evidence*. The focus shifts from understanding that something happened to examining exactly what was involved.

Item-level retrieval compared to aggregated insights

Content Search operates at the level of *individual items*. Each result represents a specific email, file, or record that can be examined directly.

This differs from *aggregated views*, which summarize data into counts or patterns. Aggregation provides an overview, but it removes the detail needed to understand specific events. **Content Search** preserves that *detail*, making it possible to examine the *exact content* involved.

Both approaches are useful, but they serve different purposes. **Aggregated insights** helps identify *where* to look. **Content Search** provides *what* needs to be examined once that focus is established.

Content Search limitations

Content Search retrieves only what matches the query and exists within the index. If the query is too *broad*, results may become difficult to manage. If it is too *narrow*, relevant data may be missed.

It also does not interpret or prioritize results. Every matching item is returned without assessing its importance or relevance. The responsibility for analysis remains with the investigator.

Finally, Content Search does not *detect risk* or *enforce controls*. It provides *access to* data rather than *decisions about* that data, representing the final step in the process as investigations move from signals and indicators to the underlying content itself.

Summary

Risk in a Copilot environment doesn't begin with alerts or incidents. It starts much earlier, in how the environment is structured. When permissions are too broad, classification is incomplete, or controls are only partially in place, those gaps don't stay contained—they shape everything that follows.

Microsoft Purview brings that structure into view. Compliance Manager establishes whether the right controls exist in the first place, turning compliance into something measurable rather than assumed. From there, Data Explorer makes sensitive data visible at scale, showing where it exists and how it is distributed across the environment. At this stage, the focus is not on activity, but on exposure.

As activity comes into focus, the perspective shifts. Insider Risk Management connects actions over time, building a picture of behavior rather than isolated events. DLP operates at the point where data is used, applying policy decisions in real time. Communication Compliance looks at what is being said, identifying messages that may introduce risk, while Activity Explorer exposes exactly what happened, step by step, with full context.

Copilot changes how that environment is experienced. Access still follows the same permission model, but retrieval becomes broader and more immediate. DSPM for AI makes this visible by highlighting where sensitive data and broad access overlap, bringing exposure into clearer focus.

When the investigation moves beyond signals, Content Search returns matching items and metadata for review or export, depending on the permissions and eDiscovery workflow in use. This is where understanding shifts from patterns and indicators to the actual content involved.

Taken together, these capabilities follow a clear path. The environment is first validated, then made visible, then observed through activity, controlled at the point of use, and finally examined in detail when required. Copilot does not alter that path—it makes the outcome of it immediately visible in every response.

In the next chapter, the focus moves from identifying broader data protection and governance risks to oversharing in SharePoint. You will look at how administrators identify shared content that may be too widely accessible, monitor risky collaboration patterns, and use governance capabilities to manage access across SharePoint sites.

Microsoft Learn reference links

The following table provides official Microsoft references for the main Microsoft Purview compliance, data discovery, insider risk, DLP, communication compliance, activity analysis, DSPM for AI, and eDiscovery topics introduced in this chapter.

Topic	What it covers	Microsoft Learn reference
Identifying Compliance Risks with Compliance Manager	Explains how Microsoft Purview Compliance Manager assesses compliance posture, tracks controls, recommends improvement actions, and measures progress through compliance scores.	`https://learn.microsoft.com/en-us/purview/compliance-manager`

Topic	What it covers	Microsoft Learn reference
Identifying Sensitive Information with Data Explorer	Explains how Data Explorer provides visibility into classified and sensitive data across Microsoft 365 by using labels, classifiers, and sensitive information types.	`https://learn.microsoft.com/en-us/purview/data-classification-data-explorer`
Identifying Risks with Insider Risk Management	Explains how Insider Risk Management uses policies, indicators, alerts, and cases to identify and investigate risky user activity patterns.	`https://learn.microsoft.com/en-us/purview/insider-risk-management`
Identifying and Responding to DLP Alerts	Explains how Microsoft Purview DLP detects sensitive information, applies policy conditions, and generates alerts when risky data activity requires review.	`https://learn.microsoft.com/en-us/purview/dlp-learn-about-dlp`
Identifying Violations in Communication Compliance	Explains how Communication Compliance analyzes communication content, including Microsoft 365 Copilot and Copilot Chat prompts and responses, for policy violations.	`https://learn.microsoft.com/en-us/purview/communication-compliance`

Topic	What it covers	Microsoft Learn reference
Identifying User Activities in Activity Explorer	Explains how Activity Explorer provides audit-derived activity views for labeled content and user interactions with sensitive data.	`https://learn.microsoft.com/en-us/purview/data-classification-activity-explorer`
Discovering and Managing AI Activity with DSPM for AI	Explains how DSPM for AI helps organizations discover AI activity, identify sensitive data exposure, and manage data security risks related to AI use.	`https://learn.microsoft.com/en-us/purview/dspm-for-ai`
Searching Data Using Purview eDiscovery Content Search	Explains how Microsoft Purview eDiscovery is used to search, retrieve, review, and manage Microsoft 365 content for investigations and legal cases.	`https://learn.microsoft.com/en-us/purview/edisc`

Table 6.1: Microsoft references for data protection and governance risk topics covered in this chapter

Together, these references support the chapter's focus on how Microsoft Purview helps organizations identify compliance gaps, locate sensitive data, analyze user activity, detect risky behavior, manage AI-related exposure, and retrieve content for investigation.

Key terms and acronyms

The following table introduces the main Microsoft Purview, compliance, data protection, activity analysis, AI exposure, and eDiscovery terms used throughout this chapter. It gives readers a quick reference as they review how data protection and governance risks are identified across Microsoft 365 and Copilot environments.

Term	Meaning
Compliance Manager	A Microsoft Purview solution that evaluates whether required controls are implemented and provides assessments, improvement actions, and compliance scores.
Compliance score	A numerical measure that reflects how fully compliance controls have been implemented and validated.
Assessment	A structured set of controls in Compliance Manager aligned to a regulation, standard, baseline, or internal compliance requirement.
Improvement action	A recommended action in Compliance Manager that identifies what must be changed or completed to improve control coverage.
Data Explorer	A Microsoft Purview tool that shows aggregated visibility into classified and sensitive data across Microsoft 365 services.
Sensitive information type (SIT)	A pattern-based definition used to identify sensitive data such as financial, personal, medical, or custom organizational information.
Sensitivity label	A Microsoft Purview label used to classify content and apply protection settings such as encryption, access restrictions, or markings.
Insider Risk Management	A Microsoft Purview solution that identifies risky user behavior by correlating activity signals over time and grouping them into alerts or cases.
Signal	An observable user or data activity that may contribute to risk analysis, such as accessing, downloading, copying, or sharing content.
Indicator	A configured condition used by Insider Risk Management to determine which signals are relevant to a risk scenario.
Risk scenario	A defined pattern of concern, such as potential data exfiltration, policy violation, or misuse of access.
Insider risk case	A structured investigation record that brings together related alerts, signals, user context, and activity patterns for review.

Term	Meaning
Data Loss Prevention (DLP)	A Microsoft Purview capability that detects sensitive information and applies policy actions to monitor, restrict, or block risky data activity.
DLP policy	A policy that defines the sensitive data, locations, conditions, users, and actions used to detect or control data loss risk.
DLP alert	A notification generated when a DLP policy match meets the configured threshold for review or escalation.
Communication Compliance	A Microsoft Purview solution that analyzes communication content, including supported Copilot prompts and responses, for policy violations.
Reviewable item	A communication, prompt, response, or message surfaced for review because it matched a Communication Compliance policy condition.
Activity Explorer	A Microsoft Purview tool that shows audit-derived activity events for labeled content and user interactions with data.
Audit event	A recorded activity from Microsoft 365 audit logs that captures what happened, who performed the action, and when it occurred.
DSPM for AI	Data Security Posture Management for AI, a Microsoft Purview capability used to identify AI activity, sensitive data exposure, and oversharing risks.
AI activity	User interactions with AI apps, including prompts and responses, can be monitored and reviewed where supported.
AI exposure	A condition where sensitive data can be accessed or surfaced through AI because of broad permissions, weak classification, or oversharing.
eDiscovery	A Microsoft Purview capability used to identify, search, review, and manage electronically stored information for investigations or legal cases.
Content Search	A search capability within the Microsoft Purview eDiscovery experience used to retrieve specific Microsoft 365 items based on query conditions.

Term	Meaning
Query	A search definition made up of keywords, locations, date ranges, participants, or other conditions used to retrieve matching content.
Indexed data	Data that has been processed into a searchable index so it can be retrieved by eDiscovery or search-based tools.

Table 6.2: Key data protection and governance risk terms and acronyms

These terms connect the chapter's terminology to the AB-900 skills measured. They also give readers a simple reference point for understanding how Microsoft Purview identifies compliance gaps, sensitive data, user activity, DLP alerts, communication violations, AI exposure, and investigation-ready content.

Exam readiness drill – chapter review questions

Apart from mastering key concepts, strong test-taking skills under time pressure are essential for acing your certification exam. That's why developing these abilities early in your learning journey is critical.

Exam readiness drills, using the free online practice resources provided with this book, help you progressively improve your time management and test-taking skills while reinforcing the key concepts you've learned.

HOW TO GET STARTED

1. Open the link or scan the QR code at the bottom of this page
2. If you have unlocked the practice resources already, log in to your registered account. If you haven't, follow the instructions in the *Free Benefits with Your Book* section in this book's *Preface* and come back to this page.
3. Once you log in, click the START button to start this chapter's quiz
4. We recommend attempting a quiz multiple times till you're able to answer most of the questions correctly and well within the time limit

5. You can use the following practice template to help you plan your attempts:

Working On Accuracy		
Attempt	**Target**	**Time Limit**
Attempt 1	40% or more	Till the timer runs out
Attempt 2	60% or more	Till the timer runs out
Attempt 3	75% or more	Till the timer runs out
Working On Timing		
Attempt 4	75% or more	1 minute before time limit
Attempt 5	75% or more	2 minutes before time limit
Attempt 6	75% or more	3 minutes before time limit

The above drill is just an example. Design your drills based on your own goals and make the most out of the online quizzes accompanying this book.

Link to this chapter's quiz

You need to unlock the online practice resources to access the link below. Check the *Free Benefits with Your Book* section in the *Preface* for detailed instructions on how to do this. You only need to unlock the resources once.

Open Quiz `https://packt.link/pqWQf`or scan the QR code

7

Identifying and Monitoring Oversharing in SharePoint in Microsoft 365

Collaboration platforms such as **SharePoint** enable organizations to store, share, and work on information at scale. As usage grows, employees collaborate with colleagues and external partners across teams and projects, increasing the risk that information may be shared more broadly than intended.

This chapter explores how administrators identify **oversharing** within **SharePoint** environments and how governance capabilities help organizations monitor and manage access to shared content.

You will learn how administrators investigate sharing activity, analyze governance reports that highlight risky collaboration sites, and apply advanced management capabilities that help ensure appropriate access to sensitive information.

This chapter primarily supports the **Identify and monitor oversharing in SharePoint in Microsoft 365** module from the *Skills Measured* section of the **AB-900** exam.

By the end of this chapter, you will be able to confidently answer questions on the following topics:

- Understanding oversharing risks in SharePoint
- Identifying the tools to troubleshoot oversharing in an organization
- Running a data access governance report in SharePoint
- Understanding features and capabilities of SharePoint Advanced Management, including restricted site access

Understanding how these capabilities work together helps organizations maintain visibility into how information is shared across SharePoint sites, identify collaboration spaces that may present governance risks, and apply controls that ensure sensitive information remains accessible only to the appropriate users.

Understanding oversharing risks in SharePoint

SharePoint plays a central role in collaboration by providing a *shared environment* where documents and information can be stored, accessed, and worked on collectively.

The same features that make collaboration easy can also create **risk.**

Sharing a document in SharePoint often takes only a few clicks. A user can send a link to a colleague, grant access to a team, or invite an external partner to review content. In fast-moving work environments, those actions are usually taken with productivity in mind rather than with security considerations.

This might happen when a document is shared with a large internal group, when access permissions are set too broadly, or when links allow people outside the organization to open content. In many cases, the person sharing the information may not realize how widely the document can be accessed.

For organizations, the consequences of oversharing extend beyond simple mistakes. Sensitive business information, financial data, or internal planning documents can reach people who were never meant to see them. In regulated industries, that exposure can create compliance issues as well as reputational damage. Even when the content itself is not highly confidential, uncontrolled sharing can make it difficult for administrators to understand who has access to important information.

Because collaboration is essential for modern work, organizations cannot simply restrict all sharing activity. Instead, administrators need ways to understand how information is being shared, where permissions may be broader than expected, and which locations in the environment may present higher risk.

This risk becomes more visible in environments that use Microsoft 365 Copilot and agents. Copilot respects the permissions, sharing settings, and policies already applied in Microsoft 365, so content that has been shared too broadly in SharePoint can become available through Copilot responses when a user already has access to it. For administrators, oversharing is therefore not only a SharePoint governance issue; it also affects whether Copilot can surface information to the right audience.

What oversharing means in SharePoint environments

In **SharePoint**, sharing information is designed to be simple. A user can open a document, select **Share**, and send a link to colleagues or external partners within seconds. That ease of sharing is one of the reasons organizations rely on SharePoint for collaboration. Teams can quickly exchange ideas, review documents together, and move projects forward without waiting for files to be emailed back and forth.

However, the same convenience that enables collaboration can also create *unintended exposure*, because sharing options are quick to use and the implications of those choices are not always obvious.

For example, when a document is shared using a broad permission setting or a reusable link, the access granted may extend further than the person sharing the file expected. A link forwarded to another colleague, or a permission applied at a folder level, can quickly widen access to that information. Over time, documents that were meant for a small project team may end up visible to large internal groups or even external collaborators.

A file that only needs to be reviewed might be shared with editing rights, allowing recipients to change the document or pass it along to others. In busy work environments, these decisions are often made quickly, without a detailed review of how access might spread across the organization.

External collaboration introduces another dimension to the issue. Organizations frequently invite partners, vendors, or contractors to work on shared documents. While this type of collaboration is common and often necessary, it can also increase the chances that content becomes visible outside the intended audience if permissions are not carefully managed.

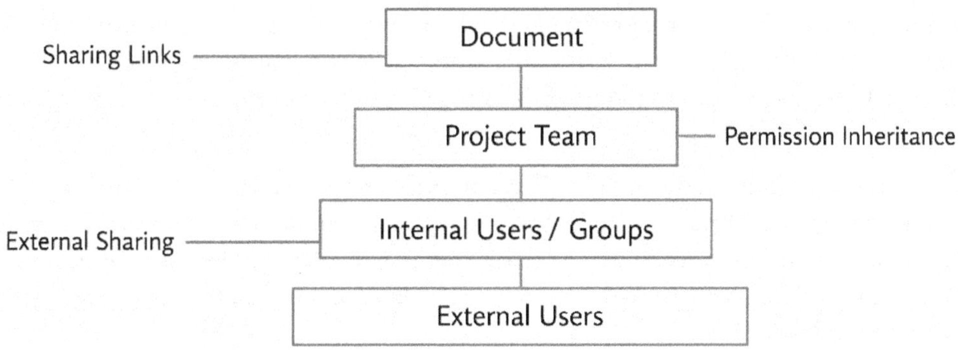

Figure 7.1: Oversharing expansion through links, permissions, and external access

Figure 7.1 illustrates how oversharing in SharePoint develops as access expands beyond the original intended audience. A document is typically shared first with a specific project team to support day-to-day collaboration. From there, access can widen as sharing links are reused or forwarded, and as permissions inherited from folders or sites grant visibility to broader internal users or groups.

Over time, the same content may also be shared externally with partners, vendors, or contractors, further extending its reach. Each individual sharing action may appear reasonable in isolation, but together these actions can gradually broaden access in ways that are difficult to track.

Common oversharing scenarios and business risks

In most cases, **oversharing** appears through everyday collaboration habits that gradually expand access to information. One common scenario involves *link-based sharing*.

A user may create a link to a document so that colleagues can review it quickly. If that link allows broad access, anyone who receives it can open the file. When the link is forwarded to other people, the audience grows without the original author realizing how widely the content has spread.

Another situation occurs when *permissions* are applied *too broadly*. For example, a document stored in a shared project folder might inherit permissions that allow an entire department to view it. While the original intention may have been to share the file with only a few people, the inherited permissions mean many more users can access the information.

Oversharing can also appear during *external collaboration*. Organizations often invite vendors, contractors, or business partners to review documents or contribute to projects. If those guests are given access to a full site or a large folder structure instead of a specific file, they may be able to see additional content that was never meant to be shared outside the organization.

These situations are rarely the result of malicious behavior. Instead, they come from the normal pace of work. Employees focus on completing tasks and sharing information efficiently, while the structure of permissions and links quietly determines who else might gain access.

From a business perspective, the impact of oversharing can be significant. Confidential documents, financial information, product plans, or internal communications may become visible to people who were never intended to see them. In regulated industries, this type of exposure can also create compliance concerns, especially if sensitive data becomes accessible outside the organization.

Because of these risks, oversharing becomes more than a technical issue. It becomes a governance challenge. Organizations must allow employees to collaborate easily while still maintaining appropriate control over who can access important information. Recognizing the common situations where oversharing occurs is the first step toward identifying and correcting those risks across the SharePoint environment.

Identifying the tools to troubleshoot oversharing in an organization

Once administrators understand how oversharing occurs, the next step is learning how to investigate it. In a large organization, thousands of documents may be shared across hundreds of sites and teams. Manually checking permissions for every file would be impractical, so administrators rely on tools that provide visibility into how permissions to information are granted and expanded throughout the environment. Without tools that expose these relationships, identifying the source of oversharing would be extremely difficult.

Microsoft 365 and SharePoint include **reporting** and **auditing** capabilities that help administrators investigate these situations.

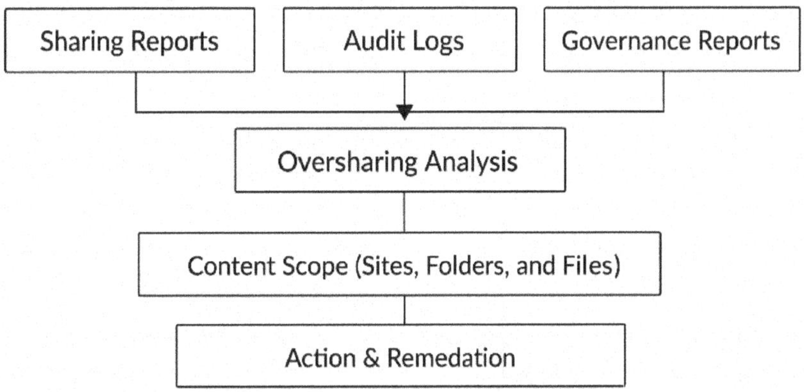

Figure 7.2: Oversharing investigation across reports, auditing, and governance insights

Figure 7.2 shows how administrators investigate oversharing by combining inputs from audit logs, sharing reports, and governance reports. These sources provide visibility into how content is accessed, shared, and managed across sites, folders, and files. By bringing these signals together, administrators can identify where access may be broader than intended.

Data Access Governance includes both snapshot and activity-based reports. Snapshot reports show the current permission or sensitivity state of SharePoint sites, while activity reports highlight recent sharing behavior, such as sites where users created many sharing links or shared content with **Everyone except external users** (**EEEU**). This helps administrators identify oversharing patterns across large environments without checking individual files one by one.

As a result, oversharing can be detected across large environments without manually checking individual files. This allows administrators to identify risky sharing patterns, such as widespread access or external exposure, and take corrective action before they develop into broader governance issues.

Sharing reports in Microsoft 365 and SharePoint

To investigate oversharing effectively, administrators need visibility into how access to documents is granted and expanded.

Sharing reports can be generated from the **SharePoint admin center** to review *sharing activity* and *external access* for selected sites. This gives administrators a practical starting point for reviewing how SharePoint content has been shared and whether external users are involved.

Microsoft 365 and SharePoint include built-in **sharing reports** that help administrators examine how access to content is granted and distributed. These reports show which documents have been shared, who currently has access to them, and whether external users are involved. Instead of manually reviewing permissions one location at a time, administrators can use these reports to quickly identify areas where sharing activity may require closer attention.

Sharing reports also provides insight into how access was granted. A document may have been shared directly with a specific user, distributed through a sharing link, or made available through permissions applied at the folder or site level. Understanding how that access originated helps administrators trace the path through which information became available to a wider audience.

In larger environments, this visibility becomes especially valuable. Collaboration across departments, projects, and external partners can create complex permission structures that evolve over time.

By using sharing reports as an investigative starting point, administrators can review sharing activity and determine whether corrective action is required. These tools do not change permissions or enforce restrictions.

This visibility allows administrators to understand how information is moving across SharePoint sites and collaboration spaces where potential exposure may exist.

Auditing and monitoring sharing activity

Auditing focuses on examining how access to information changes within the environment. Administrators can review records that show when documents were shared, which users accessed them, and whether external participants were involved. These activity records allow administrators to trace the sequence of events that led to a document becoming widely accessible.

Audit records are reviewed from the Microsoft Purview portal under Audit. This is where administrators can search for sharing and access events across Microsoft 365 workloads, including SharePoint activity.

For example, administrators may want to identify documents that were shared using broad access links or content that contains sensitive information but has been distributed outside the organization. When these situations appear, administrators can investigate further and determine whether the sharing activity aligns with organizational policies.

In large collaboration environments, reviewing activity manually is rarely practical. Administrative tools allow organizations to examine sharing behavior across many sites at once and identify unusual access patterns more efficiently. Instead of checking permissions for individual files, administrators can focus on areas where the likelihood of oversharing is higher.

By observing sharing activity over time, administrators can detect situations where access may be expanding unexpectedly and take action before sensitive information is exposed more broadly.

Running a data access governance report in SharePoint

Investigating individual sharing events is an important part of managing oversharing, but administrators also need a way to step back and evaluate risk across the entire SharePoint environment. Understanding where sensitive information exists and how broadly it is shared becomes difficult without a broader governance view.

Data Access Governance reporting provides that wider perspective. Data Access Governance reports are accessed from the **SharePoint admin center** under **Reports** | **Data access governance**. Administrators use this location to run reports that highlight risky SharePoint sites and oversharing patterns.

Rather than focusing on *individual documents*, this capability highlights *SharePoint sites* that may present higher levels of risk. By examining how information is stored, labeled, and shared across sites, administrators can identify collaboration spaces where governance attention may be needed.

One of the key benefits of governance reporting is that it helps administrators focus their attention on the most significant issues first. Instead of manually reviewing every collaboration site, reports surface patterns that suggest potential governance concerns, such as sites containing sensitive content or locations where sharing activity appears unusually broad.

A site containing regulated information or confidential business data may require stricter access controls than those used for general collaboration. Governance reports, therefore, help administrators understand where oversight is most needed and where corrective action may have the greatest impact.

By providing a structured view of how information is shared across SharePoint sites, data access governance reporting supports a more proactive approach to managing oversharing. Administrators can move beyond investigating individual sharing incidents and begin identifying systemic patterns that could expose sensitive information across the organization.

Understanding Data Access Governance (DAG) reports

As SharePoint environments grow, it becomes increasingly difficult for administrators to understand where sensitive information is stored and how widely it is shared. Individual documents may appear secure when viewed in isolation, yet across hundreds of sites and thousands of files, patterns can emerge that create governance risks. Data Access Governance reports help administrators see those patterns.

A **Data Access Governance** (**DAG**) report examines SharePoint sites and highlights situations where access to information may require closer review. Rather than focusing on individual files, these reports analyze characteristics of an entire site. For example, a report may reveal that a site contains sensitive information, that external sharing is enabled, or that permissions allow access beyond the intended audience.

Several common Data Access Governance reports help administrators recognize these risks more clearly:

- **Sharing links**: Shows links that allow access for anyone, people in the organization, or specific people shared externally
- **Content shared with Everyone except external users (EEEU)**: Highlights broad internal sharing where content is available to a wide internal audience
- **Sites with labeled files**: Identifies sites that contain files with sensitivity labels
- **Sites with too many users**: Highlights sites where the permission state may indicate broader access than intended

Data Access Governance in the SharePoint admin center can also be used to report on permissions and active sharing links for OneDrive content, helping administrators identify oversharing beyond SharePoint sites.

These reports give administrators a more specific view of how oversharing appears across SharePoint sites. Instead of only knowing that a site may present risk, administrators can see whether the concern relates to broad sharing links, wide internal access, labeled content, or excessive site permissions.

A site containing confidential material and external collaboration may require stronger controls than a site used for general internal communication. DAG reports bring those types of situations into view so administrators can evaluate whether the current sharing configuration is appropriate.

Another important aspect of these reports is visibility into site ownership and governance. In some cases, a collaboration site may remain active long after the original project has ended. If the site owner is no longer responsible for maintaining access, permissions may remain unchanged even as team membership evolves. DAG reporting highlights these situations so that administrators can ensure someone is accountable for reviewing and managing access.

By bringing together information about sensitive content, sharing activity, and site ownership, DAG reports provide a structured view of how information is governed across collaboration sites. These reports identify risk but do not change site permissions.

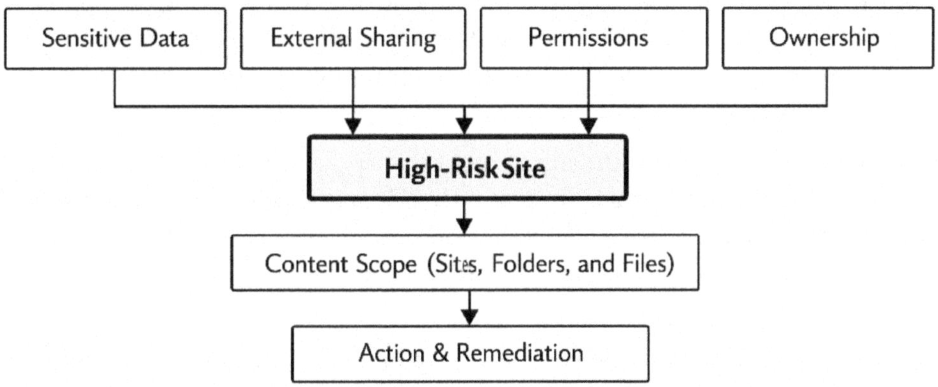

Figure 7.3: Data Access Governance risk identification model

Figure 7.3 shows how Data Access Governance reports identify sites that may present governance risks by analyzing characteristics such as sensitive data, permissions, and external sharing. Instead of focusing on individual files, the model evaluates the overall risk profile of a SharePoint site based on how information is stored, accessed, and shared.

As a result, administrators can identify high-risk sites where access may be broader than intended or where governance controls may be insufficient. This allows them to prioritize review and apply appropriate controls to reduce exposure across the environment.

Using DAG reports to identify and remediate risky sites

Once a Data Access Governance report highlights sites that may present governance concerns, administrators can begin reviewing those locations in more detail. The purpose of the report is not simply to display information, but to guide administrators toward the areas of the SharePoint environment where access to content may require closer attention.

A typical report may reveal several types of potential risk. Some sites may contain sensitive information while still allowing external access. Others may have no active owner responsible for managing permissions. In some situations, a site may simply have accumulated broad access over time as team membership and project requirements changed. Each of these conditions can increase the likelihood that information is being shared more widely than intended.

When administrators review these findings, the next step is determining whether the current configuration of the site still reflects the needs of the organization. A collaboration space that was originally created for a temporary project might still allow external partners to access documents long after the project has finished. In other cases, permissions may have expanded gradually as users shared content with additional teams or departments.

Addressing these situations often involves relatively straightforward changes. Administrators or site owners may remove unnecessary guest access, adjust sharing settings, or apply sensitivity labels that define how information should be protected. In some cases, assigning a new site owner ensures that someone is responsible for reviewing permissions and maintaining appropriate access controls in the future.

By guiding administrators toward the sites most likely to present risk, Data Access Governance reports help organizations focus their attention where it matters most. Instead of searching through every collaboration space individually, administrators can concentrate on the locations where sharing patterns, sensitive information, or ownership gaps suggest that corrective action may be needed.

While these tools help identify oversharing, organizations also need controls to limit how access is applied across collaboration sites.

Understanding the features and capabilities of SharePoint Advanced Management (including restricted access control)

While governance reports help administrators identify potential oversharing risks, organizations often need additional controls to manage access across large SharePoint environments. As collaboration platforms grow, hundreds of sites may exist across departments, projects, and external partnerships. Maintaining appropriate access across all of these locations requires tools that support continuous governance rather than occasional investigation.

SharePoint Advanced Management (SAM) provides additional capabilities designed to help administrators monitor and control access to SharePoint sites more effectively.

Data Access Governance reports identify where oversharing risks exist, while SharePoint Advanced Management provides controls such as **Restricted Access Control (RAC)** to limit and manage access to those sites.

Restricted Access Control requires users to belong to a specified Microsoft Entra security group before they can access the site, even if they already have site permissions.

These features extend the visibility and governance controls already available in SharePoint, allowing organizations to apply more structured oversight to how collaboration spaces are used.

A site created for a temporary initiative may remain active long after the original project ends. Without governance controls that monitor these changes over time, access can slowly extend beyond the original intent.

These capabilities become especially important where sensitive data is stored within collaboration sites. Finance teams, human resources departments, or research groups may use SharePoint to manage documents that require stricter oversight. Advanced management features help administrators ensure that only authorized users can access those locations.

Overview of SharePoint Advanced Management

As organizations rely more heavily on SharePoint for collaboration, administrators need ways to manage not only individual documents but also the long-term governance of entire collaboration sites. **SharePoint Advanced Management** extends the standard administrative capabilities of SharePoint by providing additional tools designed to help organizations maintain control over how sites are used and how access evolves over time.

In many environments, SharePoint sites are created frequently as teams start new projects or collaborate with external partners. Over time, these sites may accumulate documents, permissions, and sharing links that remain in place long after the original purpose of the site has changed. Without governance mechanisms to monitor these environments, it becomes difficult for administrators to determine which sites still require active oversight and which ones may present potential risks.

Key SharePoint Advanced Management capabilities include **Data Access Governance reports, Restricted Access Control (RAC), Restricted Content Discovery (RCD), site access reviews,** and **change history reports.** Together, these capabilities help administrators identify oversharing risks, limit access to sensitive sites, reduce unnecessary content discovery, review whether access remains appropriate, and understand how site settings have changed over time.

Site lifecycle management is another SharePoint Advanced Management capability used to manage inactive or poorly governed sites. For exam scenarios where SharePoint sites have fewer than the required number of owners and must be marked read-only if not remediated, choose Site lifecycle management.

Site access reviews help administrators confirm whether access to a SharePoint site still matches the current needs of the team or project. When a Data Access Governance report identifies a site with broad access, inactive ownership, or sensitive content, administrators can use a site access review to ask site owners to review who has access and remove users or groups that no longer need it. This helps prevent permissions from remaining in place long after a project, role, or collaboration requirement has changed.

This is why SharePoint Advanced Management is especially relevant for Copilot readiness. Data Access Governance reports help administrators identify sites with sensitive or overshared content, while Restricted Access Control can limit access to defined users or groups. These controls reduce the chance that broadly shared SharePoint content becomes visible through Copilot or agent-based experiences.

Together, these capabilities help administrators detect situations where access permissions have expanded unexpectedly or where collaboration sites remain active even though the original project has ended.

Instead of responding only when an issue is discovered, administrators can use these capabilities to continuously review how sites are accessed and whether permissions remain appropriate for the teams using them.

By providing greater visibility into site activity and governance conditions, SharePoint Advanced Management allows organizations to manage collaboration environments more proactively. Administrators gain a clearer understanding of how sites are being used across the organization and can ensure that access to information remains aligned with business needs and security expectations.

Summary

Collaboration platforms such as SharePoint make it easy for teams to store documents, share information, and work together across departments and organizations. Oversharing occurs when documents, folders, or entire collaboration sites become accessible to users who were not meant to see them.

In this chapter, you learned how oversharing can occur in everyday collaboration environments and why organizations need visibility into how information is being shared across sites and teams. Understanding the common ways oversharing appears—such as broad sharing links, inherited permissions, or external collaboration—helps administrators recognize where sensitive information may be exposed to a wider audience than expected.

The chapter also explored the tools administrators use to investigate sharing activity across the organization. Sharing reports and auditing capabilities provide visibility into how documents are distributed and who currently has access to them. By reviewing this information, administrators can identify situations where sharing behavior may require closer review.

Another important capability is the use of **Data Access Governance** (**DAG**) reports, which help administrators identify SharePoint sites that may present governance concerns. By focusing on these high-risk sites, administrators can take targeted actions such as reviewing permissions, adjusting sharing settings, or assigning responsible site owners.

Finally, the chapter introduced SharePoint Advanced Management capabilities that support ongoing governance of collaboration environments. Features such as Restricted Access Control, change history reports, and site access reviews help organizations maintain appropriate control over sensitive collaboration spaces while still allowing teams to work effectively.

Together, these capabilities help organizations maintain visibility into how information is shared within SharePoint environments, identify collaboration sites that may present governance risks, and apply controls that ensure sensitive information remains accessible only to the appropriate users.

In the next chapter, you will move from SharePoint governance to the core features and capabilities of Microsoft 365 Copilot and agents, including built-in Copilot functionality, agent capabilities, licensing models, configurable Copilot features, and practical use cases for Researcher, Analyst, and custom agents.

Microsoft Learn reference links

The following table provides official Microsoft references for the main SharePoint oversharing, troubleshooting, Data Access Governance, and SharePoint Advanced Management topics introduced in this chapter.

Topic	What it covers	Microsoft Learn reference
Understanding oversharing risks in SharePoint	Explains how sharing works in SharePoint and OneDrive, including external sharing, sharing links, and the risks created when content becomes accessible beyond the intended audience.	`https://learn.microsoft.com/en-us/sharepoint/external-sharing-overview`
Identifying the tools to troubleshoot oversharing in an organization	Explains how administrators use sharing reports and audit search to investigate how SharePoint content has been shared and who has access to it.	`https://learn.microsoft.com/en-us/sharepoint/sharing-reports` `https://learn.microsoft.com/en-us/purview/audit-search`
Running a data access governance report in SharePoint	Explains how Data Access Governance reports identify SharePoint sites with potentially overshared or sensitive content, including broad links, labeled files, and excessive access.	`https://learn.microsoft.com/en-us/sharepoint/data-access-governance-reports`
Understanding features and capabilities of SharePoint Advanced Management, including restricted site access	Explains SharePoint Advanced Management capabilities such as Data Access Governance reports, Restricted Access Control, Restricted Content Discovery, site access reviews, and controls that support Copilot readiness.	`https://learn.microsoft.com/en-us/sharepoint/advanced-management` `https://learn.microsoft.com/en-us/sharepoint/restricted-access-control`

Table 7.1: Microsoft references for SharePoint oversharing and governance topics covered in this chapter

Together, these references support the chapter's focus on how oversharing occurs in SharePoint, how administrators investigate sharing activity, how Data Access Governance reports identify risky sites, and how SharePoint Advanced Management capabilities help control access to sensitive collaboration spaces.

Key terms and acronyms

The following table introduces the main SharePoint oversharing, troubleshooting, Data Access Governance, and SharePoint Advanced Management terms used throughout this chapter.

Term	Meaning
SharePoint	Microsoft's collaboration platform for storing, managing, sharing, and governing documents and sites across Microsoft 365.
SharePoint site	A collaboration space used to store documents, pages, lists, permissions, and shared content for a team, project, or department.
Oversharing	A condition where documents, folders, or sites become accessible to more users or groups than originally intended.
External sharing	Sharing SharePoint or OneDrive content with people outside the organization, such as guests, partners, vendors, or contractors.
Sharing link	A link used to grant access to SharePoint or OneDrive content. The link type determines who can use it.
Inherited permissions	Permissions passed down from a parent site, library, or folder to child items such as folders or files.
Sharing report	A SharePoint report used to review shared files, folders, links, and external users associated with a site.
Audit log	A Microsoft 365 record of user and admin activities, including SharePoint sharing and access events.
Data Access Governance (DAG)	A SharePoint governance capability that identifies sites with potentially overshared or sensitive content.
DAG report	A report that surfaces risky SharePoint sites based on broad permissions, sharing links, sensitive content, or access patterns.

Term	Meaning
SharePoint Advanced Management (SAM)	A SharePoint add-on capability that provides advanced governance controls for managing site access and oversharing risk.
Restricted Access Control (RAC)	A SharePoint Advanced Management capability that limits access to a site by requiring approved group membership in addition to site permissions.
Restricted Content Discovery (RCD)	A SharePoint Advanced Management capability that limits whether selected SharePoint content appears in search, Copilot, and agentic experiences.
Site access review	A review process where site owners confirm whether current users or groups should still have access to a SharePoint site.
Copilot readiness	Preparing Microsoft 365 content, permissions, sharing settings, and governance controls so Copilot retrieves only appropriately governed content.

Table 7.2: Key SharePoint oversharing and governance terms and acronyms

These terms connect the chapter's terminology to the AB-900 skills measured and give readers a concise reference for SharePoint oversharing, troubleshooting, Data Access Governance, SharePoint Advanced Management, and Copilot readiness.

Exam readiness drill – chapter review questions

Apart from mastering key concepts, strong test-taking skills under time pressure are essential for acing your certification exam. That's why developing these abilities early in your learning journey is critical.

Exam readiness drills, using the free online practice resources provided with this book, help you progressively improve your time management and test-taking skills while reinforcing the key concepts you've learned.

HOW TO GET STARTED

1. Open the link or scan the QR code at the bottom of this page
2. If you have unlocked the practice resources already, log in to your registered account. If you haven't, follow the instructions in the *Free Benefits with Your Book* section in this book's *Preface* and come back to this page.

3. Once you log in, click the START button to start this chapter's quiz
4. We recommend attempting a quiz multiple times till you're able to answer most of the questions correctly and well within the time limit
5. You can use the following practice template to help you plan your attempts:

Working On Accuracy		
Attempt	**Target**	**Time Limit**
Attempt 1	40% or more	Till the timer runs out
Attempt 2	60% or more	Till the timer runs out
Attempt 3	75% or more	Till the timer runs out
Working On Timing		
Attempt 4	75% or more	1 minute before time limit
Attempt 5	75% or more	2 minutes before time limit
Attempt 6	75% or more	3 minutes before time limit

The above drill is just an example. Design your drills based on your own goals and make the most out of the online quizzes accompanying this book.

Link to this chapter's quiz

You need to unlock the online practice resources to access the link below. Check the *Free Benefits with Your Book* section in the *Preface* for detailed instructions on how to do this. You only need to unlock the resources once.

Open Quiz `https://packt.link/HoYJior` scan the QR code

8

Understanding Features and Capabilities of Copilot and Agents

This chapter introduces the core features and capabilities of **Microsoft 365 Copilot** and **agent-based AI**. It will compare built-in **Copilot** functionality with **agent** capabilities, understand how *licensing models* differ between **monthly** and **pay-as-you-go billing**, and identify which **Copilot** features can be *enabled* or *restricted*.

The chapter also explores practical use cases for **Researcher**, **Analyst**, and **custom agents** to help readers determine when each option is most effective.

This content aligns with the **Understand features and capabilities of Copilot and agents** sub-module within the **Perform basic administrative tasks for Copilot and agents** domain of the **AB-900 Skills Measured**.

By the end of this chapter, you will be able to confidently answer questions on the following topics:

- Comparing Built-In Capabilities of Copilot and Agents
- Comparing Copilot Monthly Licensing and Pay-As-You-Go
- Identifying Copilot Features That Can Be Enabled or Disabled
- Identifying Use Cases for Researcher
- Identifying Use Cases for Analyst
- Identifying Use Cases for Custom Agents

By mastering these foundational concepts, readers will be prepared to evaluate Copilot deployment models and select the right agent types for their organization.

Comparing built-in capabilities of Copilot and Agents

Copilot acts as a **productivity assistant** within familiar applications by generating responses at the point of interaction. Based on **prompts** and available **context**, an **output** is created in *real time* and remains tied to the *current session*.

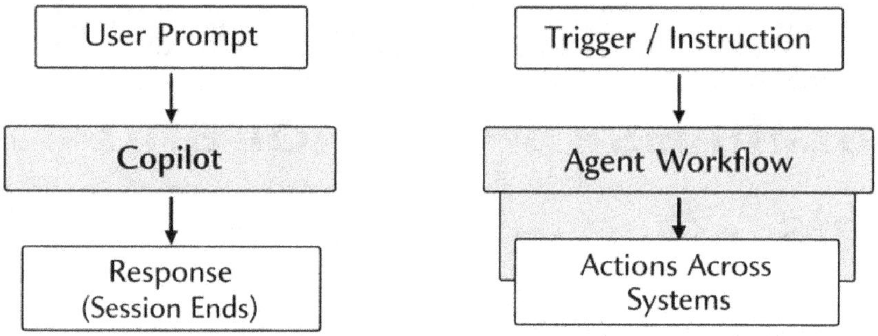

Figure 8.1: Copilot assistance compared to agent execution

Figure 8.1 illustrates this boundary by contrasting **Copilot's** *in-session* response generation with **agent** *workflows*.

Agents extend the model by continuing work beyond the response, executing predefined tasks across systems, and producing **outcomes** that persist after the initial instruction.

This shifts work from **user-driven interaction** to **system-driven execution**: **Copilot** delivers information for the user to interpret or act on, while agents can apply instructions, knowledge, and actions to support defined tasks, including workflows that may update systems or data when configured to do so.

Between general-purpose Copilot chat and custom agents, Microsoft 365 includes **specialized first-party agents** such as **Researcher** and **Analyst** that focus on **insight** rather than **workflow execution**.

Copilot and agent limitations

Copilot remains bound to the interaction context and the data it can access at that moment. Responses reflect available information and prompt clarity, so output quality shifts based on how well the request is formed and what data is accessible. No action is taken beyond generating the response, leaving execution dependent on the user.

Agents operate within the constraints of their defined scope, permissions, and configured logic. Execution follows defined boundaries and cannot extend beyond the configured scope or permissions.

Copilot remains focused on shaping information within the interaction, while agents extend that intent into execution across systems, separating decision support from operational action.

Comparing Copilot's monthly licensing and pay-as-you-go

Copilot and **agent** usage can be licensed through fixed monthly licensing or usage-based billing. For AB-900, the key distinction is not only the billing model, but which Copilot product uses that model.

Microsoft 365 Copilot uses a per-user monthly license. This gives assigned users access to Microsoft 365 Copilot experiences across Microsoft 365 apps and services, with cost based on the number of licensed users rather than each interaction.

Supported **Microsoft 365 Copilot Chat** scenarios can use **pay-as-you-go** billing through a billing policy linked to an Azure subscription. This differs from the included web-based Copilot Chat experience available with eligible Microsoft 365 subscriptions.

SharePoint agents can also use pay-as-you-go billing. The meter applies to SharePoint agent usage, not ordinary SharePoint activity such as opening documents, browsing libraries, or collaborating on files. Consumption is tied to agent interactions that retrieve, process, or analyze SharePoint content.

Copilot Studio agent usage can be billed through Copilot Credit packs or pay-as-you-go meters, depending on configuration. Bring-your-own-model configurations may be billed separately.

In the **Microsoft 365 admin center**, administrators attach pay-as-you-go billing to supported Copilot services through billing policies. Cost reporting can show Microsoft 365 Copilot Chat usage under the **m365copilotchat** tag and separately report SharePoint agent usage.

Where departmental cost visibility is required, billing and cost reporting should use the configured billing policy, Azure subscription cost data, and tags or a cost allocation structure that identifies the department.

Licensing model limitations

Per-user licensing restricts cost control to user allocation. Once a license is assigned, the cost remains fixed even if usage is low, and scaling requires adding or removing licenses rather than adjusting activity. Unused or underused licenses still contribute to total spend. Consumption-based billing introduces variability that depends on workload behavior. Increased activity raises cost without a fixed upper boundary, making spending less predictable over time. Budget control depends on managing usage patterns rather than limiting access.

Cost control, therefore, depends on how licensing is aligned to expected usage, balancing predictable spend against workload-driven variability.

Identifying Copilot features that can be enabled or disabled

Copilot availability is controlled through layered settings that determine where and how it can be used. Copilot availability depends on user assignment and service enablement working together, with environment-wide settings defining the overall scope.

For exam scenarios that ask where to prevent users from generating images with Copilot, use the Microsoft 365 admin center because Copilot image generation is controlled from Copilot settings there.

User-level access assignment controlling Copilot availability

User-level assignment determines who is permitted to use Copilot. Access is tied to identity, so only users with the appropriate assignment can initiate interactions. Without that assignment, Copilot remains unavailable regardless of service configuration.

Assignment scales access across individuals or groups. Expanding the assignment increases availability across users, while removing it immediately restricts access. Control stays aligned to identity rather than workload or service behavior.

User-level assignment defines eligibility and establishes the first condition required for Copilot use.

Service-level enablement controlling where Copilot is active

Service-level enablement determines where Copilot operates across the environment. Activation is applied at the workload level, so Copilot becomes available only within the services where it has been enabled. If a service is not enabled, Copilot does not function there, even if users have access.

Each service maintains its own activation boundary. Enabling Copilot in one workload does not extend functionality to others, keeping behavior isolated to where activation has been applied. Availability is shaped by which services are turned on rather than by user assignment alone.

Service-level enablement defines where Copilot runs and limits functionality to specific workloads within the environment.

Environment-wide compared to service-level control scope

Environment-wide controls define whether Copilot is broadly available across the organization, setting a baseline that applies across services. When restricted at this level, Copilot availability is limited regardless of individual service settings. The control acts as a top-level boundary.

Service-level controls operate within that boundary, determining where Copilot is active across specific workloads. Enabling or disabling at the service level refines availability, allowing functionality in some services while restricting it in others.

Environment-wide control establishes the overall limit, while service-level control shapes availability within that limit across individual services.

Copilot control limitations

Copilot controls vary by capability. Administrators can manage availability through licensing, service settings, billing policies, and supported scenario controls such as Copilot image generation. These controls affect whether specific capabilities are available, but they do not redesign how Copilot generates responses once a capability is allowed.

Changes apply within defined boundaries and do not override underlying service dependencies. If Copilot relies on data, permissions, or service functionality, those conditions still govern what it can access and produce. Control settings influence availability, not the internal operation of the capability.

Configuration determines where Copilot is available, while functionality within that scope remains consistent with the service and data it operates on.

Copilot control, therefore, defines availability through identity, service activation, and environment scope, without altering how the capability operates within those boundaries.

Identifying use cases for Researcher

Researcher is a first-party Microsoft 365 Copilot agent for users with a Microsoft 365 Copilot license. It is accessed from the **Agents** area in Microsoft 365 Copilot Chat, where Microsoft makes it available as a built-in agent rather than a custom agent created by the organization.

Researcher can use work content the user has access to through Microsoft 365 and Microsoft Graph, together with web content, to produce source-cited research reports.

Researcher is used when a question needs information from more than one source. It gathers and synthesizes content across organizational data and the public web, then turns that material into structured findings that show how the sources relate to each other.

Its role becomes evident when questions extend beyond a single document, message, or dataset. Researcher builds a broader picture by aggregating and consolidating content into a coherent context, allowing users to explore topics, compile findings, and gain multi-source understanding. Output emphasizes combined context rather than isolated responses, supporting research-focused tasks where breadth and connection are essential.

The capability fits scenarios where insight depends on connecting distributed information. Work shifts from retrieval to interpretation, shaping how knowledge is discovered, structured, and applied across the organization.

Multi-source content aggregation

Researcher retrieves content from multiple sources and brings it into a single working set. Data remains in its original locations, but relevant content is collected and aligned within the same context. Information that would otherwise require separate queries is surfaced together.

Cross-source content synthesis

Researcher goes beyond aggregation by combining information from different sources into a single, coherent result. Content is not only collected but interpreted together, allowing relationships, patterns, and inconsistencies across sources to be reflected in the output. The result presents a unified understanding rather than separate inputs.

Exploratory Research Scenarios

Researcher supports scenarios where the outcome is not predefined, and the direction of inquiry evolves during use. Queries begin with a broad objective, and additional context is gathered as new information is surfaced. The process adapts as relevant data points emerge across sources.

Activity progresses through discovery rather than a fixed sequence. Retrieved information influences what is examined next, allowing the scope to expand or narrow based on findings. The result reflects an evolving understanding shaped by what is uncovered during the process.

Structured output generation

Researcher organizes aggregated and synthesized content into a defined format that presents findings in a clear and usable way. Information is arranged into sections, summaries, or ordered outputs that reflect how the data relates across sources. The result moves from raw insight to structured presentation.

Structure reduces ambiguity in how information is consumed. Instead of fragmented or loosely connected results, output is shaped into a consistent format that highlights key points and supporting details. Relationships between sources are preserved within that structure.

Structured output transforms combined insight into an organized form that can be reviewed, shared, or acted upon.

Researcher limitations

Researcher depends on accessible data sources and the context provided during the request. If relevant information is not available or cannot be retrieved, the resulting output reflects only the accessible subset. Coverage is limited by data availability rather than intent.

Synthesis remains constrained by source quality and consistency. Conflicting or incomplete data affect how conclusions are formed, and output reflects those gaps or inconsistencies. Results do not extend beyond what can be supported by the underlying sources.

Execution does not occur beyond information handling. Researcher gathers, combines, and presents insight, but it does not perform actions or modify systems. Outcomes remain informational rather than operational.

Researcher produces insight within the limits of available data and does not extend into execution or system-level change.

Identifying use cases for Analysts

Analyst is a first-party Microsoft 365 Copilot agent for users with a Microsoft 365 Copilot license. It is accessed from the Agents area in Microsoft 365 Copilot Chat, where Microsoft makes it available as a built-in agent rather than a custom agent created by the organization. **Analyst** is used for structured data analysis tasks such as calculating statistics, identifying trends, finding outliers, and producing reports from attached or otherwise available structured data.

Analyst is used when a question depends on structured data rather than broad content retrieval. It works with data that can be measured, compared, grouped, or calculated, helping users understand what the dataset shows rather than simply summarizing available content.

Its role becomes evident when users need to examine trends, deviations, and relationships within a dataset. Analysts can turn raw data into interpreted findings, such as changes over time, unusual values, or comparisons between categories.

The capability fits scenarios where understanding depends on data behavior. Work shifts from reviewing values manually to interpreting patterns, outliers, and relationships that can guide the next business decision.

Structured dataset analysis

Analyst processes data that is already organized into tables, fields, and defined formats. Queries operate over that structure, allowing values to be filtered, compared, and grouped based on consistent attributes. Analysis stays grounded in the schema of the dataset.

Structured data supports repeatable evaluation. Calculations, aggregations, and comparisons produce consistent results because the underlying format does not change between runs. Output reflects measured differences and relationships rather than interpreted narrative.

Pattern, trend, and anomaly detection

Analyst examines datasets to identify recurring behavior, directional change, and deviations from expected values. Patterns emerge through repeated data relationships, trends appear as movement over time, and anomalies surface as values that fall outside normal ranges. Analysis focuses on how data behaves rather than what it describes.

Detection is driven by comparison across data points. Baselines form from historical or grouped data, and current values are evaluated against those baselines. Deviations stand out when they differ significantly from established patterns or expected ranges.

Pattern and trend analysis reveal consistent behavior over time, while anomaly detection highlights deviations that require attention.

Data-driven insight generation

Analyst produces insight directly from data relationships, calculations, and comparisons within the dataset. Results are derived from measured values rather than inferred narrative, with conclusions grounded in how the data behaves. Output reflects evidence contained within the data itself.

Insight emerges through aggregation, correlation, and evaluation of data points. Metrics, groupings, and comparisons highlight changes, relationships, and performance across the dataset. Findings are based on observed patterns rather than external interpretation.

Data-driven insight relies on quantitative evidence from the dataset, shaping conclusions through measurable relationships.

Multi-source dataset handling

Analyst works across multiple datasets that share a compatible structure, allowing data from different sources to be combined for analysis. Fields are aligned so values can be compared, joined, or aggregated across those sources. Analysis operates on the combined dataset as a single analytical surface.

Relationships between datasets are established through common attributes such as identifiers, timestamps, or categories. Joining and correlating data across sources reveals patterns that would not appear when each dataset is examined independently. Results reflect how data points relate across systems.

Multi-source handling aligns structured datasets so they can be combined and evaluated together for broader analytical coverage.

Analyst limitations

Analysis depends on structured, high-quality data with consistent formatting, which directly affects the accuracy and depth of insight.

Execution does not extend beyond analysis. **Analyst** identifies patterns, trends, and relationships, but it does not act on those findings or modify systems. Outcomes remain analytical rather than operational.

Analyst is intended for structured data analysis rather than broad unstructured research, and it does not carry out actions beyond analysis.

Some analysis scenarios involve working directly with individual files rather than structured datasets. In these cases, Code Interpreter is used to process and analyze file-based data, producing calculations, transformations, or visual outputs within the scope of that file.

For exam scenarios where an agent must analyze an Excel workbook and create charts or visualizations from that file, choose the **Code Interpreter** capability.

Identifying use cases for custom agents

Custom agents enable organizations to support specific scenarios by applying defined instructions, knowledge sources, and, where configured, actions or workflows. They can process requests, retrieve grounded information, trigger processes, or update data depending on their design and permissions.

Custom agents are also appropriate when the organization needs instructions that differ from the general chat experience or when responses must be grounded in a specific knowledge source, such as a website.

These capabilities are used where tasks must be executed consistently across systems without repeated user input.

Before comparing these capabilities visually, it's helpful to note that Researcher and Analyst are specialized Copilot capabilities focused on insight generation, not execution, while custom agents operate at the execution layer.

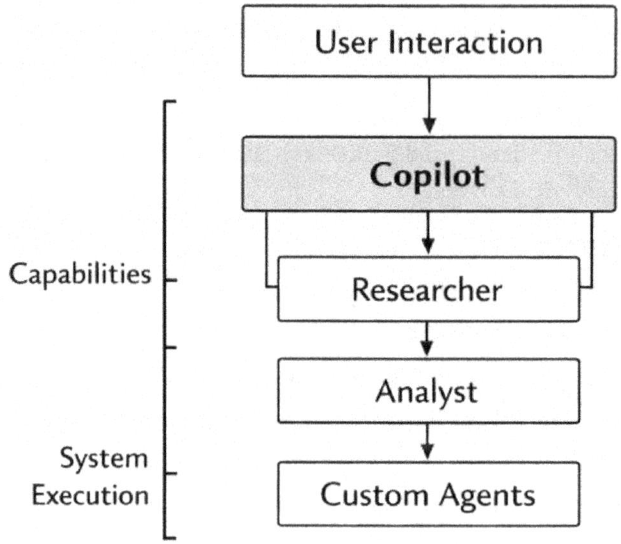

Figure 8.2: Capability placement of Copilot and agents

Figure 8.2 shows how Copilot, Researcher, Analyst, and custom agents operate at different levels, progressing from user interaction to system execution. Copilot sits closest to the user, providing general-purpose assistance during interaction. Researcher and Analyst extend that capability by focusing on information synthesis and structured data analysis, respectively, without performing actions. Custom agents operate at the execution layer, where predefined workflows carry out tasks across systems.

Execution of predefined workflows

Custom agents execute workflows that are *defined in advance*, with each step following a set sequence or condition. **Actions** are carried out according to that structure, ensuring consistent behavior each time the workflow runs. Execution does not depend on real-time interpretation but follows established logic.

Workflows progress through defined steps such as data retrieval, processing, and updates across systems. **Condition**s determine how the workflow moves forward, allowing different paths based on input or state. Activity continues until the defined sequence is completed.

Predefined workflows produce consistent, repeatable execution aligned with a specific outcome.

Automation of repetitive tasks

Custom agents *automate tasks* that *occur frequently* and follow the *same pattern each time*. Once defined, the task runs without manual repetition, reducing the need for user intervention. Execution follows the same logic on each run, producing consistent results.

Repetition shifts from *user-driven action* to *system-driven execution*. Tasks that would otherwise require repeated input are handled automatically, allowing activity to scale across users, data, or systems without additional effort. Output reflects the same operation applied consistently over time.

Automation removes *repeated manual interaction* and replaces it with consistent system execution for *recurring tasks*.

Continued task execution beyond the initial trigger

Custom agents continue executing after the initial trigger *without requiring* further user input. Once started, the workflow progresses through its defined steps, handling subsequent actions as conditions are met. Execution persists until the defined objective is reached or the workflow completes.

Activity *extends beyond* a single interaction. **Triggers** initiates the process, but *execution* moves forward independently, allowing tasks to run across time, systems, or data changes. Progress depends on workflow logic rather than ongoing user involvement.

Continued task execution shifts from a one-time interaction to ongoing operation driven by predefined logic.

Application of custom business logic

Custom agents *apply logic* that reflects specific business rules, conditions, and decision paths. Execution follows those rules, allowing actions to vary based on inputs, data states, or predefined conditions. Behavior aligns with how the organization defines its processes.

Logic introduces *conditional branching* within workflows. Different outcomes are produced depending on the data or context encountered during execution. Decisions are made within the workflow itself rather than requiring user input at each step.

Custom business logic enables workflows to adapt within defined boundaries based on inputs and conditions.

Custom agent limitations

Custom agents operate only within the workflows, permissions, and logic that have been defined. Execution *cannot extend beyond* those boundaries, so tasks outside the configured scope are not performed. Outcomes remain tied to what has been explicitly designed.

Behavior depends on the quality and completeness of the defined logic. Incomplete conditions or missing paths limit how the agent responds during execution, and results reflect those gaps. Execution follows the defined structure without adapting beyond it.

Access and data constraints further restrict operation. Agents can act only on systems and data they are permitted to use, so unavailable or restricted resources prevent execution from progressing. Results reflect both configuration and access boundaries.

Summary

This chapter introduced the core features of Microsoft 365 Copilot and agent-based AI, showing how Copilot supports user interaction while agents execute tasks across systems. It also covered licensing models, Copilot controls, and practical use cases for Researcher, Analyst, and custom agents.

Together, these concepts help organizations evaluate Copilot deployment options, select appropriate agent types, and align AI capabilities with business needs and cost considerations.

In the next chapter, you will move from basic Copilot administration to managing agents, including how agents are created, configured, shared, and controlled across Microsoft 365 Copilot and Copilot Studio.

Microsoft Learn reference links

The following table provides official Microsoft references for the main Copilot, agent, licensing, control, Researcher, Analyst, and custom agent topics introduced in this chapter.

Topic	What it covers	Microsoft Learn reference
Comparing Built-In Capabilities of Copilot and Agents	Explains how Microsoft 365 Copilot and agents support different interaction and execution patterns, including built-in Copilot experiences and agent-based extensions.	`https://learn.microsoft.com/en-us/microsoft-365/copilot/extensibility/agents-overview`

Topic	What it covers	Microsoft Learn reference
Comparing Copilot Monthly Licensing and Pay-As-You-Go	Explains how Microsoft 365 Copilot pay-as-you-go billing works for supported services such as Microsoft 365 Copilot Chat and SharePoint agents, including Azure subscription-based metering.	`https://learn.microsoft.com/en-us/microsoft-365/copilot/pay-as-you-go/overview`
Identifying Copilot Features That Can Be Enabled or Disabled	Explains how administrators manage Copilot agents and capabilities, including enabling, disabling, assigning, blocking, or removing agents in the Microsoft 365 admin center.	`https://learn.microsoft.com/en-us/microsoft-365/admin/manage/manage-copilot-agents-integrated-apps`
Identifying Use Cases for Researcher	Explains how Researcher works as a Microsoft 365 Copilot agent for complex, multi-step research tasks that use work content and web content to produce source-cited reports.	`https://learn.microsoft.com/en-us/microsoft-365/copilot/researcher-agent`
Identifying Use Cases for Analyst	Explains how Analyst is provided as a Microsoft 365 Copilot agent and used for structured analysis tasks such as identifying patterns, trends, and insights from data.	`https://learn.microsoft.com/en-us/microsoft-365/copilot/copilot-agent-install`

Topic	What it covers	Microsoft Learn reference
Identifying Use Cases for Custom Agents	Explains how custom agents extend Microsoft 365 Copilot through declarative agents, custom engine agents, instructions, knowledge, and actions for organization-specific scenarios.	`https://learn.microsoft.com/en-us/microsoft-365/copilot/extensibility/agents-overview`

Table 8.1: Microsoft references for Copilot and agent capability topics covered in this chapter

Together, these references support the chapter's focus on how Copilot and agents differ, how monthly and pay-as-you-go models affect access and billing, how Copilot and agent capabilities can be controlled, and when Researcher, Analyst, or custom agents are the appropriate option.

Key terms and acronyms

The following table introduces the main Copilot, agent, licensing, control, Researcher, Analyst, and custom agent terms used throughout this chapter.

Term	Meaning
Microsoft 365 Copilot	A Microsoft 365 AI experience that helps users generate, summarize, reason over, and work with information through prompts and available organizational context.
Agent	An AI capability that can use instructions, knowledge, and actions to perform a defined task or support a specific business scenario.
Built-in Copilot capability	A Copilot feature provided as part of the Microsoft 365 Copilot experience without the organization building a custom agent.
Custom agent	An agent created or configured for a specific organizational purpose, workflow, knowledge source, or business process.
Researcher	A first-party Microsoft 365 Copilot agent used for multi-source research, synthesis, and source-cited report generation.

Term	Meaning
Analyst	A first-party Microsoft 365 Copilot agent used for structured data analysis, trend identification, comparison, calculation, and anomaly detection.
Microsoft 365 Copilot license	A per-user monthly license that gives assigned users access to Microsoft 365 Copilot experiences.
Pay-as-you-go (PAYG)	A usage-based billing model where eligible Copilot or agent activity is charged based on consumption rather than a fixed per-user license.
Microsoft 365 Copilot Chat	A Copilot chat experience that can use pay-as-you-go billing for supported agent and work data scenarios.
SharePoint agent	An agent associated with SharePoint content that can use pay-as-you-go billing when users interact with it.
Copilot credits	Capacity used by Copilot Studio and agent experiences, supplied through prepaid capacity or pay-as-you-go billing depending on configuration.
Billing policy	A configuration that links supported Copilot pay-as-you-go usage to billing through an Azure subscription.
Feature enablement	The process of making a Copilot or agent capability available to users or groups.
Feature disablement	The process of restricting or turning off a Copilot or agent capability for users, groups, or the organization.
Agent assignment	The process of making an agent available to selected users or groups.
Agent blocking	An administrative control used to prevent an agent from being available or used in the organization.
Microsoft 365 admin center	The admin portal, where administrators manage Microsoft 365 services, users, billing, Copilot settings, and agent availability.
Microsoft Graph	The Microsoft 365 data and relationship layer that Copilot and some agents use to access permitted organizational context.

Term	Meaning
Source-cited report	A structured Researcher output that includes references to the sources used to support the findings.
Structured data	Data organized into rows, columns, fields, or tables so it can be measured, compared, grouped, or analyzed.
Trend	A pattern of movement or change in structured data over time or across categories.
Anomaly	A value or pattern in structured data that differs from expected behavior or normal ranges.
Workflow	A defined sequence of steps that an agent follows to complete a task or process.
Business logic	The rules and conditions that determine how a custom agent behaves during a workflow.

Table 8.2: Key Copilot and agent capability terms and acronyms

These terms connect the chapter's terminology to the AB-900 skills measured and give readers a concise reference for Copilot and agent differences, licensing models, feature controls, Researcher, Analyst, and custom agent use cases.

Exam readiness drill – chapter review questions

Apart from mastering key concepts, strong test-taking skills under time pressure are essential for acing your certification exam. That's why developing these abilities early in your learning journey is critical.

Exam readiness drills, using the free online practice resources provided with this book, help you progressively improve your time management and test-taking skills while reinforcing the key concepts you've learned.

HOW TO GET STARTED

1. Open the link or scan the QR code at the bottom of this page
2. If you have unlocked the practice resources already, log in to your registered account. If you haven't, follow the instructions in the *Free Benefits with Your Book* section in this book's *Preface* and come back to this page.

3. Once you log in, click the START button to start this chapter's quiz
4. We recommend attempting a quiz multiple times till you're able to answer most of the questions correctly and well within the time limit
5. You can use the following practice template to help you plan your attempts:

Working On Accuracy		
Attempt	**Target**	**Time Limit**
Attempt 1	40% or more	Till the timer runs out
Attempt 2	60% or more	Till the timer runs out
Attempt 3	75% or more	Till the timer runs out
Working On Timing		
Attempt 4	75% or more	1 minute before time limit
Attempt 5	75% or more	2 minutes before time limit
Attempt 6	75% or more	3 minutes before time limit

The above drill is just an example. Design your drills based on your own goals and make the most out of the online quizzes accompanying this book.

Link to this chapter's quiz

You need to unlock the online practice resources to access the link below. Check the *Free Benefits with Your Book* section in the *Preface* for detailed instructions on how to do this. You only need to unlock the resources once.

Open Quiz `https://packt.link/vD1vT`or scan the QR code

9

Performing Basic Administrative Tasks for Copilot

This chapter covers the core administrative tasks required to manage Microsoft 365 Copilot in an organization.

It also explains how to **manage prompts** throughout their lifecycle, including saving, sharing, scheduling, and deleting.

Copilot features are enabled and managed through the **Microsoft 365 admin center**, where administrators control availability at the user and service level rather than through security, compliance, or monitoring tools.

This content focuses on the **Perform basic administrative tasks for Copilot** sub-module within the Perform basic administrative tasks for Copilot and agents domain of the AB-900 Skills Measured.

By the end of this chapter, you will be able to confidently answer questions on the following topics:

- Assigning Copilot licenses
- Monitoring and managing pay-as-you-go billing policies
- Monitoring Copilot usage and adoption
- Managing prompts in Copilot

These skills equip readers with the essential administrative capabilities required to operationalize Copilot effectively and support secure, governed AI adoption.

Assigning Copilot licenses

Licenses control who can use Copilot, defining which users are allowed to interact with it and setting the boundary for AI usage.

The system differentiates between **entitled** and **non-entitled** users. Licensed users gain access to Microsoft 365 Copilot features included with that license, while users without the license cannot use those licensed Microsoft 365 Copilot experiences.

This separation establishes governance at the **identity level**, ensuring that access is *intentional, controlled,* and *aligned* with organizational policies and readiness.

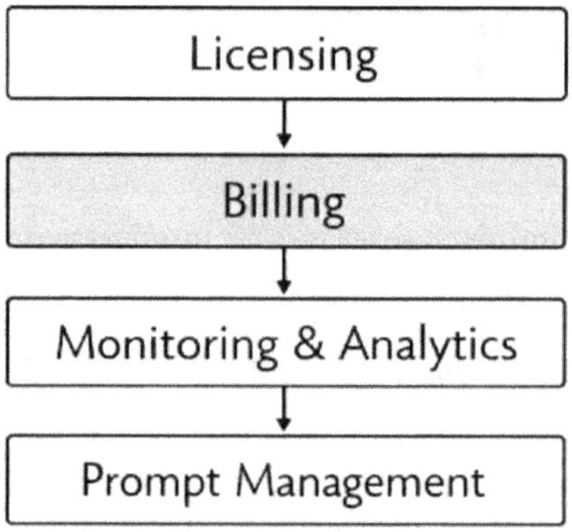

Figure 9.1: Administrative layers for managing Copilot

Figure 9.1 shows the layered administrative controls used to manage Microsoft 365 Copilot.

In addition to licensing-based access control, administrators manage Copilot through independent layers that govern cost, visibility, and procedural use. Billing governs how usage is charged through pay-as-you-go consumption models, controlling cost rather than behavior. Monitoring and analytics provide visibility into usage and adoption patterns without enforcing restrictions. Prompt management governs how prompts are created, shared, scheduled, and retired, supporting governance and accountability.

Where to find this: In the **Microsoft 365 admin center**, Copilot licenses can be assigned from **Billing** | **Licenses** | **Microsoft 365 Copilot**, or from **Users** | **Active users** | **Licenses**.

License assignment as the control for Copilot access

The system evaluates assigned identities in real time, granting access to entitled users and continuously enforcing access boundaries to prevent unauthorized interactions.

In practice, this ensures that only approved personnel generate AI responses. Analysts and administrators can rely on license enforcement to maintain consistent access control, minimizing the risk of unregulated AI activity within the tenant.

Individual license assignment behavior

Individual license assignment applies directly to a single user identity. When a license is assigned, the system flags that user as entitled to Copilot capabilities, allowing AI interactions immediately. Unassigned users cannot invoke any Copilot functionality.

This operates at the identity level, where each user's account is checked against assigned licenses and access is enforced automatically.

For individually assigned licenses, entitlement comes directly from the user's assigned license. Other controls, such as service plans, admin settings, and separately assigned group-based licenses, may still affect the overall availability of Copilot experiences.

Operationally, administrators can control access on a per-user basis, granting AI capabilities to specific individuals without impacting others. This direct mapping ensures precise governance, limiting exposure and reducing the risk of unapproved Copilot activity.

Group-based license assignment and inheritance behavior

Licenses can be assigned to groups, automatically extending access to all group members.

When a user joins a licensed group, license assignment is applied based on group membership after the change is processed. When a user leaves the group, the inherited license is removed after the membership and licensing updates are processed.

The system enforces inheritance hierarchically. Each member's identity is checked against group licenses, and overlapping assignments are resolved by the system to prevent conflicts. Individual licenses remain independent, so a user can retain access even if group membership changes.

Operationally, group-based assignment simplifies governance at scale. Administrators manage access consistently across multiple users, reducing administrative overhead while maintaining controlled exposure. Inheritance ensures that entitlements accurately reflect dynamic organizational membership.

Copilot licensing limitations

Copilot licenses control access but do not govern the behavior or capabilities of the AI itself.

Assigned users may access the Microsoft 365 Copilot capabilities made available to them through licensing, service plans, and admin configuration.

Licensing checks whether the user is entitled to use the capability, but Copilot interactions remain governed by permissions, service policies, data protection controls, DLP, and responsible AI safeguards.

Operationally, administrators must recognize that licensing sets the perimeter, not the operational rules. Governance relies on licenses to define who can engage with Copilot, while additional controls—such as usage monitoring, activity policies, or role assignments—manage actual feature behavior.

Individual and group-based assignments define entitlement, while inheritance ensures dynamic, consistent application across teams. Limitations clarify that licensing controls availability, not feature behavior, signaling where additional governance and monitoring must intervene.

Monitoring and managing pay-as-you-go billing policies

Pay-as-you-go billing charges are based on actual Copilot usage, so costs increase or decrease depending on how much the service is used rather than being fixed in advance.

Continuous monitoring of usage and billing policies allows administrators to correlate operational behavior with expenditure, anticipate budget impact, and ensure spending aligns with organizational expectations.

Operationally, pay-as-you-go requires active oversight. Administrators can track usage-driven accumulation, review budget notifications, and compare consumption against expected spending. Understanding this linkage between AI activity and financial outcomes supports resource planning, budget management, and informed decision-making across the organization.

Where to find this: In the **Microsoft 365 admin center**, pay-as-you-go billing policies are managed from **Copilot** | **Billing & usage** | **Billing policies**.

Pay-as-you-go: a consumption-based billing model

Pay-as-you-go charges reflect *actual usage* rather than fixed licensing. Supported pay-as-you-go Copilot usage is *metered* and contributes to the billing total.

Billed amounts are typically updated daily, in some cases more frequently, and can take up to 24 hours to appear in Microsoft Cost Management.

Usage events are collected and reflected through billing and cost reporting rather than appearing instantly. This model contrasts with fixed licensing, where the cost is static regardless of user behavior.

Operationally, administrators gain transparency into how AI is consumed across the tenant. They can correlate usage with spending trends, anticipate budget impact, and plan resource allocation based on observed behavior.

Usage-driven cost behavior in pay-as-you-go

Costs accumulate based on the meter used by the supported Copilot service or scenario. Higher eligible usage increases charges, while lower usage reduces consumption-based costs.

Usage events are collected and reflected through billing and cost reporting rather than appearing instantly. Billed amounts are typically updated daily, sometimes more frequently, and can take up to 24 hours to appear in Microsoft Cost Management.

Operationally, administrators can track patterns of AI engagement and identify areas of higher consumption. Usage-driven behavior highlights teams or users with higher usage, allowing proactive cost review and informed decisions about adoption, budgeting, and billing configuration.

Billing policy controls for pay-as-you-go usage

Billing policies define how pay-as-you-go consumption is monitored and reported. Policies can connect eligible Copilot usage to an Azure subscription and support budget notifications, but they do not enforce a hard spending cap or stop usage automatically. When configured, budget thresholds are reached, administrators receive notifications so they can review spending and decide whether action is needed.

Where departmental cost visibility is required, billing and cost reporting should use the configured billing policy, Azure subscription cost data, and tags or a cost allocation structure that identifies the department.

The system tracks consumption against configured budget thresholds and can generate notifications when those thresholds are reached. Exceeding a budget does not block further usage, stop the service, or stop billing. To stop pay-as-you-go billing entirely, an administrator must disconnect the pay-as-you-go service.

Operationally, administrators use these controls to monitor spending rather than enforce a fixed cap. Budget notifications reduce the risk of unnoticed cost increases, but administrators still need to review usage and take action if spending needs to be reduced or stopped.

Pay-as-you-go billing limitations

Pay-as-you-go controls consumption costs but does not restrict the type or volume of Copilot features a user can access once usage begins. Users can continue using supported Copilot features after a budget threshold is reached, and licensing or billing controls do not change how Copilot features behave.

The mechanism provides financial visibility rather than enforcement. The system monitors usage against budget thresholds and can trigger alerts, but it does not apply caps, stop usage, or modify operational AI capabilities.

Operationally, administrators must recognize that pay-as-you-go only governs expenditure, not usage patterns. Predictable budgeting requires combining billing controls with monitoring and usage policies to manage both financial and operational risk effectively.

Monitoring Copilot usage and adoption

Monitoring Copilot usage and adoption provides visibility into how AI capabilities are used across users, applications, and features, distinguishing between enabled users and active users to reflect actual adoption.

Administrators can analyze interactions across teams, applications, and periods, identifying areas of high engagement as well as gaps where usage is low or inconsistent. Copilot Analytics and related reporting surfaces can show adoption and usage patterns across users, apps, and selected Copilot activities, helping administrators understand where usage is high or low.

Limitations of monitoring clarify that visibility alone does not enforce behavior, signaling where governance, policies, and supplemental oversight must intervene.

Where to find this: In the **Microsoft 365 admin center**, Copilot usage reports are available from **Reports** | **Usage** | **Microsoft 365 Copilot**.

Enabled and active users as core adoption metrics

Enabled and active users represent the baseline for Copilot adoption. Enabled users have entitlement through licensing, while active users engage with Copilot features during defined periods. Tracking both categories differentiates potential access from actual operational usage.

The mechanism collects interaction data from licensed accounts and correlates it with activity logs. Each session or action updates metrics for active participation, while enabled-only accounts remain recorded as available but inactive. This ensures that adoption metrics reflect both opportunity and realized engagement.

Operationally, administrators can identify gaps between licensed entitlement and real usage. Teams with high enabled but low active counts may require training or communication, while areas with consistent active engagement indicate successful adoption and integration into workflows.

Usage analysis across users, applications, and time

Usage analysis aggregates Copilot activity across multiple dimensions to provide a comprehensive view of adoption. The system collects session data, feature interactions, and application engagement, then correlates them with user identities over time. Patterns emerge, showing how usage varies by individual, team, and application context.

The mechanism continuously processes event logs and telemetry to generate time-based and user-based summaries. Each interaction contributes to metrics such as frequency, duration, and feature utilization, creating a multi-dimensional dataset for administrators to analyze. This evaluation identifies both heavy and light usage trends.

Operationally, administrators can analyze adoption behavior, enabling resource planning and targeted interventions. Understanding usage over time highlights peaks, lulls, and application preferences, supporting decisions on training, policy adjustments, and feature rollout strategies.

Monitoring surfaces for Copilot usage visibility

Monitoring surfaces provide the interface and tools through which Copilot activity is observed. Data from user interactions, feature usage, and application engagement are aggregated and presented via dashboards, reports, and analytics surfaces. These surfaces consolidate signals to give administrators a clear picture of adoption patterns.

The system collects telemetry from Copilot sessions and translates it into visualizations and summaries. Each interaction contributes to metrics that populate charts, tables, and trend analyses, enabling continuous oversight of usage across the organization. This ensures administrators can identify anomalies, adoption gaps, or high-usage segments efficiently.

Operationally, these surfaces allow teams to make data-driven decisions. Visibility into usage patterns informs training needs, highlights areas for policy adjustment, and provides evidence for cost and resource planning related to AI engagement.

Copilot Analytics for feature-level insights

Copilot Analytics spans several reporting surfaces rather than a single report. For AB-900, the main surfaces to recognize are the Microsoft 365 admin center usage reports, found under **Reports** | **Usage** | **Microsoft 365 Copilot**, and the Copilot Dashboard in Viva Insights.

For exam scenarios that ask for detailed Teams Copilot metrics, such as meeting hours summarized by Copilot or meeting actions taken with Copilot, use the Copilot Dashboard in Viva Insights.

The Microsoft 365 admin center shows reports such as Copilot usage and Copilot Chat usage, while Viva Insights provides broader Copilot adoption and impact reporting. Access to Copilot Dashboard and Viva Insights reporting depends on the required licensing, service plans, roles, and configuration.

The system processes telemetry from all Copilot interactions, mapping usage to specific features and correlating it with users and applications. Metrics such as frequency, duration, and depth of feature use are generated, highlighting which capabilities are most utilized and which remain underused.

Operationally, administrators can identify high-impact features and assess training needs for underutilized functionality. Feature-level insights support decisions on workflow optimization, resource allocation, and targeted adoption initiatives, ensuring Copilot capabilities are leveraged effectively across the organization.

Copilot usage monitoring limitations

Monitoring tracks access and interaction, but does not control how users engage with Copilot features. While metrics capture sessions, commands, and feature-level usage, the system cannot enforce operational behavior or modify how AI responses are generated.

Operationally, administrators rely on monitoring to guide adoption strategies and identify patterns, but additional governance layers—such as policies, training, or role assignments—are required to influence behavior. Understanding these limitations ensures that visibility is combined with active controls for comprehensive oversight.

Managing prompts in Copilot

Prompts move through different stages, including saving, sharing, scheduling, execution, and deletion. Prompt Gallery is the Microsoft 365 Copilot surface where users discover, save, reuse, and share prompts. It includes Suggested, Your Prompts, and Teams views, so users can discover recommended prompts, return to prompts they saved, and share prompts with a Teams team. **Scheduled prompts** is the Microsoft 365 Copilot feature used to run prompts at a defined time or recurrence from the Copilot Chat scheduled prompts page.

Operationally, administrators can manage supported controls for scheduled prompts and rely on audit, compliance, and user governance processes to oversee how prompts are used. These controls reduce risk but do not guarantee prompt quality or prevent every unintended repeated action.

Limitations clarify that while lifecycle and governance controls manage procedural compliance, they do not evaluate content quality or prevent errors in AI outputs. Combining monitoring, governance, and policy enforcement provides a complete framework for safe and accountable prompt usage.

Where to find this: In Microsoft 365 Copilot Chat, **Prompt Gallery** is used to discover, save, reuse, and share prompts, while **Scheduled prompts** is used to manage prompts that run at a defined time or recurrence.

Prompt lifecycle management

Prompt lifecycle management governs the creation, retention, scheduling, and deletion of prompts.

Saved, shared, and scheduled prompts can have lifecycle states such as creation, reuse, sharing, scheduling, execution, and deletion, depending on the feature used.

The system evaluates prompt metadata, execution history, and scheduling parameters to maintain an accurate lifecycle record. Changes such as edits, rescheduling, or deletion update the system, ensuring the current status reflects actual operational conditions.

Operationally, administrators can monitor prompt usage over time, identify active or dormant prompts, and maintain control over AI-driven actions. Lifecycle management prevents uncontrolled accumulation of prompts, supports auditing, and ensures that operational workflows rely on current and valid instructions.

Risks from prompt sharing and repeated execution

When prompts are shared across users or teams, there is a higher risk of unintended or repeated AI actions. Repeated execution or duplication can lead to inconsistent outputs, increased resource usage, or unintended exposure of sensitive data.

Prompt activity may be logged or surfaced through supported audit and compliance experiences, but administrators still need to review usage patterns to identify repeated or distributed use that may create risk.

Each interaction is logged to maintain accountability, but the system cannot inherently prevent misuse or overuse solely through sharing controls.

Operationally, administrators must monitor prompt distribution and repeated execution to reduce errors and manage exposure. Understanding these risks ensures that prompts are shared intentionally, supporting reliable AI outputs while limiting potential operational or compliance issues.

Governance controls for prompt lifecycle management

Prompt governance depends on the controls available for each prompt feature. Prompt Gallery supports saving, reuse, and sharing, while Scheduled Prompts has admin controls for feature availability and compliance. These controls should be combined with audit, Purview, and user training where oversight is required.

Permissions and policies are applied at the identity and group level, monitoring prompt actions and logging changes. Edits, executions, or deletions trigger audit records, and access controls prevent unauthorized users from modifying or executing prompts outside established policies.

Operationally, administrators maintain structured oversight of prompt activity, ensuring that AI-driven actions adhere to organizational standards. Governance reduces the risk of misuse, preserves accountability, and supports auditing and reporting requirements.

Prompt management limitations

Prompt management governs creation, sharing, scheduling, and deletion, but cannot control the content quality or execution outcomes of AI responses. While lifecycle tracking enforces procedural compliance, the system does not prevent errors, inappropriate outputs, or unintended consequences from prompt execution.

Operational boundaries are enforced at the administrative and identity level. Saved, shared, and scheduled prompts may be governed through the controls available to those features, while prompt-related activity can be reviewed through supported audit and compliance mechanisms.

Operationally, administrators must combine prompt lifecycle management with monitoring, training, and policy enforcement to maintain control over AI interactions. Understanding these limitations clarifies where governance must supplement monitoring to mitigate operational and compliance risks.

Summary

This chapter covered the core administrative tasks required to manage Microsoft 365 Copilot, including license assignment, pay-as-you-go billing policies, usage monitoring, and prompt lifecycle management. Together, these capabilities enable organizations to operationalize Copilot effectively while supporting secure, governed AI adoption.

In the next chapter, the focus moves from administering Microsoft 365 Copilot to administering agents, including how user access is configured, how agents are created and approved, and how agent usage and lifecycle status are monitored across the Microsoft 365 admin center and Power Platform admin center.

Microsoft Learn reference links

The following table provides official Microsoft references for the main Copilot license assignment, pay-as-you-go billing, usage monitoring, adoption reporting, and prompt management topics introduced in this chapter.

Topic	What it covers	Microsoft Learn reference
Assigning Copilot licenses	Explains how administrators assign Microsoft 365 Copilot licenses to users through the Microsoft 365 admin center, including license assignment from Billing or Active users.	`https://learn.microsoft.com/en-us/microsoft-365/copilot/microsoft-365-copilot-setup`
Monitoring and managing pay-as-you-go billing policies	Explains how pay-as-you-go billing is configured for Microsoft 365 Copilot services, how billing policies are attached to an Azure subscription, and how usage-based costs are monitored.	`https://learn.microsoft.com/en-us/microsoft-365/copilot/pay-as-you-go/setup`
Monitoring Copilot usage and adoption	Explains how administrators use Microsoft 365 admin center reports and Copilot Analytics to monitor Copilot usage, adoption, active users, and engagement trends.	`https://learn.microsoft.com/en-us/microsoft-365/admin/activity-reports/microsoft-365-copilot-usage`
Managing prompts in Copilot	Explains how Prompt Gallery and scheduled prompts allow users to save, share, reuse, schedule, and delete prompts in Microsoft 365 Copilot.	`https://learn.microsoft.com/en-us/microsoft-365/copilot/copilot-prompt-gallery` `https://learn.microsoft.com/en-us/microsoft-365/copilot/scheduled-prompts`

Table 9.1: Microsoft references for Copilot administration topics covered in this chapter

Together, these references support the chapter's focus on how administrators assign Copilot access, manage usage-based billing, monitor adoption, and understand prompt lifecycle features such as saving, sharing, scheduling, and deleting prompts.

Key terms and acronyms

The following table introduces the main Copilot licensing, pay-as-you-go billing, usage monitoring, adoption, and prompt management terms used throughout this chapter.

Term	Meaning
Microsoft 365 Copilot license	A per-user license that gives an assigned user access to Microsoft 365 Copilot features.
License assignment	The process of assigning a Microsoft 365 Copilot license to a user so they can access Copilot features.
Individual license assignment	Assigning a Copilot license directly to a single user account.
Group-based license assignment	Assigning licenses to a group so eligible members receive Copilot access through group membership.
Entitled user	A user who has been assigned the required license and can access Microsoft 365 Copilot.
Pay-as-you-go (PAYG)	A usage-based billing model where eligible Copilot activity is charged based on consumption rather than a fixed monthly license.
Billing policy	A configuration that connects supported Copilot pay-as-you-go usage to billing through an Azure subscription.
Azure subscription	The billing container used to charge supported pay-as-you-go Copilot usage.
Consumption	The amount of eligible Copilot usage that contributes to pay-as-you-go billing.
Budget alert	A notification triggered when pay-as-you-go spending reaches configured budget thresholds.
Microsoft Cost Management	The Azure cost management experience used to review and analyze pay-as-you-go usage and charges.

Term	Meaning
Copilot usage report	A Microsoft 365 admin center report that shows Copilot activity, enabled users, active users, and adoption trends.
Enabled user	A user who has access to Copilot through licensing or assignment.
Active user	A user who has actually used Copilot during a reporting period.
Adoption	The extent to which licensed users actively use Copilot across the organization.
Copilot Analytics	Microsoft reporting experiences that help organizations analyze Copilot readiness, adoption, usage, and business impact.
Prompt	A natural language instruction or request entered into Copilot.
Prompt Gallery	The Microsoft 365 Copilot feature where users can discover, save, reuse, and share prompts.
Saved prompt	A prompt stored by a user for later reuse.
Shared prompt	A prompt made available to other users or a team through supported Copilot prompt-sharing features.
Scheduled prompt	A prompt configured to run at a defined time or recurrence.
Prompt deletion	Removing a saved or scheduled prompt when it is no longer needed.

Table 9.2: Key Copilot administration terms and acronyms

These terms connect the chapter's terminology to the AB-900 skills measured and give readers a concise reference for Copilot license assignment, pay-as-you-go billing policies, usage and adoption monitoring, and prompt management.

Exam readiness drill – chapter review questions

Apart from mastering key concepts, strong test-taking skills under time pressure are essential for acing your certification exam. That's why developing these abilities early in your learning journey is critical.

Exam readiness drills, using the free online practice resources provided with this book, help you progressively improve your time management and test-taking skills while reinforcing the key concepts you've learned.

HOW TO GET STARTED

1. Open the link or scan the QR code at the bottom of this page
2. If you have unlocked the practice resources already, log in to your registered account. If you haven't, follow the instructions in the *Free Benefits with Your Book* section in this book's *Preface* and come back to this page.
3. Once you log in, click the START button to start this chapter's quiz
4. We recommend attempting a quiz multiple times until you're able to answer most of the questions correctly and well within the time limit
5. You can use the following practice template to help you plan your attempts:

Working On Accuracy		
Attempt	**Target**	**Time Limit**
Attempt 1	40% or more	Till the timer runs out
Attempt 2	60% or more	Till the timer runs out
Attempt 3	75% or more	Till the timer runs out
Working On Timing		
Attempt 4	75% or more	1 minute before time limit
Attempt 5	75% or more	2 minutes before time limit
Attempt 6	75% or more	3 minutes before time limit

The above drill is just an example. Design your drills based on your own goals and make the most out of the online quizzes accompanying this book.

Link to this chapter's quiz

You need to unlock the online practice resources to access the link below. Check the *Free Benefits with Your Book* section in the *Preface* for detailed instructions on how to do this. You only need to unlock the resources once.

Open Quiz `https://packt.link/pUx2mor` scan the QR code

10

Performing Basic Administrative Tasks for Agents

This chapter covers the essential administrative tasks needed to manage **agent-based AI** within **Microsoft 365**. Readers will learn how to configure user access to agents, create new agents, and understand the approval flows required before agents become available in the organization.

The chapter also explains how to monitor agent usage, operational insights, and lifecycle status through the **Microsoft 365 admin center** and the **Power Platform admin center**.

This content primarily focuses on the **Perform basic administrative tasks for Copilot and agents** module from the *Skills Measured* section of the **AB-900** exam.

By the end of this chapter, you will be able to confidently answer questions on the following topics:

- Identifying How to Configure User Access to Agents
- Creating an Agent
- Understanding the Agent Approval Process
- Monitoring Agents Using Admin Centers

These capabilities ensure that organizations can deploy, govern, and maintain agents effectively as part of a secure and controlled AI environment.

Identifying how to configure user access to agents

Agents act on behalf of users or processes, so controlling access is essential to keep activity safe and predictable. Access is controlled by three layers working together: licensing determines who can use agents, roles define what actions they can perform, and the environment limits where those actions can occur.

Where to find this: Agent access and availability are managed through the **Microsoft 365 admin center** and related agent management settings.

Users who create or use **agents** in **Microsoft 365 Copilot experiences** commonly require a **Microsoft 365 Copilot license**, while administrative access is controlled through roles such as AI Administrator, Global Administrator, and Global Reader for view-only scenarios. **Copilot Studio authoring** may also depend on the appropriate Power Platform environment permissions.

The separation of user authorization from agent capabilities ensures operational boundaries are enforced. Agents execute actions only when licensing, role, and environmental conditions are all satisfied. Unauthorized interactions are blocked, preserving system integrity and maintaining strict visibility over operational activity.

Operationally, these controls shape monitoring, investigation, and management workflows across the tenant. Access restrictions determine which agents are visible in administrative views, what activity is logged, and which resources remain protected. By linking licensing, roles, and environmental scope, administrators can ensure that agents operate safely, predictably, and only within intended boundaries while supporting necessary operational tasks.

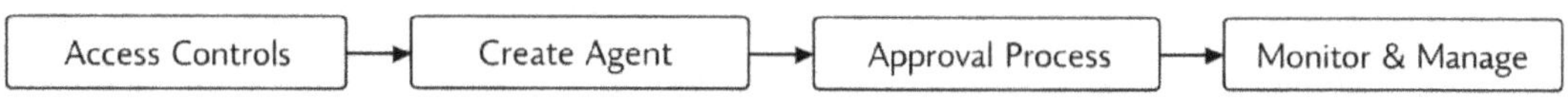

Figure 10.1: Agent lifecycle management stages

Figure 10.1 illustrates the high-level lifecycle used to manage agents in Microsoft 365. After access controls define who is permitted to work with agents, agent creation defines instructions, configuration, and knowledge sources, but does not make the agent operational. The approval process governs whether an agent can be deployed, acting as the release gate without altering its behavior. Once deployed, monitoring and management provide visibility into usage, operational performance, and lifecycle status.

Licensing controls access to agents

Licenses determine which users are authorized to interact with agents. Only users with the required license types can create, use, or assign agents. This restriction prevents unlicensed users from accessing operational capabilities or sensitive data.

For Microsoft 365 Copilot experiences, users who create or use agents commonly require a Microsoft 365 Copilot license, while Copilot Chat may be available through eligible Microsoft 365 or Office 365 plans, and metered agent scenarios may use pay-as-you-go credits.

These restrictions impact operational workflows and monitoring. Only authorized users contribute to agent activity logs, and alerts or operational insights reflect interactions within the licensed population.

Role assignment controls agent management permissions

Roles define what management operations a user can perform on agents. Assigning a role grants explicit permissions such as creating, editing, or deleting agents while preventing actions outside the assigned scope.

Agent administration uses roles such as AI Administrator and Global Administrator for management, while Global Reader supports view-only review; Copilot Studio authors may also require appropriate Power Platform environment roles.

Role enforcement separates administrative capability from general access. Users without the appropriate role cannot modify agents or affect their configuration, even if they have licenses.

These controls influence operational workflows and auditing. Only users with proper roles appear in management logs and agent activity reports, ensuring that all modifications are traceable and aligned with governance requirements.

The environment defines agent scope and data access

The environment limits where agents can operate and what resources they can reach. Each agent inherits boundaries from the assigned environment, including accessible systems, data sets, and operational contexts.

Environmental enforcement separates agent activity across organizational or security domains. Agents cannot access resources outside their designated environment, preventing cross-domain operations that could expose sensitive information.

This control affects monitoring, investigation, and operational workflows. Logs, alerts, and visibility reflect only activity within the scoped environment, ensuring auditability and reducing risk exposure while agents perform their tasks.

Combined licensing and role requirements for agent access

Agent access requires both the appropriate license and the assigned role. Even if a user holds a license, they cannot perform management actions unless their role grants the necessary permissions.

The combination enforces operational boundaries at multiple layers. Licensing gates who can interact with agents, while roles determine what actions are allowed, ensuring agents operate only under authorized supervision.

These dual controls shape visibility, monitoring, and operational workflows. Activity logs, alerts, and management reports reflect interactions that meet both licensing and role criteria, preventing unauthorized or accidental changes while maintaining traceable governance.

Agent access limitations

Access to agents is constrained by licensing, role assignments, and environmental scope. Users lacking any of these prerequisites cannot interact with agents, preventing unauthorized execution or data exposure.

These limitations enforce operational boundaries across the tenant. Agents appear and act only within the confines set by combined access controls, ensuring that activity remains traceable and compliant with governance policies.

The restrictions impact monitoring and investigation workflows. Logs, alerts, and operational dashboards reflect only authorized interactions, and any attempts to bypass access controls are inherently blocked, reducing risk while maintaining system integrity.

Creating an agent

Creating an agent involves defining its purpose and operational availability within the organization.

Where to find this: Agents can be created by using **Agent Builder** in **Microsoft 365 Copilot** for simpler natural-language agent creation, or by using **Copilot Studio** for more advanced agents that require richer configuration, actions, connectors, or environment-level control. **Agent Builder** provides a guided experience for defining instructions and knowledge sources, while Copilot Studio provides a fuller authoring environment for designing, testing, and managing more advanced agents.

Instructions dictate the agent's actions, configuration determines its structure and capabilities, and creation methods govern when and where the agent becomes active.

Knowledge sources inform responses, ensuring agents operate predictably and provide accurate outputs. Testing ensures that instructions and configuration align with intended behavior, while editing and updates preserve functionality and maintain visibility.

Agents differ from Copilot in how they operate. While Copilot generates responses to user prompts within applications, agents execute tasks across systems based on defined instructions and workflows.

Operationally, a structured creation workflow ensures agents execute only within their defined scope, reduces the risk of misconfiguration, and supports governance by clearly separating conceptual design from activation and usage.

Instructions define agent behavior

Instructions provide the operational logic that governs how an agent responds to inputs and executes tasks. Each instruction maps a user intent or trigger to a sequence of actions, controlling agent behavior in predictable ways.

The instruction set separates task definition from execution environment. Agents act only according to the instructions assigned, preventing arbitrary or unintended operations.

These controls affect monitoring, auditing, and operational workflows. Agent activity reflects the instructions provided, enabling traceability of outcomes, predictable performance, and alignment with intended operational goals.

Configuration defines agent structure and capabilities

Configuration determines how an agent is built, including its components, operational logic, and resource access. Each configuration defines the agent's scope, enabling specific functions while restricting unintended operations.

The configuration separates structural design from behavioral instructions. Even if instructions change, the underlying configuration enforces consistent capabilities and operational boundaries.

These controls impact monitoring, operational management, and auditing. Logs, performance metrics, and visibility reflect the configuration constraints, ensuring agents operate reliably and within defined limits.

Creation methods define how agents are instantiated

Creation methods determine how an agent moves from design to operational deployment. These methods control when and where an agent becomes active and which initial settings or templates it inherits.

Instantiation separates build-time parameters from runtime behavior. Agents are only active in environments and contexts allowed by their creation method, preventing unintended activation or access.

This directly affects monitoring and how governance is applied. Deployment logs, availability status, and execution metrics reflect creation constraints, ensuring agents execute only as intended while maintaining traceable activity.

Knowledge sources ground agent responses

Knowledge sources provide the information and context that agents use to generate responses. They determine the content an agent can reference, ensuring outputs are accurate, relevant, and aligned with operational requirements.

Grounding separates response content from agent instructions. Even with identical instructions, differing knowledge sources result in distinct outputs, constraining the agent to authorized and validated information.

These controls impact monitoring, auditing, and investigation. Responses are traceable to specific sources, allowing verification, reducing misinformation risk, and supporting operational compliance.

Testing validates behavior and knowledge before deployment

Testing evaluates whether agents perform as intended under operational conditions. It verifies that instructions, configuration, creation methods, and knowledge sources interact correctly to produce expected outcomes.

Validation separates intended functionality from unintended behavior. Only agents that pass tests proceed to deployment, preventing operational errors or misaligned responses from reaching active environments.

These controls affect monitoring and governance workflows. Logs, test results, and validation records provide traceable evidence of agent readiness, ensuring operational reliability and alignment with organizational policies.

Editing modifies the agent and resharing controls visibility

Editing updates an agent's instructions, configuration, or knowledge sources, altering how it behaves in operational contexts. Resharing defines which users or groups can view or use the modified agent, controlling exposure across the tenant.

These controls separate the agent's operational logic from its distribution. Modifications affect only the agent's behavior once published, and resharing ensures visibility aligns with governance policies.

Operational workflows and monitoring reflect changes made through editing and resharing. Logs track who performed edits, which elements were updated, and which users gained or lost access, maintaining auditability and secure management.

Agent creation limitations

Agent creation is restricted by licensing, role assignments, environment scope, and platform constraints. Users cannot instantiate agents outside these boundaries, preventing unauthorized or unsupported deployments.

Limitations separate conceptual design from operational execution. Even valid instructions and configurations cannot bypass access or scope controls, enforcing predictable and secure deployment.

These controls affect monitoring, governance, and operational workflows. Logs, deployment records, and visibility reports reflect only permitted agent creations, ensuring accountability, traceability, and alignment with organizational policies.

Understanding the agent approval process

Agent approval governs the transition from creation to deployment, ensuring that each agent meets organizational standards, complies with policies, and does not introduce unmanaged risk.

Where to find this: Agent approval is reviewed through the **Microsoft 365 admin center agent management** experience. Administrators use the **Requests** workflow to review submitted agents and decide whether to publish or reject them. Approval controls whether the agent becomes available to users, but it does not rebuild the agent or change the instructions, knowledge sources, or permissions defined during creation.

The system checks what was built against the approval criteria. An agent may be fully constructed, configured, and tested, but it cannot access tenant resources or perform actions until approval conditions are satisfied. This separation maintains a clear boundary between creation and operational authority.

Operationally, approval decisions control release eligibility, enforce governance boundaries, and influence visibility in administrative and monitoring workflows. By integrating approval into the agent lifecycle, administrators can ensure that only compliant, policy-aligned agents become active, preserving security and operational integrity across the organization.

Governance defines approval criteria

Approval conditions specify the criteria an agent must meet before deployment. Policies evaluate factors such as compliance, testing outcomes, and configuration alignment to ensure agents adhere to organizational standards.

These conditions separate authorized deployment from agent readiness. Even fully built and tested agents cannot proceed unless they satisfy governance requirements, preventing unauthorized or non-compliant activity.

Approval conditions impact monitoring, operational oversight, and auditability. Logs and reports reflect whether agents meet the defined criteria, ensuring that only agents aligned with governance policies become active.

Approval controls release, not build or access

Approval determines whether an agent can be deployed, but it does not change the agent's instructions, configuration, or access permissions. Agents retain their defined capabilities and scope regardless of approval status.

This separation enforces governance without modifying underlying behavior. Build and access controls remain intact, ensuring that operational boundaries set during creation and configuration persist.

The control affects monitoring and audit workflows. Logs and dashboards reflect which agents have been released while maintaining traceable records of the approval process, supporting compliance and accountability.

Approval transitions to monitoring after deployment

Once an agent is approved and deployed, ongoing monitoring tracks its activity, behavior, and compliance. Approval marks the point at which operational oversight begins, ensuring that only sanctioned agents are observed and logged.

The transition separates pre-deployment governance from active monitoring. Agents cannot be monitored until approval is granted, preserving the integrity of operational workflows and preventing unapproved activity from generating data.

These controls impact visibility, investigation, and audit workflows. Logs, alerts, and operational dashboards reflect only approved agents, allowing security and compliance teams to analyze activity with confidence in the agent's authorization status.

Monitoring agents using admin center

Once agents are deployed, the system begins tracking how they are used, how they perform, and how they change over time, providing continuous visibility into their behavior.

Where to find this: Agent monitoring is reviewed across the **Microsoft 365 admin center**, **Copilot Studio**, and the **Power Platform admin center**.

In the **Microsoft 365 admin center**, tenant-level agent usage reporting is available from **Reports** | **Usage** | **Microsoft 365 Copilot** | **Agents**, including adoption, active users, and active agents.

In **Copilot Studio**, administrators can use the **Analytics tab** for individual agents to review performance, satisfaction, and session metrics. **Copilot Studio** | **Analytics tab**.

In the **Power Platform admin center**, administrators can review analytics for consumption-based and pay-as-you-go agents. **Power Platform admin center** | **analytics for consumption-based/pay-as-you-go agents**.

Continuous monitoring identifies drift, anomalies, or changes in behavior that could impact visibility, security, or resource management.

By maintaining a lifecycle perspective, administrators can ensure agents continue to function as intended, detect issues proactively, and preserve the integrity and reliability of AI-driven workflows.

Monitoring begins after deployment

Systems track all operational activity, capturing interactions, execution patterns, and task outcomes.

This initiation separates pre-deployment governance from active observation. Agents remain unmonitored until deployed, ensuring that only sanctioned activity is recorded and analyzed.

Monitoring affects visibility, auditing, and operational oversight. Logs and dashboards reflect active agent behavior, supporting investigation, compliance, and resource management.

Usage monitoring tracks adoption and interactions

Usage monitoring captures how users interact with agents, including frequency, task execution, and engagement patterns. This data reveals adoption trends and highlights which agents are actively utilized.

Monitoring separates operational activity from administrative configuration. Only interactions by authorized users and within assigned environments contribute to usage metrics, ensuring accurate representation of agent adoption.

These controls impact operational oversight and investigation workflows. Usage logs inform decisions on agent effectiveness, optimization opportunities, and resource allocation, while maintaining traceability of user-agent interactions.

Operational monitoring evaluates performance and reliability

Operational monitoring tracks agent execution efficiency, response times, error rates, and task completion success. It identifies performance deviations that could affect workflows or system stability.

This monitoring separates runtime evaluation from design and deployment. Agents continue to function under observed conditions, and anomalies trigger operational awareness without altering their configured behavior.

These controls influence visibility, incident response, and resource management. Logs and metrics provide actionable insights into agent reliability, enabling timely intervention and maintaining tenant operational integrity.

Lifecycle monitoring manages agents over time

Lifecycle monitoring observes agents from deployment through decommissioning. It tracks operational health, relevance, and compliance with policies throughout the agent's active period.

This monitoring separates ongoing evaluation from creation and approval processes. Agents continue to be assessed against operational and governance standards to detect drift or changes in effectiveness.

These controls impact visibility, resource planning, and risk management. Logs and reports provide historical insights, enabling decisions on retention, updates, or retirement of agents while maintaining accountability and traceability.

Monitoring identifies drift, risks, and resource impact

Ongoing monitoring detects deviations from expected agent behavior, potential security risks, and resource consumption patterns. It highlights operational anomalies that could affect performance or compliance.

This monitoring separates detection of operational issues from deployment or design. Agents remain functional, but deviations trigger visibility into drift and risk, allowing proactive management.

These controls influence investigation, resource planning, and governance. Logs, alerts, and reports provide actionable insights on agent health, risk exposure, and system impact, enabling timely mitigation while maintaining traceable oversight.

Agent monitoring limitations

Agent monitoring provides visibility into usage, performance, and lifecycle events, but it does not control agent behavior or prevent operational issues. While monitoring surfaces highlight activity, anomalies, and resource consumption, they do not enforce policy or restrict execution. Monitoring alone cannot prevent misuse, drift, or unintended outcomes.

Operationally, administrators must combine monitoring with access controls, approval processes, and governance policies to maintain effective oversight. Visibility supports informed decision-making, but control requires additional mechanisms beyond monitoring alone.

Summary

This chapter examined the core administrative tasks required to manage agents within Microsoft 365. It explained how user access to agents is configured, including access models and assignment scope. The chapter also described the agent creation workflow and the approval processes that help ensure agents are deployed in a controlled manner.

The chapter concluded by exploring how agents are monitored using the Microsoft 365 admin center and the Power Platform admin center. Together, these administrative capabilities enable organizations to deploy, govern, and maintain agents effectively as part of a secure and well-managed AI environment.

As you finish this book, the key lesson is that Microsoft 365 and Copilot administration work best when the pieces are understood together. Identity, licensing, data protection, governance, agents, and monitoring all shape how users access information and how organizations keep that access controlled. With that foundation, you can approach AB-900 questions by recognizing which Microsoft 365 capability is being tested and which administrative control best fits the situation.

Microsoft Learn reference links

The following table provides official Microsoft references for the main agent access, creation, approval, monitoring, and lifecycle topics introduced in this chapter.

Topic	What it covers	Microsoft Learn reference
Identifying How to Configure User Access to Agents	Explains the prerequisites, licensing, admin roles, and policy controls required to configure access to agents in Microsoft 365.	`https://learn.microsoft.com/en-us/microsoft-365/copilot/agent-essentials/agent-prerequisites`
Identifying How to Configure User Access to Agents	Explains how administrators manage agents and configure agent-related controls in the Microsoft 365 admin center.	`https://learn.microsoft.com/en-us/microsoft-365/admin/manage/manage-copilot-agents-integrated-apps`
Creating an Agent	Explains how Agent Builder in Microsoft 365 Copilot provides a simpler natural-language experience for creating agents.	`https://learn.microsoft.com/en-us/microsoft-365/copilot/extensibility/agent-builder-build-agents`
Creating an Agent	Provides the main Microsoft Copilot Studio documentation for creating, configuring, publishing, and managing more advanced agents.	`https://learn.microsoft.com/en-us/microsoft-copilot-studio/`
Creating an Agent	Explains how knowledge sources provide the data and context an agent can use to generate grounded responses.	`https://learn.microsoft.com/en-us/microsoft-copilot-studio/knowledge-copilot-studio`
Understandin g the Agent Approval Process	Explains how administrators review submitted agent requests in the Microsoft 365 admin center and choose whether to publish or reject them.	`https://learn.microsoft.com/en-us/microsoft-365/copilot/agent-essentials/agent-lifecycle/agent-copilot-studio-requested`

Topic	What it covers	Microsoft Learn reference
Understanding the Agent Approval Process	Explains how agents built by users can be shared, managed, and submitted for organizational availability.	`https://learn.microsoft.com/en-us/microsoft-365/copilot/extensibility/agent-builder-share-manage-agents`
Monitoring Agents Using Admin Centers	Explains how administrators review agent usage, adoption, active users, and active agents from Microsoft 365 admin center reports.	`https://learn.microsoft.com/en-us/microsoft-365/admin/activity-reports/microsoft-365-copilot-agents-new`
Monitoring Agents Using Admin Centers	Explains how agent access, sharing, publishing, and governance settings are managed through the Microsoft 365 admin center.	`https://learn.microsoft.com/en-us/microsoft-365/copilot/agent-essentials/m365-agents-admin-guide`

Table 10.1: Microsoft references for agent administration topics covered in this chapter

Together, these references support the chapter's focus on configuring user access to agents, creating agents, understanding approval workflows, and monitoring agent usage and lifecycle status through admin centers.

Key terms and acronyms

The following table introduces the main agent access, creation, approval, monitoring, and lifecycle terms used throughout this chapter.

Term	Meaning
Agent	An AI capability configured to answer questions, support tasks, or help users complete work based on defined instructions, knowledge sources, and available actions.
Agent Builder	The simpler agent creation experience in Microsoft 365 Copilot allows users to create agents using natural language.

Term	Meaning
Copilot Studio	The fuller authoring environment used to create, configure, test, publish, and manage more advanced agents.
Microsoft 365 admin center	The admin center is used to manage Microsoft 365 services, including agent availability, agent requests, usage reports, and organization-level agent controls.
Power Platform admin center	The admin center is used to manage Power Platform environments that support Copilot Studio authoring and environment-level administration.
Microsoft 365 Copilot license	A per-user license is commonly required for users who create or use agents in Microsoft 365 Copilot experiences.
AI Administrator	An administrative role used to manage Microsoft 365 Copilot and AI-related settings, including agent-related administration.
Global Administrator	A highly privileged administrative role that can manage tenant-wide Microsoft 365 settings, including agent-related controls.
Global Reader	A read-only administrative role that can view Microsoft 365 settings and reports without making configuration changes.
Environment	A Power Platform boundary that helps define where Copilot Studio agents are created, managed, and governed.
Instructions	The behavior guidance that defines what an agent should do, how it should respond, and how it should handle user requests.
Knowledge source	Information connected to an agent so it can ground responses in relevant and approved content.
Agent creation	The process of defining an agent's purpose, instructions, knowledge sources, configuration, and availability before it is submitted or published.
Agent testing	The process of checking whether an agent responds as intended before it is made available to users.
Agent approval	The governance process used to decide whether an agent can be released or made available for organizational use.

Term	Meaning
Requests workflow	The Microsoft 365 admin center workflow where submitted agents can be reviewed before they are made available to users.
Publish	The approval action that makes a reviewed agent available for organizational use.
Reject	The approval action that prevents a submitted agent from being made available to users.
Agent monitoring	The process of reviewing agent usage, adoption, lifecycle status, and operational behavior after deployment.
Agent usage report	A Microsoft 365 admin center report used to review agent adoption, active users, active agents, and usage trends.
Active agent	An agent that has recorded usage or activity during a reporting period.
Active user	A user who has interacted with an agent during a reporting period.
Lifecycle status	The current operational state of an agent, such as created, submitted, published, monitored, updated, or retired.

Table 10.2: Key agent administration terms and acronyms

These terms connect the chapter's terminology to the AB-900 skills measured and give readers a concise reference for configuring user access to agents, creating agents, understanding approval workflows, and monitoring agents through admin centers.

Exam readiness drill – chapter review questions

Apart from mastering key concepts, strong test-taking skills under time pressure are essential for acing your certification exam. That's why developing these abilities early in your learning journey is critical.

Exam readiness drills, using the free online practice resources provided with this book, help you progressively improve your time management and test-taking skills while reinforcing the key concepts you've learned.

HOW TO GET STARTED

1. Open the link or scan the QR code at the bottom of this page
2. If you have unlocked the practice resources already, log in to your registered account. If you haven't, follow the instructions in the *Free Benefits with Your Book* section in this book's *Preface* and come back to this page.
3. Once you log in, click the START button to start this chapter's quiz
4. We recommend attempting a quiz multiple times until you're able to answer most of the questions correctly and well within the time limit
5. You can use the following practice template to help you plan your attempts:

Working On Accuracy		
Attempt	**Target**	**Time Limit**
Attempt 1	40% or more	Till the timer runs out
Attempt 2	60% or more	Till the timer runs out
Attempt 3	75% or more	Till the timer runs out
Working On Timing		
Attempt 4	75% or more	1 minute before time limit
Attempt 5	75% or more	2 minutes before time limit
Attempt 6	75% or more	3 minutes before time limit

The above drill is just an example. Design your drills based on your own goals and make the most of the online quizzes accompanying this book.

Link to this chapter's quiz

You need to unlock the online practice resources to access the link below. Check the *Free Benefits with Your Book* section in the *Preface* for detailed instructions on how to do this. You only need to unlock the resources once.

Open Quiz `https://packt.link/AumxT` or scan the QR code

11

Unlock Your Exclusive Benefits

Your copy of this book includes the following exclusive benefits:

Follow the guide below to unlock them. The process takes only a few minutes and needs to be completed once.

Unlock this Book's Free Benefits in 3 Easy Steps

Step 1

Keep your purchase invoice ready for *Step 3*. If you have a physical copy, scan it using your phone and save it as a PDF, JPG, or PNG.

For more help on finding your invoice, visit `https://www.packtpub.com/en-us/unlock?step=1`.

> Note
>
> **Note**: If you bought this book directly from Packt, no invoice is required. After *Step 2*, you can access your exclusive content right away.

Step 2

Scan the QR code or go to `packtpub.com/unlock`.

On the page that opens (similar to *Figure 11.1* on desktop), search for this book by name and select the correct edition.

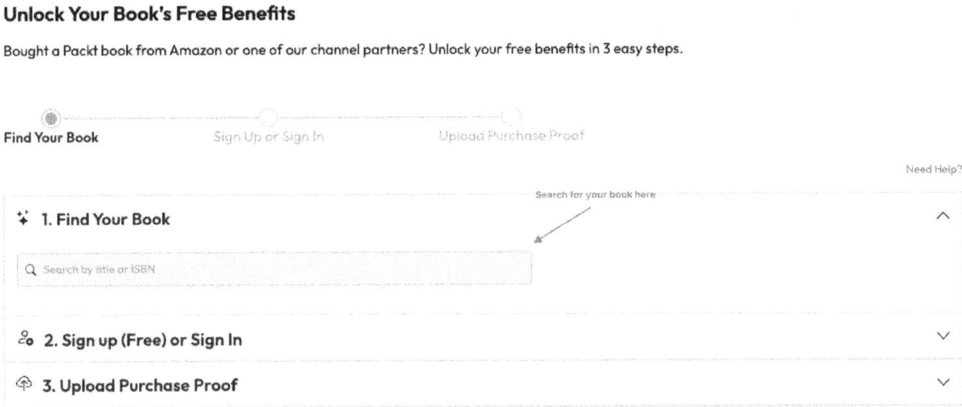

Figure 11.1: Packt unlock landing page on desktop

Step 3

After selecting your book, sign in to your Packt account or create one for free. Then upload your invoice (PDF, PNG, or JPG, up to 10 MB). Follow the on-screen instructions to finish the process.

Need Help

If you get stuck and need help, visit `https://www.packtpub.com/unlock-benefits/help` for a detailed FAQ on how to find your invoices and more. This QR code will take you to the help page.

> Note
>
> **Note**: If you are still facing issues, reach out to `customercare@packt.com`.

packtpub.com

Subscribe to our online digital library for full access to over 7,000 books and videos, as well as industry leading tools to help you plan your personal development and advance your career. For more information, please visit our website.

Why subscribe?

- Spend less time learning and more time coding with practical eBooks and Videos from over 4,000 industry professionals
- Improve your learning with Skill Plans built especially for you
- Get a free eBook or video every month
- Fully searchable for easy access to vital information
- Copy and paste, print, and bookmark content

At www.packtpub.com, you can also read a collection of free technical articles, sign up for a range of free newsletters, and receive exclusive discounts and offers on Packt books and eBooks.

Other Books You May Enjoy

If you enjoyed this book, you may be interested in these other books by Packt:

Agentic AI with Microsoft Foundry

Balamurugan Balakreshnan, Sina Fakhraee, Jay Padhya, Minsoo Thigpen

ISBN: 978-1-80667-395-7

- Configure and navigate Microsoft Foundry projects
- Build copilots using GPT and OpenAI models
- Apply prompt engineering and fine-tuning techniques
- Implement retrieval-augmented generation (RAG)
- Create intelligent agents with the Agent Framework
- Connect enterprise data and external APIs securely
- Orchestrate multi-agent workflows and automation
- Evaluate, monitor, and deploy responsible AI systems

Microsoft Copilot in Azure

David Rendón, Steve Miles

ISBN: 978-1-83620-025-3

- Set up and configure Microsoft Copilot in the Azure Portal
- Deploy and manage Azure Kubernetes Service (AKS) and App Services using Copilot
- Integrate Copilot with Azure Functions, Blob Storage, and Azure SQL
- Secure resources using Microsoft Defender for Cloud and compliance policies
- Monitor cloud workloads and troubleshoot issues using Copilot diagnostics
- Leverage AI-driven cost optimization and performance recommendations
- Strengthen cloud security posture using AI-enhanced threat detection and remediation
- Master prompt engineering techniques to get the most accurate and effective results from Copilot

Workflow Automation with Microsoft Power Automate

Aaron Guilmette

ISBN: 978-1-83664-963-2

- Build cloud flows using triggers, connectors, and actions
- Use Copilot and generative AI to create and edit flows
- Automate desktop tasks with Power Automate for Desktop
- Create approval processes for Teams, Slack, and email
- Connect Power Automate to Dataverse, Forms, and SQL
- Implement error handling, monitoring, and troubleshooting
- Govern and scale automations using best practices

Packt is searching for authors like you

If you're interested in becoming an author for Packt, please visit `authors.packt.com` and apply today. We have worked with thousands of developers and tech professionals, just like you, to help them share their insight with the global tech community. You can make a general application, apply for a specific hot topic that we are recruiting an author for, or submit your own idea.

Share your thoughts

Now you've finished *Microsoft 365 Copilot and Agent Administration Fundamentals*, we'd love to hear your thoughts! Scan the QR code below to go straight to the Amazon review page for this book and share your feedback or leave a review on the site that you purchased it from.

`https://packt.link/r/1807306518`

Your review is important to us and the tech community and will help us make sure we're delivering excellent quality content.

Index

A

Agents, versus Copilot
- built-in capabilities 190
- licensing model limitations 191, 192
- limitations 190
- monthly licensing 191
- pay-as-you-go 191

Analyst **195**
- anomaly detection 196
- data-driven insight generation 196
- limitations 197
- multi-source dataset handling 196
- structured dataset analysis 196
- use cases, identifying 195

access checks **122**

access management
- simplifying, with groups 77

access restrictions **123**

agents **190**
- access limitations 224
- approval process 227, 228
- configuration, for structure and capabilities 225
- creating 224
- creation limitations 227
- creation methods, for instantiation 225
- editing updates 226
- instructions, for behavior 225
- knowledge sources, for grounding agent responses 226
- licensing and role requirements, combining for access 224
- licensing controls access 223
- lifecycle monitoring 230
- management permissions, controlled by role assignment 223
- monitoring, limitations 231
- monitoring, with admin center 228, 229
- operational monitoring 230
- resharing, for controlling visibility 226
- scope and data access 223
- testing, for validating behavior and knowledge before deployment 226
- usage monitoring 229
- user access, configuring to 222

app permission policies **38**

app registrations **80, 81**

application identities **50**

attack techniques **57**

audit logs **84**
- reviewing, for administrative and configuration activity 85, 86

auditing **176**

authentication **49**
- factors 52, 53
- methods 52
- multi-factor authentication (MFA) 52
- passwordless authentication 53
- purpose 50
- versus authorization 51

authorization **51, 54**
- purpose 54
- role-based access control (RBAC) 54

B

breaking inheritance **28**

C

Communication Compliance **104**

Communication site **26**

Content Search **159**
- content retrieval 161
- data searching with 159, 160
- filtering, with conditions 161
- filtering, with keywords 161
- filtering, with locations 161
- indexed data, in Microsoft 365 services 161
- item-level retrieval, compared to aggregated insights 162
- limitations 162
- query-based data retrieval, across Microsoft 365 160

Copilot **190**
- grounding controls 128
- limitations 118
- Microsoft 365 data sources 117
- policy-aligned response generation 127
- prompt filtering 127
- prompt-driven data retrieval 118
- retrieval flow, across Microsoft 365 services 115, 116
- security control limitations 125
- system messages 128

Copilot Analytics
- for feature-level insights 213

Copilot Studio agent **191**

Copilot availability **192**
- environment-wide controls 193
- limitations 193
- service-level enablement 192
- user-level access assignment 192

Copilot licenses
- assigning 208, 209
- group-based license assignment 209
- individual license assignment 209
- inheritance 209
- limitations 209

Copilot usage
- active users 212
- adoption 212
- analysis 212
- enabled users 212
- monitoring 212
- monitoring, limitations 214
- surfaces, monitoring for visibility 213

channels **34, 35**
- private channels 36
- shared channels 36
- standard channels 35

classification **100 - 102, 123**

compliance risks and recommendations
- identifying, with Compliance Manager 138, 139

conditional access **70, 71**

conditional access policies **70 - 73**
- access controls 72
- assignments 72
- conditions 72

configuration objects
- in Exchange Online admin center 16, 17
- in Microsoft Teams admin center 32, 33
- in SharePoint admin center 24

custom agents **197**
- continued task execution 199
- custom business logic application 199
- limitations 199
- predefined workflows execution 198
- repetitive tasks automation 199
- use cases, identifying 197

custom domains **8, 11 - 13**

D

DNS records **12**

Data Access Governance (DAG) reports **178, 179**
- risky sites, identifying with 179
- running, in SharePoint 177

Data Explorer **100, 106**
Data Loss Prevention (DLP) **104, 124**
data classification **100**
data governance **98**
data lifecycle governance **104**
default groups
 members 29, 30
 owners 29, 30
 visitors 29, 30
default permission groups **29**
default tenant domain **8 - 11**
device identities **50**
direct license assignment **4**
distribution groups **77**
distribution list **22, 23**
document libraries
 identifying 26, 27
domain verification **11**
domains **8**

E

Entra ID **3 - 5**
Exact Data Match (EDM) **101**
Exchange Online **3 - 5, 8**
Exchange Online admin center
 configuration objects 16, 17
eDiscovery **106**
encryption **123**
enterprise applications **80, 81**
enterprise guardrails **126**

F

folder-level permissions **32**
folders **27**
 identifying, within libraries 27, 28

G

grounding **126**
grounding controls
 in Copilot 128
group-based license assignment **3, 4**
groups **74 - 76**
 access management, simplifying 77
 distribution groups 77
 Microsoft 365 groups 77
 permissions, managing within 55
 security groups 76
guardrails **125**

I

Identity Secure Score **82, 83**
 using 84
Insider Risk Management **104**
identities **49, 50**
 application identities 50
 device identities 50
 service identities 50
 user identities 50
identity objects **74**
 groups 74 – 76
 user identity 74, 75
identity providers (IDPs) **50, 68**
inherited permissions **28**
input filtering **126**
intent **115**
item-level permissions **32**

J

just-in-time (JIT) privileged access **82**

L

library-level permissions **31**
license assignments **3**
licenses **3**
licensing **3**

M

MX record **12**
Microsoft 365 **98**
Microsoft 365 admin center **3, 7, 8**
Microsoft 365 groups **77**

Microsoft 365 license **5**

Microsoft 365 permissions model **121, 122**

Microsoft 365 tenant **7, 8**

Microsoft Defender **49**
- risk detection 124, 125

Microsoft Defender XDR
- alert correlation 59
- capabilities 58
- incidents 59
- investigation and response capabilities 59
- security signals 58
- telemetry 58

Microsoft Defender for Endpoint (MDE) **103**

Microsoft Entra **49**
- applications 69
- capabilities 68 – 70
- features 68 – 70
- groups 69
- Identity Secure Score 69
- roles 69
- users 69

Microsoft Entra admin center
- URL 68

Microsoft Entra tools
- sign-in issues, investigating 87

Microsoft Graph **118, 119**
- as data aggregation layer 119
- limitations 120
- prompt grounding 120

Microsoft Purview **49, 98, 123**
- capabilities 99, 100
- classification 100
- data classification 100
- data compliance 99
- Data Explorer 100
- data governance 98, 99
- Data Loss Prevention (DLP) 124
- data security 99
- Exact Data Match (EDM) 101
- for data protection 123
- retention rules 105
- sensitive information types (SITs) 101
- sensitive information, detecting 100
- sensitivity labels 102, 103
- trainable classifiers 101

Microsoft Purview Activity Explorer **153**
- activity events 154
- activity timelines, for investigation 154, 155
- audit-derived activity events 153, 154
- event-level activity, compared to aggregated data insights 155
- limitations 155
- user activities, identifying 152, 153
- user interactions, with data 154

Microsoft Purview Communication Compliance **150**
- conditions, for non-compliant communication content 151
- limitations 152
- message content analysis, across communication channels 151
- policy violations, identifying 150
- structured review workflows, for investigation 152
- violations, as reviewable items 151

Microsoft Purview Compliance Manager **138, 139**
- compliance posture, through control-based assessments 139
- compliance posture, versus detection and enforcement 141
- compliance risks and recommendations, identifying 138, 139
- compliance score 140
- control responsibility 140
- improvement actions, for control gaps 140

Microsoft Purview DLP **147**
- alerts, for sensitive data events 149

alerts, identifying 147
alerts, responding to 147
enforcement actions, for data protection 149
limitations 149
policy conditions, based on classification signals 148
policy matches, for classified or sensitive data 148

Microsoft Purview DSPM for AI 155, 156
AI access, to data 157
AI Activity, discovering 155, 156
AI Activity, managing 155, 156
AI exposure scenarios, for sensitive data 158
data exposure, from AI access 157
exposure risk, from classification and access 157, 158
governance, through classification and access 158, 159
limitations 159

Microsoft Purview Data Explorer 141, 142
aggregated insights, from classified data 143
classification signals, from labels and sensitive information types 142
classified data distribution, across services 143
limitations 143
sensitive information, identifying 141

Microsoft Purview Insider Risk Management 144
behavioral patterns, from correlated activity signals 146
investigation and management cases 146
limitations 147
risk scenarios and policies 146
risks, identifying 144
signals and indicators, from user activity 145
user-centric risk model 145

Microsoft Purview eDiscovery
data searching, with Content Search 159, 160

Microsoft Purview risk lifecycle 138

Microsoft Teams 3 - 5, 8

Microsoft Teams admin center
configuration objects 32, 33

m365copilotchat 191

mailbox types 17
comparing 21, 22
resource mailbox 20, 21
shared mailbox 19, 20
user mailbox 17 – 19

meeting policies 37

members 29, 30

messaging policies 38

modern threat landscape 56

multi-factor authentication (MFA) 52

O

organization profile settings 13, 14

organization-wide settings 13

organizational container 8

oversharing, in SharePoint 173
risks 172
scenarios and business risks 174

oversharing, troubleshooting in organization
tools 175

owners 29, 30

P

Privileged Identity Management (PIM) 81, 82

Prompt Gallery 214

passwordless authentication 53

patterns 101

pay-as-you-go billing 210
limitations 211
policy controls 211

usage-driven cost behavior 211

permission trimming **120**

permissions **28, 31, 116, 122**
Copilot enforcement 122
folder-level permissions 32
inheritance 28
item-level permissions 32
library-level permissions 31
managing, within groups 55
site-level permissions 31

policy checks **126**

policy rules **127**

policy-aligned response generation
in Copilot 127

private channels **36**

privileged accounts **81**

privileged role activation
controlling 82
monitoring 82

prompt filtering
in Copilot 127

prompt grounding
with Microsoft Graph 120

prompt lifecycle management **215**
governance controls 215

prompt management
limitations 216

prompt-driven data retrieval
in Copilot 118

prompts **115, 116, 214**
repeated execution, risks 215
sharing, risks 215

protection policies **123**

R

Researcher **193**
cross-source content synthesis 194
exploratory scenarios 194
limitations 195
multi-source content aggregation 194
structured output generation 194
use cases, identifying 193, 194

Restricted Access Control (RAC) **181**

Restricted Content Discovery (RCD) **181**

resource mailbox **20, 21**

response generation **127**

response shaping **128**

responses **116**

responsible AI **128**
principles 125, 126

retention **104**

retention labels **105 - 107**

retention policies **104 - 106**

retention rules **105**

risk detection
with Microsoft Defender 124, 125

role-based access control (RBAC) **54**
advantages 55

roles **28**

S

SharePoint
DAG reports, running 177
external collaboration 173
oversharing 173, 174
oversharing risks 172
oversharing scenarios and business risks 174

SharePoint Advanced Management (SAM) **180**
features and capabilities 180
overview 181, 182

SharePoint Online **3 - 5, 8**

SharePoint admin center
configuration objects 24

SharePoint agents **191**

SharePoint site types **25**
Communication site 26
Team site 25, 26

scheduled prompts **214**

security alerts **57**

security groups **76**

security investigation **57**

security token **78**

sensitive data 98
sensitive information 100
sensitive information types (SITs) 101
sensitivity labels 102, 103, 106, 107, 123
data protection, supporting 103, 104
service identities 50
service plan 5
service principal 80
shared channels 36
shared mailbox 19, 20
sharing reports 176
sign-in issues
investigating, with Microsoft Entra tools 87
resolving 87
sign-in logs 84
reviewing, in Microsoft Entra 84, 85
sign-in results 87
single sign-on (SSO) 78
site-level permissions 31
standard channels 35
system messages
in Copilot 128

T

Team site 25, 26
Teams policy types 36, 37
app permission policies 38
meeting policies 37
messaging policies 38
teams 33, 34
tenant-level settings 8
tenant-wide access and sharing settings 14, 15
threat detection 57
threat intelligence 56, 57
threat protection 56
tools, for troubleshooting oversharing in organization 175, 176
auditing 176
monitoring 177
sharing reports 176
traditional perimeter-based security 46, 47
trainable classifiers 101

U

user access
configuring, to agents 222
user identities 50
user identity 74, 75
as data access context 117
user mailbox 17 - 19
user-based license assignment 3

V

visitors 29, 30

W

workloads 3

Z

Zero Trust 46
core principles 48
in Microsoft 365 49
Zero Trust security model 47

www.ingramcontent.com/pod-product-compliance
Lightning Source LLC
LaVergne TN
LVHW060030210926
848481LV00013B/3829